The TIME LIFE
Complete ☀ Gardener

Three Seasons
of Bloom

By the Editors of Time-Life Books
ALEXANDRIA, VIRGINIA

Contents

Cover: *Yellow, pink, and red primroses, orange globeflowers,
and other perennials announce early summer in this Eugene,
Oregon, garden. In the insets, crocuses in the snow of earliest
spring and chrysanthemums amid autumn leaves extend the
limits of the flowering season.* **Endsheets:** *Spring rhododendrons
embellish a patio in Falls Church, Virginia.* **Half title page:**
*A mixed border of chrysanthemums, sage, and marigolds blooms
into late summer in Lancaster, Pennsylvania.* **Title page:** *Another Pennsylvania garden showcases summer-flowering lilies,
daylilies, and nasturtiums.*

The Consultants

C. Coleston Burrell is a garden designer, writer, photographer, and lifelong plantsman. He is president of Native Landscape Design and Restoration, Ltd., of Minneapolis, Minnesota, a firm specializing in the creation of environmentally appropriate gardens and restorations. He has gardened for more than 32 years and has graduate degrees in horticulture and landscape architecture.

Barbara W. Ellis is a horticulturist, gardener, and author. A graduate of Kenyon College and Ohio State University's School of Horticulture, she is a former managing editor of garden books at Rodale Press, as well as director of publications for the American Horticultural Society and editor of *American Horticulturist* magazine and newsletter. She gardens in eastern Pennsylvania.

Sally Roth is a naturalist, gardener, writer, and editor in New Harmony, Indiana. She is a contributing editor for *Fine Gardening* magazine. Her work has also appeared in Rodale's *Illustrated Encyclopedia of Gardening and Landscaping Techniques* and Taylor's *Guide to Fruits and Berries*. She is author of two forthcoming books: Taylor's *Guide to Ornamental Grasses* (1997) and *Natural Landscaping* (1997).

The Ever-Blooming Garden

Gardens that display color through a long growing season are common; much rarer is a garden that does it with three seasons of flowers. This book will show you how to have such a garden for your own.

The five gardens on the following pages demonstrate how a little planning can produce a garden adorned with blooms of one kind or another through the seasons, every season like a new act in a play about flowers. Each garden is in a different region of the country, and each is shown flowering in the different seasons; a plot plan and plant list allow you to re-create any of these gardens.

Floral Bounty in Colorado

For this garden of alpine plants on the western fringe of the Great Plains adjoining the Rocky Mountains, the spring-summer-fall blooming season is relatively short. The front part of the garden occupies a dry strip in sandy soil running between the street and the sidewalk (see the plot plan, page 8). The rest of the garden is a 25-foot-wide bed that wraps around the house, replacing a conventional lawn.

The garden in spring, photographed here, sets a pastel theme for the year. In the front, pale yellow *Scutellaria alpina* 'Lupulina' (skullcap) contrasts with purple *Salvia* (sage) and clear blue *Linum perenne* (perennial flax). Low-growing pink and red *Dianthus* x *allwoodii* (Allwood pink) at the front and middle echoes the bearded iris in the back. At center, a local native, beardtongue, combines with more traditional midwestern plantings of golden yellow *Eschscholzia californica* (California poppy), pink *Centaurea,* and purple *Allium christophii.*

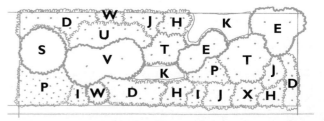

Penstemon palmeri
Background plants should be tall and provide strong lines. Beard-tongues contrast and balance the soft, horizontal lines of the spreading plants in the front bed.

Oenothera missourensis
Ozark sundrops provide the central, vibrant color of the summer garden, the patches of yellow guiding the eye to other, softer-toned flowers.

The Garden in Summer

As spring drifts into summer, the garden's pastel theme intensifies. Rosy *Goniolimon tataricum* (statice) and feathery pink clouds of *Limonium latifolium* (sea lavender) across the middle create a mist of pink against which the bright patches of several varieties of pinks left over from spring, recently blooming *Dianthus nardiformis* (late pink), and deep pink *Callirhoe involucrata* (poppy mallow), ignite the front of the border. At the rear, the robust silvery foliage and red spikes of *Agastache mexicana* (Mexican giant hyssop) can reach to 5 feet tall by the end of the summer. The clear yellow blossoms of *Oenothera missourensis* (Ozark sundrops) appear in mid-summer and carry late into the season, when the fragrant, pink, nodding clusters of *Lycoris squamigera* (magic lily) suddenly emerge to usher in the shorter days of fall.

This garden's textural features, too, become amplified in summer as the fine-leaved plants with small, delicate flowers now contrast dramatically with emerging larger-leaved plants. The lush effect has a pleasing balance of colors, textures, and sizes. ■

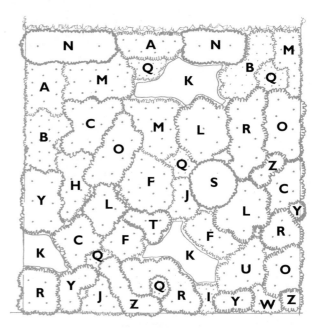

NOTE: "G" is underplanted throughout the front bed.

Lavatera thuringiaca
Tree mallows provide a tall back border of pastel flowers that echo the pink and purple tones dominating the garden in fall.

Crocus speciosus
Delicate flowers massed in broad plantings create a carpet of color that leads the eye to the islands of chrysanthemums, asters, and sedums found farther back in the beds.

The Garden in Fall

The pastel color theme of the garden deepens in fall, and the layers of plantings become lower and more compact. At the back, the clear pink of *Lavatera thuringiaca* (tree mallow) picks up the pink-petaled daisy flowers of a group of 'Clara Curtis' chrysanthemums in the middle of the border. Flanking them is *Aster ericoides* (heath aster), a tough native plant with finely textured rayed flowers that mirror the mums' blossoms. A mass planting of deep purple *Crocus speciosus* (fall crocus) glows among spreading stonecrops such as the red-flowered, purple-leaved *Sedum* 'Rosy Glow' and the pink-flowered, silver-blue *S.* 'Vera Jameson'. They make a durable ground cover, with flowers that last until the first snow. ∎

Plant List

A. *Agastache mexicana* (Mexican giant hyssop) (20)

B. *Allium christophii* (stars-of-Persia) (39)

C. *Aster ericoides* (heath aster) (15)

D. *Callirhoe involucrata* (poppy mallow) (21)

E. *Centaurea dealbata* (knapweed) (5)

F. *Chrysanthemum* 'Clara Curtis' (chrysanthemum) (27)

G. *Crocus speciosus* (fall crocus) (many)

H. *Dianthus* x *allwoodii* (Allwood pink) (19)

I. *Dianthus* 'Little Jock' (pink) (25)

J. *Dianthus nardiformis* (pink) (21)

K. *Eschscholzia californica* (California poppy) (by seed)

L. *Goniolimon tataricum* (statice) (17)

M. *Iris* hybrids (bearded iris) (36)

N. *Lavatera thuringiaca* (tree mallow) (6)

O. *Limonium latifolium* (sea lavender) (17)

P. *Linum perenne* (perennial flax) (17)

Q. *Lycoris squamigera* (magic lily) (49)

R. *Oenothera missourensis* (Ozark sundrops) (22)

S. *Penstemon palmeri* (beardtongue) (2)

T. *Penstemon strictus* (stiff beardtongue) (15)

U. *Salvia jurisicii* (sage) (19)

V. *Salvia officinalis* (sage) (2)

W. *Salvia sclarea* (clary) (3)

X. *Scutellaria alpina* 'Lupulina' (skullcap) (3)

Y. *Sedum* 'Rosy Glow' (stonecrop) (12)

Z. *Sedum* 'Vera Jameson' (stonecrop) (7)

A Spring Garden in Maryland

This formal garden uses strong horizontal and vertical elements to frame the loose and billowing beauty of the seasons. The long, straight, horizontal influence of the lawn and the upright line of arborvitae trees backing the borders are a year-round presence that gives constancy to the ever-changing garden over the seasons. Carefully placed statues punctuate those lines to reinforce and unify the whole and lure a curious visitor down the extended length of the borders.

Within this framework is a carefully orchestrated symphony of bloom. Beginning in spring, a 200-foot expanse of Japanese and Siberian iris mingles with magenta clouds of *Hesperis matronalis* (dame's rocket) and waves of white 'May Queen' oxeye daisies *(Chrysanthemum leucanthemum)*. 'Duchesse de Nemours' peonies the color of apple blossoms soften the hot pink of the dame's rocket. At the edge of the border, the bright faces of pansies and the intense blue of lobelia carry the garden through the summer. This mingling of diverse hues and heights softens the garden's linear aspects with harmonious clouds of color and texture.

This is the spring garden in its semiformal splendor: varied but orderly, with a judicious repetition of plant groups that conveys a reassuring predictability but with a hint of surprise. It invites the visitor to return and witness the flowers of seasons to come. ■

Coreopsis verticillata
'Moonbeam' tickseeds provide pastel yellow areas that allow the eye to rest amid the garden display of vibrantly colored larkspurs, lilies, and yarrows.

Echinacea purpurea
Wherever they are placed in the garden, purple coneflowers attract attention. Outstanding on their own, they harmonize well with their neighbors when combined with other boldly colored flowers in a planting.

The Garden in Summer

This well-planned garden changes personality with the seasons. It moves from offering a gracious spring welcome of pink and purple pastels and cool white to the jaunty look of brightly colored cottage-style flowers in a warm summer rainbow of yellow, pink, and blue. All the while, the design maintains the subtle tension between the formality of its structure and the loose exuberance of its informal plants. For example, 'Golden Sunburst Strain' trumpet lilies, *Achillea filipendulina* 'Moonshine' (yarrow), *Rudbeckia* 'Goldsturm' (black eyed-Susan), and *Coreopsis verticillata* 'Moonbeam' (tickseed) enliven the border with patches of sunny yellow. Pink *Echinacea purpurea* (purple coneflower), 'Stargazer' lilies, and *Alcea rosea* 'Chater's Doubles' (hollyhock) replace the fading pink peonies, while white oxeye daisies, climbing white 'New Dawn' roses at the end of the border, and deep blue *Consolida* 'Giant Imperial Series' (larkspur) tone down the bright colors. ■

The Garden in Fall

Color brightens the mood of the autumn garden to keep the atmosphere from becoming somber. The formal lawn and the arborvitae hedge have provided a constant green framework over the seasons, against which the colors of the flowers can play. Now the floral color theme has shifted with the season to reflect the cheeriest of autumn's reds, yellows, oranges, and purples.

Bunches of black-eyed Susans and tall clusters of *Heliopsis scabra* 'Golden Plume' (false sunflower) left over from summer provide the yellows; bronzy orange appears with the blooms of *Helenium autumnale* 'Brilliant' (sneezeweed). The mix is sweetened with pink *Phlox carolina* 'Rosalinde' (thick-leaf phlox) and purple coneflowers carried over from summer, and deepened with the rich hue of *Aster novae-angliae* 'Purple Dome'. ■

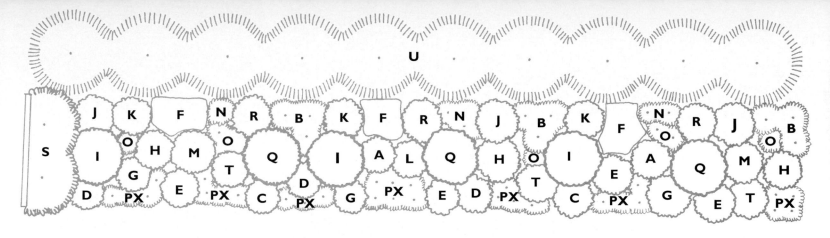

Plant List

A. *Achillea filipendulina* 'Moonshine' (yarrow) (2)

B. *Alcea rosea* 'Chater's Doubles' (hollyhock) (9)

C. *Aster novae-angliae* 'Purple Dome' (New England aster) (2)

D. *Chrysanthemum leucanthemum* 'May Queen' (oxeye daisy) (4)

E. *Chrysanthemum* x *superbum* 'Snow Lady' (Shasta daisy) (3)

F. *Consolida ambigua* 'Giant Imperial Series' (larkspur) (by seed)

G. *Coreopsis verticillata* 'Moonbeam' (tickseed) (3)

H. *Echinacea purpurea* (purple coneflower) (3)

I. *Helenium autumnale* 'Brilliant' (sneezeweed) (3)

J. *Heliopsis scabra* 'Golden Plume' (false sunflower) (3)

K. *Hesperis matronalis* (dame's rocket) (3)

L. *Iris* 'Frosted Plum' (Japanese iris) (1)

M. *Iris* x *sibirica* 'Caesar's Brother' (Siberian iris) (2)

N. *Lilium* 'Golden Sunburst Strain' (trumpet lily) (6)

O. *Lilium* 'Stargazer' (Oriental lily) (6)

P. *Lobelia erinus* 'Crystal Palace' (lobelia) (15)

Q. *Paeonia* 'Duchesse de Nemours' (peony) (3)

R. *Phlox carolina* 'Rosalinde' (thick-leaf phlox) (3)

S. *Rosa* 'New Dawn' (climbing rose) (2)

T. *Rudbeckia fulgida* var. *sulivantii* 'Goldsturm' (black-eyed Susan) (3)

U. *Thuja occidentalis* 'Nigra' (American arborvitae) (10)

V. *Tulipa* 'Attila' (triumph tulip) (48)

W. *Tulipa* 'White Dream' (triumph tulip) (48)

X. *Viola* x *wittrockiana* 'Jolly Joker' (pansy) (14)

NOTE: "V" and "W" are underplanted in groups of six throughout the front of the bed.

Aster novae-angliae
New England asters create islands of restful blue-purple in the beds now dominated by the golds and reds of false sunflowers, sneezeweeds, and black-eyed Susans.

A Northwestern Garden in Summer

This garden in Eugene, Oregon, is a journey through both space and time. A cozy path winds down a corridor of extravagant color, bringing the visitor up close to the flowers and passing from an open area of bright sunlight to the shady enclosure of a gazebo. The path winds, too, through the seasons, with plants carefully selected to shine from spring through fall.

This garden takes advantage of the temperate, English-style climate of the Pacific Northwest, with its cool, rainy winters and long, warm summers that bring still more rainfall. In this photograph the garden is in its summer heyday, reveling in plants suited for the long season. *Delphinium* and two hardy perennial sages send up purple and blue spikes the whole summer. Beginning in late spring, 2-foot *Allium christophii* (stars-of-Persia) produces umbels of pinkish flowers up to 10 inches across, pairing with the salmon-pink trumpets of *Alstroemeria* (Peruvian lily). Large-scale foliage plants like *Acanthus spinosus* (bear's-breech) and *Stipa gigantea* (feather grass) come into bloom this time of year. The purple flower stalks of *Acanthus* can reach a height of 4 feet above its bold spiny leaves, and produce a gorgeous contrast to the tawny haze of the feather grass's 8-foot-tall inflorescences.

These are also good cutting flowers, making them as prized indoors as out. Yarrows, with their golden, flat-topped flower clusters, green-and-pink tinged *Astrantia* (masterwort), delphiniums, and Peruvian lilies make long-lasting cut flowers. Later in the season *Catananche caerula* (Cupid's-dart), yarrows, and alliums make excellent dried flowers for a fall bouquet. ∎

Helleborus orientalis
The nodding, pastel flowers of Lenten roses reinforce the relaxed theme of the springtime garden, providing blossoms that draw attention without dominating the landscape.

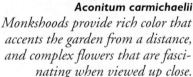

Pulmonaria 'Roy Davidson'
The lungworts, with their cool blue flowers and deep green leaves plashed with silvery white dots, accent the walkway.

Aconitum carmichaelii
Monkshoods provide rich color that accents the garden from a distance, and complex flowers that are fascinating when viewed up close.

The Garden inSpring

The rains of spring bring an early awakening of bloom and an infusion of fresh flower colors and textures along the garden path. Low-growing perennials and bulbs spread through the garden in drifts—many of them ephemerals that will disappear at the end of spring to make room for summer flowers.

Earliest of them all is *Helleborus orientalis* (Lenten rose), with pink flowers that will last through spring. Appearing at the same time are delicate *Soldanella alpina* (glacier alpenclock) with pale blue flowers, and its taller relative, the yellow *Primula elatior* (oxlip primrose). Two wild bulbs, *Erythronium revolutum* (mahagony fawn lily) and *Anemone nemorosa* (European wood anemone), and the woodland *Epimedium grandiflorum* (bishop's hat) find their way here and there.

Later in the spring, blue and pink *Pulmonaria* (lungwort) flowers rise above their speckled leaves, and *Geranium psilostemon* (cranesbill) open their pink blossoms, which last into summer. ∎

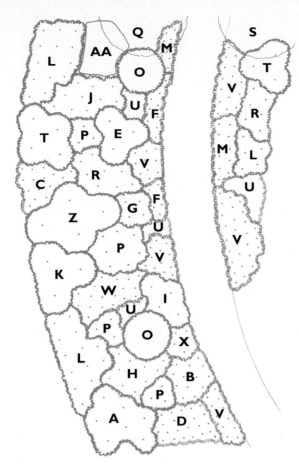

NOTE: "N" and "Y" are underplanted throughout.

Plant List

A. *Acanthus spinosissimus* (bear's-breech) (7)

B. *Achillea filipendulina* (fern-leaf yarrow) (13)

C. *Aconitum carmichaelii* (monkshood) (15)

D. *Allium christophii* (stars-of-Persia) (23)

E. *Alstroemeria* **Ligtu Hybrids** (Peruvian lily) (3)

F. *Anemone nemorosa* 'Alba' and 'Rosea' (15)

G. *Aster* x *frikartii* 'Wonder of Staffa' (Frikart's aster) (4)

H. *Astrantia major* 'Rosensymphonie' (masterwort) (11)

I. *Catananche caerulea* (Cupid's-dart) (4)

J. *Clematis recta* 'Recta Purpurea' (clematis) (10)

K. *Dahlia* 'Bishop of Llandaff' (dahlia) (3)

L. *Delphinium* 'Magic Fountain Series' (delphinium) (32)

M. *Epimedium grandiflorum* (bishop's hat) (20)

N. *Erythronium revolutum* (mahogany fawn lily) (many)

O. *Geranium psilostemon* (cranesbill) (2)

P. *Helleborus orientalis* (Lenten rose) (17)

Q. *Hydrangea anomala* ssp. *petiolaris* (climbing hydrangea) (1)

R. *Kniphofia* 'Little Maid' (red-hot poker) (14)

S. *Lonicera periclymenum* var. *serotina* (woodbine) (1)

T. *Nicotiana sylvestris* (woodland tobacco) (7)

U. *Primula elatior* (oxlip primrose) (82)

V. *Pulmonaria* 'Roy Davidson' (lungwort) (76)

W. *Salvia pratensis* (meadow clary) (19)

X. *Salvia* x *superba* 'Earl Friesland' (violet sage) (5)

Y. *Soldanella alpina* (glacier alpenclock) (many)

Z. *Stipa gigantea* (feather grass) (4)

AA. *Verbena bonariensis* (vervain) (by seed)

Nicotiana sylvestris
In addition to its visual interest in the back border, woodland tobacco also fills the garden with an unforgettable perfume.

The Garden in Fall

In fall, this garden reaches full height, with plants that will bloom until the very end of the season. The feather grass is in its majesty, towering at 8 feet, while beyond it at the back of the border stands *Nicotiana sylvestris* (woodland tobacco), the tallest of its genus at 6 feet. Its down-facing pendulous, fragrant white trumpets can be seen across the garden, and it contrasts beautifully with the rigid form of *Verbena bonariensis* (vervain), 4 feet tall with rose-violet flower clusters at the ends of stiff, twiggy branches. Deep red 'Bishop of Llandaff' dahlias have contrasting bronze-red leaves, and grow to 3 feet. They started to bloom in summer, and now add depth to the garden's color, along with the emerging deep purple spikes of *Aconitum carmichaelii* (monkshood). Daisy-like violet *Aster frikartii* blooms complement the shaggy yellow flowers of *Kniphofia* 'Little Maid' (red-hot poker). ■

Summer Flowers in a Western Garden

This inviting garden in Rancho Santa Fe, California, uses simple but elegant man-made structures and decorative features to orient its myriad textures, forms, and colors in a complex garden planting. With careful three-season planning, it becomes greater than the sum of its parts. In this photograph, it reveals a sprawling summer bounty.

A wooden pergola in the background provides strong vertical and horizontal lines that give direction to the riot of plants around it. The scattered patches of white-and-blue 'Round Table' delphiniums, *Digitalis* (foxglove), green-tinged *Zantedeschia aethiopica* (calla lily), and 'Husker Red' beardtongues echo the vertical lines of the pergola's pillars. The spreading clumps of yellow *Cotula coronopifolia* (brass-buttons), dianthus, deep-pink *Geranium cinereum* var. *subcaulescens*, scarlet *Geum* 'Mrs. Bradshaw', and *Fragaria vesca* 'Semperflorens' (woodland strawberry) create horizontal lines that softly match those of the pergola's rafters.

Indeed, this garden can be a little overwhelming at first. As shown on the plot plan on page 21, it is unusually large—20 feet deep and 15 feet wide—and is divided in half by a low stone retaining wall. Masses of spreading plants such as *Myosotis sylvatica* (forget-me-not) in spring and shrub verbenas in fall help to fill out the space, with room at the front allowed for smaller, more delicate specimens to be viewed up close. In this way, a large garden presents many smaller tableaux that encompass a world of their own. ∎

Wisteria sinensis
Chinese wisteria vines soften the hard lines of the pergola, visually tying the structure to the rest of the planting.

Myosotis sylvatica
The pastel blue flowers of forget-me-nots float through the garden like a musical theme, with daffodils and pinks providing a colorful counterpoint.

Plant List

A. *Artemisia arborescens* 'Powis Castle' (artemisia) (1)

B. *Cistus* x *purpureus* (purple rock rose) (1)

C. *Convolvulus mauritanicus* (ground morning-glory) (2)

D. *Cotula coronopifolia* (brass-buttons) (by seed)

E. *Delphinium* Round Table Series (Pacific delphinium) (6)

F. *Dianthus* 'Agatha' (pink) (4)

G. *Dianthus* 'Anthony' (pink) (3)

H. *Dierama pulcherrimum* 'Puck' (wandflower) (15)

I. *Digitalis purpurea* (foxglove) (9)

J. *Fragaria vesca* 'Semperflorens' (woodland strawberry) (5)

K. *Gaillardia* x *grandiflora* 'Yellow Queen' (blanket flower) (18)

L. *Geranium cinereum* var. *subcaulescens* (cranesbill) (2)

M. *Geum coccineum* 'Mrs. Bradshaw' (geum) (4)

N. *Helichrysum* 'Limelight' (licorice plant) (3)

O. *Lantana camara* (yellow sage) (5)

The Garden in Spring

The garden begins in spring with a finer, softer identity, while its ornaments impose a measure of constancy on the low-lying shifts of spring plants. The rugged texture of the pergola is softened by the wisteria's graceful leaves and pendant clusters of lilac flowers, which last for three weeks. Forget-me-nots and 'King Alfred' daffodils make pockets of brilliant blue and yellow in front of the retaining wall. In their midst are bright red pinks among the contrasting spring foliage of arrow-shaped calla leaves, swordlike *Watsonia*, and the deep green, waxy leaves of a young *Magnolia grandiflora*, which will not bloom for several years to come. When the forget-me-nots have finished flowering at the start of summer, they are pulled out to make room for summer plants, their seeds scattered for next spring.

In the upper part of the garden, taller plants play against each other. The pewter gray foliage of *Artemesia* 'Powis Castle' and *Lavandula stoechas* (Spanish lavender) sets off the rosy red blooms of *Polygala* x *dalmaisiana* (milkwort). Dangling flower bells of *Dierama pulcherrimum* 'Puck' (wandflower) and the early-summer blooms of *Polianthus tuberosa* 'The Pearl' (tuberose) add fragrance and touches of white. Taken together, these varied plants form an unorthodox prelude of color, texture, and form that sets the stage for the summer symphony to come. ∎

P. *Lavandula stoechas* (Spanish lavender) (4)

Q. *Linaria maroccana* 'Fairy Lights' (toadflax) (by seed)

R. *Magnolia grandiflora* (southern magnolia) (1)

S. *Mirabilis jalapa* (four-o'clock) (6)

T. *Myosotis sylvatica* (forget-me-not) (by seed)

U. *Narcissus* 'King Alfred' (daffodil) (60)

V. *Penstemon digitalis* 'Husker Red' (beardtongue) (7)

W. *Polianthes tuberosa* 'The Pearl' (tuberose) (23)

X. *Polygala* x *dalmaisiana* (milkwort) (1)

Y. *Rosa* 'Swan Lake' (climbing rose) (1)

Z. *Watsonia pyramidata* (bugle lily) (6)

AA. *Wisteria sinensis* 'Purpurea' (Chinese wisteria) (2)

BB. *Zantedeschia aethiopica* (calla lily) (5)

Note: "T" and "U" are underplanted throughout the garden.

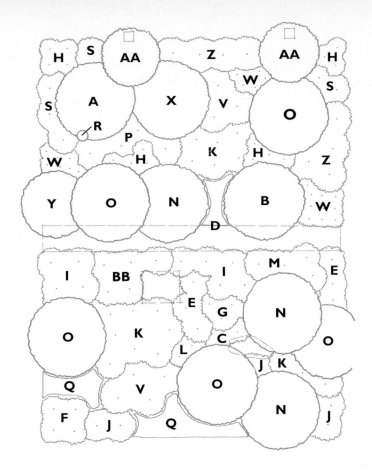

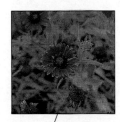

Gaillardia x grandiflora
Blanket flowers are exceptionally brilliant in color. Careful placing will insure that they punctuate rather than overpower the planting.

The Garden in Fall

Autumn in southern California is usually is warm and breezy, and the weather is reflected in the carefree yellow, white, and red flowers blooming in the garden in this season. *Gaillardia* x *grandiflora* 'Yellow Queen' (blanket flower), red with yellow-tipped petals, nestles against *Lantana camara* (yellow sage), with its uniquely scented flowers. *Helichrysum* 'Lime Light' (licorice plant) adds a cool white counterpoint with its silvery foliage and clusters of white flowers.

In the background, dependable *Mirabilis jalapa* (four-o'clock) in bright fuchsia-pink rise up between the extraordinarily fragrant waxy white flowers of tuberoses, which can overwinter safely in this Zone 9 garden. More blanket flowers and shrub verbenas in the upper garden tie the two halves together. ■

Lantana camara
Yellow sage gives the fall garden an infusion of fresh color. It also has aromatic foliage. When it is grown next to a path, the scent is released as passers-by brush the plants.

Autumnal Grace Down South

Perennials, flowering shrubs, and ornamental grasses form the framework of an informal three-season design in this North Carolina garden. Filling in that framework and extending the garden's long period of bloom, countless annuals romp at will, sometimes allowed to self-seed. By autumn, as shown here, the garden has marshaled late-season flowers and a spectrum of other fall hues to achieve an extravaganza of color.

The shrubs and ornamental grasses at the back of the bed are constants of color and texture, but they have added seasonal interest as well. The shrubs bloom in late spring, and the grasses in late summer, adding to their year-round appeal. In fall, the *Cotinus coggygria* 'Purpureus' (smoketree) and the *Berberis thunbergii* var. *atropurpurea* 'Helmond Pillar' (Japanese barberry) take on red and orange colors typical of the season. The *Sambucus nigra* 'Aurea' (European elder), which has pale, greenish yellow foliage the rest of the year, now carries black berries. Grasses like *Miscanthus sinensis* 'Gracillimus' and ruddy *Pennisetum* 'Rubrum' have tawny-red, arched inflorescences that glow in the sun.

Perennials have been spaced to allow room to spare for the showy annuals seeded or planted among them. By autumn, low-growing annuals in seasonal colors, such as zinnias, 'Jewel Series' nasturtiums (*Tropaeolum majus*), and *Verbena canadensis* (rose verbena), sprawl at the front and fill in the spaces between larger plants. The deep purple leaves of 'Blackie' sweet-potato vines stand out in high contrast to the brilliant orange and red of cosmos and *Gomphrena globosa* (globe amaranth). Shrubby *Leonotis leonurus* (lion's-ear) carries bright whorls of orange tubular flowers almost into winter. This three-season garden is taking a last curtain call and giving a quiet hint of next year's flowers. ∎

The Garden in Spring

In spring, the European elder comes into bloom with creamy fragrant blossoms held against young, pale yellow foliage that darkens with age. Nearby, exotic *Eucomis comosa* (pineapple flower) a bulb that is perennial in this Zone 8 garden, raises curious yellowish flower heads above strappy green leaves.

Then other annuals and bulbs heat up the spring color scheme. The vivid red flowers of the perennial corm *Crocosmia* 'Aurantiaca' unfurl on wiry stems next to the unusual maroon-hued *Iris sibirica* 'Sparking Burgundy'. To this unconventional pairing are added Erysimum 'Orange Bedder' (wallflower), a biennial whose seeds can be sown directly into the garden the previous fall, and the carnival colors of purple-and-orange pansies. Together with petunias, the wallflowers and pansies will carry the garden into summer. ■

Plant List

A. *Berberis thunbergii* var. *atropurpurea* 'Helmond Pillar' (Japanese barberry) (1)

B. *Brassica* 'Red Giant' (mustard) (3)

C. *Cosmos sulphureus* (yellow cosmos) (by seed)

D. *Cotinus coggygria* 'Purpureus' (smoketree) (1)

E. *Crocosmia* x *crocosmiiflora* 'Aurantiaca' (montbretia) (6)

F. *Cucurbita pepo* var. *ovifera* (ornamental gourd vine) (by seed)

G. *Dahlia* x *hybrida* 'G.F. Hamerick' (dahlia) (10)

H. *Erysimum* 'Orange Bedder' (wallflower) (by seed)

I. *Eschscholzia californica* (California poppy) (by seed)

J. *Eucomis comosa* (pineapple flower) (9)

K. *Gomphrena globosa* (globe amaranth) (by seed)

L. *Gomphrena haageana* 'Strawberry Fields' (globe amaranth) (by seed)

Iris sibirica
Siberian irises combine desirable contrasting features, notably sharp and upright simple leaves paired with soft, complex flowers that appear to float over the foliage.

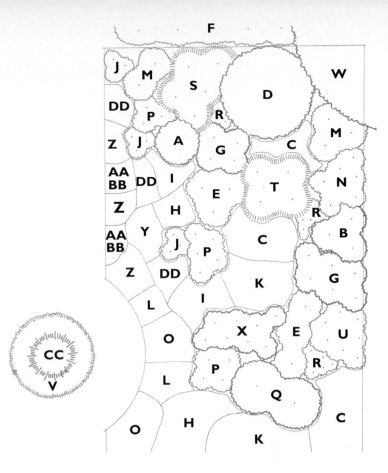

M. *Helianthus angustifolius* (swamp sunflower) (5)

N. *Hemerocallis* 'Alcazar' (daylily) (7)

O. *Ipomoea batatas* 'Blackie' (sweet-potato vine) (by seed)

P. *Iris sibirica* 'Sparkling Burgundy' (Siberian iris) (12)

Q. *Leonotis leonurus* (lion's-ear) (2)

R. *Lilium* 'Connecticut Yankee' (Asiatic lily) (14)

S. *Miscanthus sinensis* 'Gracillimus' (eulalia) (5)

T. *Pennisetum setaceum* 'Rubrum' (fountain grass) (4)

U. *Penstemon digitalis* 'Husker Red' (beardtongue) (8)

V. *Petunia integrifolia* (violet-flowered petunia) (by seed)

W. *Sambucus nigra* 'Aurea' (European elder) (1)

X. *Sedum alamosanum* 'Mediovariegatum' (sedum) (8)

Y. *Tropaeolum majus* 'Jewel Series' (nasturtium) (by seed)

Z. *Verbena canadensis* (rose verbena) (by seed)

AA. *Viola* x *wittrockiana* 'Jolly Joker' (pansy) (by seed)

BB. *Viola* x *wittrockiana* 'Scarlet Clan' (pansy) (by seed)

CC. *Yucca flaccida* (yucca) (1)

DD. *Zinnia angustifolia* (zinnia) (by seed)

Yucca flaccida

The strong lines of a yucca can dominate plants of softer texture in a bed, yet when used as a specimen plant in a place of honor it becomes the focal point for the entire flower garden.

Cotinus coggyria

For subtle, ethereal color umatched by any other plant, the purple smoke tree is a wonderful choice.

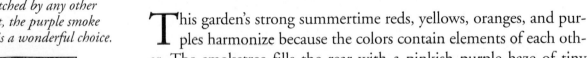

The Garden in Summer

This garden's strong summertime reds, yellows, oranges, and purples harmonize because the colors contain elements of each other. The smoketree fills the rear with a pinkish purple haze of tiny flowers that pick up the rosy tint of *Penstemon digitalis* 'Husker Red', with its burgundy-green foliage that will turn scarlet in fall. A deeper red appears in the blooms of *Dahlia* 'G. F. Hamerick'. Nearby, the orangy red reflexed petals of *Lilium* 'Connecticut Yankee' and the yellow bells of 'Alcazar' daylilies echo the orange-and-yellow of California poppy, an annual that self-sows vigorously in mild climates like this one. At their feet is a rich, purplish black carpet of 'Blackie' sweet-potato vines, also started by seed. Across the gravel path, fragrant *Yucca flaccida* blossoms rise above stiff, pointed leaf blades, ringed by a border of purple petunias that keep blooming through the heat of summer and into fall. ■

Creating an Ever-Blooming Garden

Alive with color, an ever-blooming garden produces a succession of flowers from late winter to late autumn. But creating a design for such a glorious garden takes step-by-step planning. The plan must accommodate not only your tastes and preferences, but also the unique conditions of your landscape, including soil, climate, and topography. Patterns of sun and shade vary by season, so they must be part of the plan.

A special planting technique called layering makes maximum use of space for a dense array of blooms. Gardeners who relish a changing palette can develop color patterns calculated by the season. The color of bark and berries, and even the color of your house, can become part of the visual plan. In these pages, you'll discover the essential tools, materials, and skills for creating a garden that blooms throughout the seasons.

Bands of Late-Summer Color
Unified by ribbons of repeated colors, this garden in Sharon, Connecticut, features deep purple petunias and heliotrope, red cosmos and cuphea, and hot pink zinnias and verbenas radiating along the path. Sun-yellow helianthus adds height and late-season interest.

Continuous Bloom by Design

One of the best things about gardening is anticipation, and that's what makes a three-season flowering garden so special. There's always something new coming into bloom, from late winter through spring and summer, right up to the first killing frost of fall. Perennials, annuals, and bulbs provide most of the color, but flowering shrubs, vines, and trees also add interest and provide structure in all seasons.

Planning is the key to achieving a three-season garden full of bloom, and this book will show you, step by step, a system that works. No special skills or tools are required, just a willingness to think on paper before you dig into the soil.

You'll start with the big picture, making a sketch of your entire property so you can analyze your existing plantings and identify the areas where garden beds and splashes of color will matter most. Then you'll narrow the focus of that master plan, breaking the big picture into smaller areas and finally into individual snapshots—beds of manageable size that you can develop one at a time.

With the help of the Seasonal Garden Planner at the end of this section, you'll get a clear, at-a-glance picture of the cycles of bloom in your plan. Your plan and the Seasonal Planner will make it easy to fill your garden in all three seasons with waves of color. You'll learn to get the most out of every inch of space, by planting intensively and by choosing combinations that follow one another, season after season. When the early daffodils fade, forget-me-nots planted over the bulbs step right in to fill the space, and when the forget-me-nots become tired, the fresh foliage of hardy geraniums gives them a shoulder to lean on and adds a wave of deep pink flowers.

By starting with the big picture and then tightening your focus onto individual beds and plant combinations, you can create a landscape that's full of flowers and anticipation, from the first crocuses of spring to the last asters of autumn. ∎

Color by Design
A ubiquitous backdrop of green and pewter foliage balances islands of colorful flowers that escort this Del Mar, California, garden through the seasons. Spring is highlighted with cascades of blue cinerarias and pink and red climbing roses that gently yield to the summertime gold and lavender of daylilies and mallows. In fall the yellow, pink, and blue flowers of lavender cotton, lamb's ears, and rosemary complement the reblooming roses.

Sketching Your Garden

A rough drawing of your property is the base map for all planning, and it's also a permanent record of the "before" look of the landscape. You can make your map in any season, but winter is probably the best time to start, since the entire structure of your property is more visible then. For measuring spaces, you'll need a 100-foot tape measure and possibly a helper. For drawing maps of various parts of the property, you'll need a pencil, eraser, straightedge, and a few large sheets of quarter-inch-grid graph paper. For small to medium-size areas, convert each foot of real distance to ¼ inch. For example, a 60-foot property boundary will be 15 inches long on the graph-paper grid. If the areas are large, use a 1-yard-to-¼-inch scale.

Tip

You can locate true north by using your wristwatch as a makeshift compass. Hold the watch so that the hour hand points to the sun. South will be exactly halfway between the hour hand and 12, going the shorter way around the dial. For North, simply turn 180 degrees.

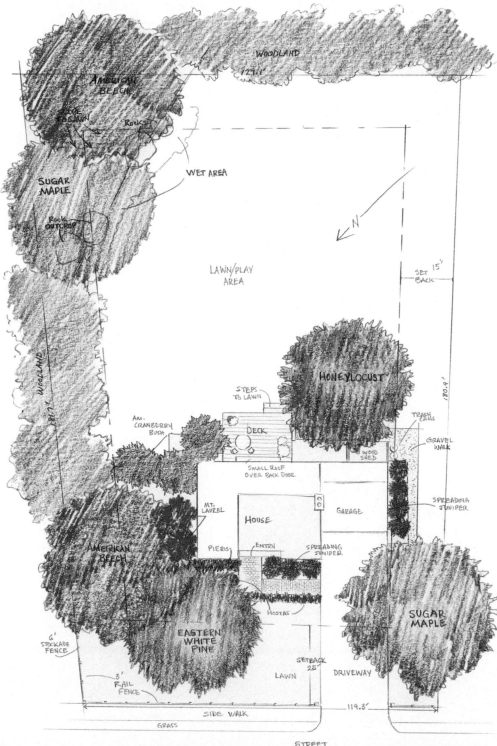

1 **Start your base map** by drawing in property boundaries and the outline of your house. Mark the important views from inside your house through the living room, bedroom, and kitchen windows. Note the views from a deck and from the front porch. Finally, indicate the views to your house from street-side and from neighboring houses. Then mark the views you would like to screen with plantings.

2 **Draw in the outbuildings** and other permanent landscape features, such as utility poles, fences, sheds, and play equipment, and mark existing trees. Draw the permanent walkways and traffic patterns.

3 **Note the obvious growing conditions** that will affect your plan, such as wet and dry spots and windy areas. These notes will be important when it comes time to select plants for beds in these areas.

4 **Indicate permanent colors** already in the landscape, starting with the color of your house, to coordinate plant colors. Also note the locations and colors of any evergreens so you can plan complementary companion plantings. If you have existing perennial beds or shrubs that you want to keep, note their general colors as you have observed them through the seasons.

Using Your Base Map

aking a base map sets the foundation of your plans for a garden of three-season bloom, but it's only a start. Your next step is to add overlays to record conditions in your garden and sketch designs for new plantings. To make an overlay, tape a sheet of tracing paper to the base map and make a new drawing on it.

Mapping Sun and Shade

For a lavish display of three-season bloom, it's vital to know where you have sun and shade, because few plants bloom well in full shade; most need full sun or partial shade. To get an exact picture, draw shade patterns at 10 a.m., 1 p.m., and 4 p.m. on your overlay; make separate overlays for spring, summer, and fall. You will find that summer sun produces the smallest shade patterns, while the patterns for spring and fall will be roughly the same. Some computer programs for landscape design, which can plan plant combinations and give a picture of

your maturing landscape, also include a feature that tracks sun and shade through the seasons.

Plotting Seasonal Plantings

After you map the shade, begin sketching beds, in sunny areas if possible, on separate overlays. Play with layouts, shapes, and colors until the overall effect is what you're looking for. When you are satisfied, you can photocopy your base map and overlays together to serve as a permanent record.

Finally, focus on the spots where you will concentrate the three seasons of bloom. To make it easier to draw specific plans, create a larger version of these parts of the base map on a new sheet of graph paper by doubling all measurements or by enlarging the original on a photocopier. Use this as a basis for planning, marking on the overlays the specific plant combinations, as shown on page 31. Start with the spring plan, and repeat the process for summer and fall. ∎

Assessing the Elements of Your Garden

In the second stage of mapping, make a base map focusing on a selected part of your property—a part where you plan to have a collection of three-season plantings. Here, the back of the property sketched on page 29 has been drawn to scale on graph paper. Important permanent features such as trees, the deck, existing beds, and the garden boundaries are indicated directly on the grid.

This base map forms the foundation over which various overlays can be made, such as the sun and shade map discussed above. The overlay here shows prevailing winds, views into the garden, and the uses to which various parts of the garden are put. Existing plants have been drawn in colored pencil. A sunny site within view of the deck and nestled against a rock outcropping is identified as the site for a new three-season flower bed.

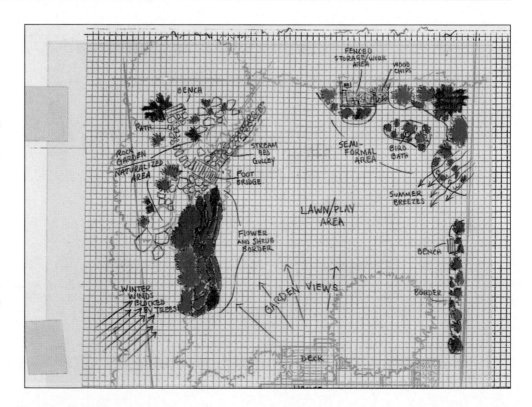

Planning the Three-Season Border

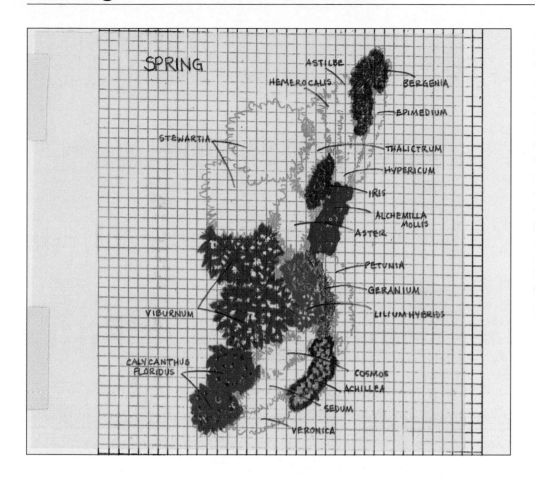

SPRING

ASTILBE
HEMEROCALIS
BERGENIA
EPIMEDIUM
STEWARTIA
THALICTRUM
HYPERICUM
IRIS
ALCHEMILLA MOLLIS
ASTER
PETUNIA
GERANIUM
VIBURNUM
LILIUM HYBRIDS
CALYCANTHUS FLORIDUS
COSMOS
ACHILLEA
SEDUM
VERONICA

In the final step in mapping your seasonal flower garden, make overlays for each of the three seasons on an enlarged plot plan. This step serves a dual purpose: The overlays, which can easily be discarded in case of mistakes, help you to sketch out combinations and also give you a record of bloom from season to season. In the plan at left, plants blooming in spring are clearly labeled; colors on the map indicate the distribution of flower colors across the bed, and reveal a pink-and-red color theme. Shade-tolerant viburnum and stewartia at the back of the bed form a backdrop for summer and fall blooms to come. For more on this process, see pages 32-33.

Four Basics of Garden Design

Keep the following principles in mind when selecting combinations of plants for your design for three seasons of bloom, using a plot plan like the one above and the Seasonal Garden Planner at the end of this section to obtain the combinations of shape and color you want for each season.

Balance
Think of your garden plan as a seesaw, with the fulcrum at an imaginary midpoint. Your task is to design your planting scheme so that plants on both sides of the garden will have equal visual weight—so that the seesaw is level—making for a restful, balanced scene. You can achieve this through strict symmetry, by planting the same plants in the same arrangement on both sides of the garden. Alternatively, you can make an asymmetrical, but still balanced, plan using tall, slender plants on one side, for example, and a mass of heavy, low-growing plants on the other.

Proportion
Scale and proportion are measures of relative size. All plantings should take into account the relative sizes of plants in a group, and the relative size of that group to the larger whole. Take visual cues from the dominant objects in your garden—your house, trees, or other features—and chose plants neither too tall nor too short in relation to them.

Repetition
Repeating a plant, color, form, or texture unifies the design by establishing a common reference point. The eye is smoothly drawn from point to point in an established rhythm, and the garden feels harmonious.

Contrast
An emphatic form, such as a vertical fan of iris leaves, or a strong color that pops out from its surrounding scheme, or a startling texture of foliage or blossoms, works to catch the eye and give shape and dimension to a design. Juxtapose light and dark colors, rough and smooth surfaces, large and small shapes, to give your planting greater definition so that plants are discernible from each other and plantings hold their own in the larger landscape.

Developing a Succession of Bloom

Success with a three-season plan depends on plant partnerships and a sequence of bloom that will keep your garden interesting throughout the better part of a year. In such a plan, the bloom period of some plants will overlap from one season to another, but most of the colors that are dominant in spring will give way to summer hues, and these will shift again when summer's heat ebbs in fall. The Seasonal Garden Planner (page 36-37) and separate overlays to attach to your base plan will help you coordinate the whole design.

How do I decide where to place plants in my design?

You can organize a planting by height. Place the tallest plants at the back of a border or in the center of a bed you wish to view from all sides. Stair-step the plants down, finishing with the lowest ones at the front or around the outside of the bed.

Making Plant Partnerships

The process of making plant partnerships takes some of the guesswork out of filling a three-season garden with color groups that work. The system is as easy as selecting the right scarf for your sweater or the right tie for your shirt, as one plant suggests the next, which leads to a third. For instance, a favorite summer-blooming red daylily may prompt you to choose a feathery-leafed, mahogany-accented *Coreopsis basalis*, which then might be backed by an elegant clump of *Miscanthus sinensis* 'Purpurascens' (red-tipped flame grass).

Each of these color clusters begins with one or two primary plants with strong characteristics that carry the color scheme for that season, and can be repeated in places throughout the garden to establish a unifying rhythm. A cluster could be based on a large shrub with a strong form and lovely flowers, or a tree with brilliant fall foliage. Or it could be a perennial or bulb, an annual like a towering orange *Cosmos sulphureus*, a flowering vine, or a clambering rose.

Next, select two or three plants to complement the primary plants. These should bloom at the same time and share the same cultural requirements as the primary plants, but they should also help create a composition. Use the design basics on page 31 to guide your choices. Complementary plants should be proportional in size to the primary plants. They should repeat some colors, textures, or forms of the primary plants, as well as contrasting with some others. (Blues and yellows are typical contrasting colors.) And together they should make a balanced arrangement.

Finally, fill in the composition with subordinate plants to unify the elements. Choose plants that provide softer color echoes of the primary plants and occupy the empty spaces; groundcovers are useful for this purpose.

Plotting a Succession of Bloom

Planning for a succession of bloom also begins with some primary plants. They might already exist in your garden or they might be new ones that you are particularly fond of, but they should always be interesting over more than one season. For example, you might have a handsome *Viburnum plicatum* (doublefile viburnum), which has showy white spring flowers and lustrous purple-red autumn foliage; let it become the cornerstone for a three-season progression of complementary bloom. Using the Seasonal Garden Planner and the encyclo-

The Ever-Blooming Garden

This garden in the Northwest glows in **summer** with mounds of chartreuse lady's-mantle flowers and shining, deep red daylily blossoms. Complementing them are the soft pink spires of astilbe, the blues and purples of a climbing clematis, and the frosty white flowers of climbing rose that serve to cool the composition.

In **spring** this garden opens with white and yellow daffodils, softly scented orange azaleas, magenta rhododendrons, and pinkish white magnolia blossoms. The astilbe bridges spring and summer with fluffy pink flowers that support the pastel color scheme of spring and complement the bold red daylilies that follow.

A handsome Japanese maple anchors the arrangement in the back, its mahogany foliage setting the color scheme for **fall**, as the azalea foliage will turn reddish orange, and fall-blooming purple loosestrife will come into flower. Cool pink yarrow will tone down the hot colors.

pedia at the back of this book, you might add a drift of miniature daffodils for early spring, spiky blue Siberian iris for early summer color, and finish with wine-colored chrysanthemums to play off the viburnum's fall foliage.

Make design sketches on scrap pieces of tracing paper taped over the base plan as you plot your plant choices on the Garden Planner: The sketch will show where the plants are in relation to one another, and the Planner keeps track of when they bloom. Together, they will show you if there are gaps in flowering. Then you might add some late-blooming yellow daylilies to the above plan for mid-summer color, and a bunch of yellow-eyed Shasta daisies to bridge summer and fall.

Concentrate on one season at a time. When you think you have a complete plan for one season, transfer it onto a permanent tracing-paper overlay and tape it to the base plan of the garden bed. Then attach a second sheet of tracing paper over the first. Draw the foliage that will be present in the next season, and fill the spaces in between with new companion plants. Repeat the process for the third season. ■

Bursting into Spring
Iris spikes create a splash of vivid purple among yellow ranunculus and daisies in this spring California garden of mixed perennials and bulbs.

▲ SPRING

▲ FALL

Getting the Most Bloom

Planning for successive seasons of bloom through the use of map overlays is one way to get a broad and continuous array of flowers in your garden. Another is to select particular plants known for having long periods of bloom that overlap from one season to the next. A third way is to enrich the soil and install plants in a tight pattern according to your understanding of their underground root structures—a process called layering—so that you are able to concentrate more plants than usual in the same space and make sure that a fair number of them will be in bloom at all times between late winter's thaw and late autumn's frost.

Choosing Plants with Long Periods of Bloom

Most shrubs, perennials, and bulbs are in flower for only a few weeks, but some, such as *Echinacea purpurea* (purple coneflower) and *Coreopsis verticillata* 'Moonbeam' (threadleaf coreopsis), can keep blooms coming for months. These make good primary plants in partnerships that bridge the seasons.

Annuals and tender perennials such as wax begonias, impatiens, petunia, and *Tagetes* (marigold) also have long-lasting blooms, but their continuous presence can become monotonous. It is better to use them sparingly to give your garden variety by adding color between clumps of perennials.

If a plant is known as a "rebloomer," it will make an initial spectacular show of bloom in spring and then put in a second, less showy, floral display in fall. Bearded irises such as yellow 'Lady Emma' and fragrant purple 'Autumn Bugler', for example, can be expected to rebloom in fall, pairing beautifully with lavender asters. Roses that flower again, which are said to be "remontant," include the white 'Blanc Double de Coubert', yellow 'Reve d'Or', and red 'Blaze'.

Some cultivars of a given species of perennial or bulb bloom earlier or later than the species, just as some species bloom at a different time than others in the same genus. For example, try *Narcissus* 'Mount Hood' or 'February Gold' for early spring bloom, followed by *N.* 'Romance' and 'Las Vegas' in mid-spring, and ending with *N.* 'Cheerfulness' in late spring. You can find early-, mid-, and late-season lilies, tulips, peonies, daylilies, irises, and Oriental poppies, for example.

Layering Plants to Pack in Flowers

In nature, plants adapt to available space by growing in layers. They cluster together at several different heights and

Perennials from Spring to Fall

Certain perennial genera are made up of species and cultivars whose flowers emerge at different times from early spring to late fall. You can plant selections from genera such as those listed below in such a way that their flowers will be represented in your garden over the entire growing season.

PLANT	COLOR	BLOOM TIME
Anemone (windflower)		
A. sylvestris	Snow white	Spring and fall
A. tomentosa	Pale pink	Summer
A. x *hybrida* 'Pamina'	Antique rose	Fall
Campanula (bellflower)		
C. portenschlagiana	Blue-violet	Spring to summer
C. persicifolia	Lilac blue, white	Summer
C. poscharskyana	Pale blue	Summer to fall
Gentiana (gentian)		
G. acaulis (stemless gentian)	Sky blue	Late spring
G. septemfida (crested gentian)	Dark blue	Summer
G. andrewsii (closed gentian)	Porcelain blue	Fall
Hemerocallis (daylily)		
H. 'Stella d'Oro'	Golden yellow	Late spring to fall
H. 'Nanuet'	Sunset red	Summer
H. 'Lacy Queen'	Rose-peach	Late summer to fall
Scabiosa (pincushion flower)		
S. 'Butterfly Blue'	Lavender blue	Spring to fall
S. caucasica 'Fama'	Bright blue	Summer
Sedum (stonecrop)		
S. acre (golden-carpet)	Sun yellow	Spring
S. spectabile (showy stonecrop)	Rose-pink	Late summer
S. 'Autumn Joy'	Antique red	Fall
Veronica (speedwell)		
V. 'Goodness Grows'	Navy blue	Spring to fall
V. austriaca ssp. *teucrium*		
'Crater Lake Blue'	Porcelain blue	Summer

widths above ground, while their varying root structures make the same accommodations below ground. You can use their timeless strategy in your garden to grow more plants in the same space, which not only increases your opportunities to watch new flowers in new colors appearing week after week and month after month, but also allows you to have blooms emerging at every level, from the soil surface to the tree canopy.

Such planting also makes for good design, as it enables you to unify the garden along the surface and from the ground up and capitalize on various plants' strengths and weaknesses. Try, for example, planting lavender, lamb's ears, or thyme under a shrub rose. Not only do the shorter plants thrive in the space beneath their tall companion, but they also help conceal the rose bush's leggy stems.

Underground, closely placed plants must also have compatible root systems (below) so that each plant has room to grow and get its share of water and soil nutrients. Be sure to group plants that have the same fertility, light, and moisture requirements. A good way to keep them all happy in a crowded situation, and get the best flowering performance, is by double digging the soil—loosening it to a depth of as much as 24 inches so that each plant gets the best possible start. ■

Compatible Root Systems

You can get a higher concentration of plants in the same space by combining different root systems that leave room for each other—for example, plants having broad, shallow root systems and plants with deeper-rooted ones. Tap-rooted columbine and tuberous anemone, with its shallow roots, can nestle close together. The iris's rhizomes and the yarrow's fibrous root clump, however, need more room; they will partner well with a deeply planted bulb, such as the allium. The list at right indicates the root systems of common flowers.

Plants by Root System

BULBS, CORMS, AND TUBERS

Dahlia (dahlia)

Liatris (gay-feather)

Lilium (lily)

Tulipa (tulip)

RHIZOMES

Iris (iris)

Mertensia ciliata (mountain bluebells)

TAPROOTS

Aquilegia canadensis (columbine)

Echinacea (purple coneflower)

Platycodon grandiflorus (balloon flower)

FIBROUS CROWNS

Alchemilla mollis (lady's-mantle)

Geranium (cranesbill)

Phlox paniculata (summer phlox)

FIBROUS CLUMPS

Achillea (yarrow)

Monarda (bee balm)

Physostegia virginiana (obedience)

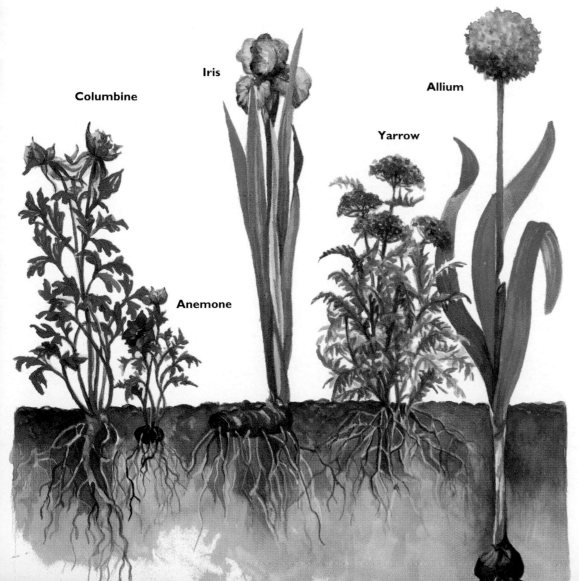

Columbine · Iris · Anemone · Yarrow · Allium

The Seasonal Garden Planner

A seasonal garden planner is a design tool that allows you to evaluate the combined visual effect of the plants you have selected for your garden. You can also use it to see at a glance which plants will be in bloom in each part of every season. Begin by photocopying the chart on the next page for a supply of blank forms.

List your plant selections in the left-hand column of a form, as shown below. Then shade in the space in the appropriate seasonal column for each plant's bloom time, using a colored pencil or marker that matches its flower color. This will give you a clear picture of the hues in your garden at any given time.

To make it easy to spot color gaps or imbalances in your plan, list plants chronologically according to their bloom time, but don't worry if you later remember others you want to add.

Helping the Design Mature

Throughout the growing season, be on the lookout for new plants that will enrich your three-season display. If your neighbors have an abundance of blooms at a time when your garden has mostly foliage, ask what they're growing. More than likely they'll be happy to share the name of the plant, and they may even offer to give you divisions or cuttings.

While perennials or shrubs are maturing, don't hesitate to fill in the spaces between them with annuals. Not only will the annuals provide much-needed bloom, they'll also shade the soil and help control weeds. ■

Tip

Take photographs of your garden at various times during the growing season and record the day and year of each photo. When you arrange them chronologically, you will have a unique guide to help with next year's design.

PLANT	SPRING			SUMMER			FALL			NOTES
	Early	Mid	Late	Early	Mid	Late	Early	Mid	Late	

The Season of Fresh Flowers

Spring begins in the garden weeks before the calendar makes it official. To a gardener who has impatiently waited out winter, a planting of the earliest bloomers—say, buttery yellow winter aconites and a flurry of snowdrops beneath star magnolias—is a welcome sight. Early flowers are usually low growing, but they stand out well against the bare ground of the garden. Soon they're joined by a wave of daffodils and then tulips, which in turn make good mates for emerging spring perennials such as phlox and brunnera. As the season progresses, azaleas, viburnums, and other shrubs add another layer of bloom, topped by flowering crab apples and serviceberry trees. The spring palette is a varied one, with plenty of white flowers, many blues and pastels, and enough vivid brights to add punch to any garden.

The Fresh Hues of Spring
A grass path in this Connecticut landscape leads past columbines at left, blue forget-me-nots, and billowing rhododendrons in a graceful arc of color and texture crowned by the white-flowering dogwood—an idyllic demonstration of the layering of spring flower colors.

Bulbs: Harbingers of Spring

Bulbs are of four types: corms, such as crocus; tubers, such as anemones; rhizomes, such as irises; and the familiar onionlike true bulbs, such as narcissus. Although they bloom throughout the growing year, their flowers especially dominate the early spring garden, getting a jump on the season by taking advantage of the increasing length of sunlight to burst into bloom before overhanging trees and shrubs fill out with foliage. After their flowers fade, they manufacture and store nutrients for next year's growth and then revert to a dormant state.

Bulbs of the Spring Season

Small bulbs, collectively called the minor bulbs, are the first to bloom. They include such favorites as multicolored crocuses, bluish white *Puschkinia*, yellow *Eranthis* (winter aconite), and pure-white *Galanthus* (snowdrop)—all of which appear in the waning months of winter. Wild woodland spring bulbs include pink hardy cyclamen, *Arisaema triphyllum* (Jack-in-the-pulpit), *Trillium* (wake-robin), and brown-speckled *Erythronium* (trout lily). Later in spring you can see alliums, *Convallaria* (lily-of-the-valley), and anemones in red, blue, and pink. Once established, these bulbs reseed freely and thrive with little care, carpeting the ground with blooms.

Later-blooming minor bulbs make superb partners with daffodils and tulips, perennials, annuals, and biennials, and grow comfortably under spring-blooming shrubs and trees. For instance, blue *Anemone blanda* (Grecian windflower) makes a complementary pairing with miniature *Narcissus* 'Minnow' or 'Tête-à-Tête' (daffodil). *Scilla siberica* (Siberian squill) can look like a pool of blue encircling the yellow-flowering *Cornus mas* (cornelian cherry).

Some spring bulbs are so versatile that they have become indispensable. Daffodils bloom from early to late spring in sunny yellows, oranges, and creamy whites, with accents of pink, orange, and green. Extend their bloom time by choosing cultivars that flower in each part of the season, and choose species of different heights. Cluster these bulbs closely, letting a few stray ones trail off at the edges of the grouping for a natural look. Plant them in flower beds, in open lawn that can wait until late spring for its first mowing, or in woodland gardens. In smaller gardens, interplant daffodils with minor bulbs under peonies and phlox.

Low-Growing Companions

Diminutive bulbs with their small flowers, as in the list at right below, make excellent companions for taller daffodils and tulips, and they all naturalize well. For a drift of color, plant them in groups. Many of these lovely bulbs self-sow readily, or can be propagated by division once they are established. After they finish flowering, plant shallow-rooted annuals among them to conceal their ripening foliage. A number of these plants, including several that are North American wildflowers, are endangered in their native habitats as a result of overcollecting. Never dig up wild plants to transplant to the garden. Specialty bulb catalog mailers and wildflower nurseries that are known for being environmentally responsible are the best sources for the plants listed here.

▼ *Crocuses, winter aconites, and snowdrops emerge through the previous year's fallen leaves to create the first bright spots of early spring.*

Arisaema triphyllum
(Jack-in-the-pulpit)

Chionodoxa luciliae
(glory-of-the-snow)

Crocus tomasinianus
(crocus)

Cyclamen hederifolium
(baby cyclamen)

Eranthis hyemalis
(winter aconite)

Fritillaria meleagris
(checkered lily)

Galanthus nivalis
(common snowdrop)

Hyacinthoides hispanica
(Spanish bluebell)

Puschkinia scilloides
(striped squill)

Scilla siberica
(Siberian squill)

Trillium grandiflorum
(white wake-robin)

Tulips, another essential spring bulb, vary greatly in hue—from pastels to hot colors to dramatic near-black—and can play a role in any spring color scheme. Their overlapping bloom times make it possible to enjoy their eye-catching forms—from pointed lily-flowered types to the extravagant parrots—in your garden from early spring until early summer. Plant them in stately clusters of a dozen or more, to stand informally with daffodils or *Muscari* (grape hyacinth), or to punctuate drifts of low-growing perennials such as *Phlox subulata* (moss pink), *Cerastium tomentosum* (snow-in-summer), or *Aurinia* (basket-of-gold). Or plant a mass of the same type and color of tulip for an elegant formal effect.

Because bulb plants exist above ground only temporarily, it is essential to plan for the time when they will retreat and leave bare spots in the garden. Situate them in drifts between the crowns of later-blooming perennials such as columbines and hardy geraniums, or between biennials like *Hesperis matronalis* (dame's rocket) or *Digitalis* (foxglove). Pansies and violets, for example, look lovely next to elfin 'Jack Snipe' or 'Hoop Petticoat' daffodils.

Spread drifts of early-booming bulbs under flowering azaleas, *Cercis canadensis* (redbud), and dogwoods so that the trees' new blooms deflect attention from the bulbs' withering foliage. Place brilliantly colored crocus or stately *Fritillaria imperialis* (crown imperial) amid ground covers like *Lamium* (dead nettle) or *Vinca* (periwinkle) so that the ground will not be bare after they disappear. A ground cover also keeps the bulbs' blossoms clean of splashing mud from spring rains. ∎

Layering Bulbs for a Succession of Bloom

Bulbs' compact root structures allow them to be tightly grouped, increasing the chance for one or another to be in bloom at any time. The crocus and anemone at right nestle close to an iris rhizome. The daffodil at center and the lily at left also can grow in tight quarters by virtue of their greater planting depths.

Cultivating Spring Bulbs

Spring-blooming bulbs are a varied group that will thrive in rich soil with ample spring moisture. Most are native to regions where the soil dries out in summer, and so a summer dry spell triggers them to become dormant. They require relatively little care and maintenance once they are put into the ground in the fall, provided some attention is paid to getting them planted right. Timing is important, as is giving the bulbs the right soil and nutrients. After they have bloomed, a simple maintenance regime will keep them healthy and ready to flower again each spring.

Tulips are especially particular about their growing conditions if they are to rebloom the next year. They need a cold spell of at least two months in winter in soil with good drainage, followed by ample sun and moisture in the spring and a dry summer dormancy. Even under the best of conditions, hybrid tulip bulbs do not readily come back for a second year of flowering, but you can successfully perennialize them in Zones 3 to 7 if you plant them 8 to 10 inches deep in loamy soil. On the other hand, species tulips such as *Tulipa kaufmanniana, T. fosterana*, and *T. greigii* will bloom year after year.

Minor bulbs such as snowdrops are apt to reseed and reappear wherever the conditions are hospitable. Caring for them is simple: A natural mulch of fallen leaves will enrich the soil and protect the plants from extreme cold. In formal garden settings, an annual top dressing of compost will keep them healthy.

Is there a way to keep tulip blooms in my garden longer?

The deeper you plant a tulip bulb, the later it will flower. Thus, you can have two rounds of bloom from the same variety. Plant a batch 6 to 8 inches deep. Plant another batch 4 inches deep. Then, in spring, about the time the first round fades, a second wave of bloom will grace your garden.

Planting Your Bulbs

Spring-blooming bulbs are planted in the fall to give them their required cold period through the winter, which prepares them to bloom when the soil temperature rises in the spring. You can order spring-flowering bulbs from catalogues for mailing at the end of summer, and from garden centers and nurseries beginning in August. Order early to assure yourself of the best selection. Until you are ready to plant, store them in a cool place either packed in fresh sawdust or moist peat, or simply in a paper bag. If you're planting late in the fall, try soaking the bulbs for 24 hours beforehand to help them root faster—an important consideration in the North, where a cold snap may unexpectedly freeze the ground overnight.

The general rule for planting most bulbs is to bury them three times as deep as the bulb is high to ensure that they bloom on time and are not damaged by freezing. Exceptions are bearded iris and *Lilium candidum* (Madonna lily). Plant bearded iris with the top half of the rhizome showing; plant Madonna lily bulbs just below the soil surface. Take care not to damage existing plantings as you dig. At planting time, mix a 9-9-6–type fertilizer into the soil at the rate recommended on the package, and then top dress with the same formula when the foliage emerges in the spring.

Tulip and crocus bulbs are particularly delectable to burrowing animals such as squirrels, voles, and mice. Protect them by lining the planting holes with sharp-edged gravel or hardware cloth, or plant the bulbs in upright tin cans open at both ends. Interplanting bad tasting daffodils with tulips and snowdrops with crocuses can also reduce damage.

After the Flowers Fade

When the bulbs have finished blooming, they begin to set seed and to absorb energy through their foliage to store nutrients for survival during dormancy. Snip off the heads of daffodils and hybrid tulips so that the bulbs' energy can go into food storage rather than making seeds; any seedling they produce would likely be inferior anyway. But allow the seedheads to develop on the minor bulbs, the wild forms of tulips and daffodils, and woodland bulbs such as trout lilies. These eventually will self-sow to make lovely drifts of color.

Resist the temptation to tie up or cut off the bulbs' ripening foliage until it has become yellow and the plant is no longer effectively photosynthesizing. At that point, gently tug the leaves out of the soil, or clip them off. Then top-dress the clumps with rich compost to ensure an adequate supply of nutrients to keep bulbs thriving. ■

Grouping Bulbs for Dazzling Color

Tulips, hyacinths, and daffodils are clustered with pansies in this garden in the Northeast to create complementary pockets of bloom. Deadheading such bulbs after their flowers fade will encourage healthier blooms the following spring.

Using Annuals to Fill the Gaps

Annuals are ideal for a splash of color when bulbs have faded. Their fibrous roots don't interfere with the bulbs, and their foliage isn't as dense as that of many perennials, so the bulb leaves have room to mature.

Cynoglossum amabile (Chinese forget-me-not), shown here, makes an excellent bulb companion. It blooms fast from seed sown in fall or very early spring, and keeps flowering after bulbs have faded. 'Mystery Rose' adds a new twist to the sky-blue flowers of the species. The shorter 'Avalanche' has pure white blossoms. All three are perfect for an attractive pastel color scheme.

Blue, purple, pink, or white *Lobelia erinus* (edging lobelia) is a good choice for later-spring gardens. Start it indoors or buy it in bloom. Plant while bulbs are still in flower, and its solid carpet of color will distract the eye when the bulbs begin to flag.

In earliest spring, when there is still a possibility of a cold snap, interplant with hardy annuals from the list at right.

Cold-tolerant annuals

Antirrhinum majus (snapdragon)

Centaurea cyanus (cornflower)

Clarkia concinna (red-ribbons)

Eschscholzia californica (California poppy)

Lobularia maritima (sweet alyssum)

Papaver rhoeas (corn poppy)

Viola x *wittrockiana* (pansy)

▼ *Chinese forget-me-nots flowering amid tulips*

The Perennials of Spring

The earliest spring perennials, such as *Helleborus* (hellebore) and *Pulmonaria* (lungwort), appear at the same time as the first of the bulbs and flowering shrubs and trees. At this stage, later-blooming perennials—peonies and *Dianthus* (pink), for instance—are just emerging as small crowns. As interplanted bulb blooms begin to fade, the emerging foliage of the perennials will fill the space the bulbs are vacating. Their flowers rise to the garden's middle level, picking up tints from shrubs and trees in the garden's higher layers.

Companions for Perennials

You can create enchanting combinations of spring bulbs and perennials in either sun or shade. In a lightly shaded spot, try a mix of minor bulbs—snowdrops and Greigii tulips, for example—with pinkish early-blooming *Helleborus orientalis* (Lenten rose), *Primula* (primrose) in various colors, and pink and blue lungworts. In a woodland, plant native *Mertensia virginica* (Virginia bluebells) and trillium with *Aquilegia* (columbine), *Uvularia* (merrybells), and *Dicentra* (bleeding heart). The upright form of tulips in a rock garden contrasts well with cascades of phlox and *Arabis* (rock cress). For formal beds and borders, combine neat arrangements of tulips and daffodils with the looser forms of columbines, bleeding hearts, and *Doronicum* (leopard's bane).

Underplant shrubs and flowering trees with spring perennials. For example, for a pink color theme, plant rosy moss pink or early *Astilbe japonica* 'Europa' under deep pink azaleas or a 'Cherokee Chief' dogwood. Or place clusters of yellow leopard's bane or *Aurinia saxatilis* (basket-of-gold) near a *Hamamelis* (witch hazel) to pick up the color of its golden, threadlike blossoms.

Late-Spring Perennials

While the earliest perennials bloom low to the ground, later-blooming ones give the garden more stature and deeper color as the weather warms. Rich pinks may appear, such as pink *Dicentra eximia* (wild bleeding heart), peonies, and 'Mrs. Perry' Oriental poppies. The deep purples of *Salvia* (sage), *Baptisia* (false indigo), *Brunnera*, and *Erigeron* 'Azure Fairy' (fleabane) also can enrich the soft palette of late spring.

Look for contrasting forms and flowers. Play off the feathery foliage and relaxed habit of bleeding heart with a sturdy, shiny-leaved plant like *Bergenia*, for instance. Or juxtapose the pink buds and dangling blue bells of *Mertensia virginica* with the similar-colored flowers of *Campanula* (bellflower) or same-shaped flowers of lungwort.

The second wave of spring bloom carries the garden from spring into summer. You may find it necessary to curb the burgeoning foliage of this explosion of growth to ensure that the garden looks as good in summer as it does in spring. Thin out stems and stake tall or top-heavy stems to make sure they don't flop early in the season, or else they may suffocate or stunt the flowers that are due to succeed them. ∎

The Ever-Blooming Garden

Old-fashioned foxgloves tower regally in **spring** over bright white daisies in this garden in the Northeast. The biennial foxgloves, with their bell-shaped blooms and rosettes of slightly crinkled leaves, are reminiscent of a cottage garden. While their pinks and lavenders are nicely echoed in the flowers behind them, the fluffy peonies and rhododendrons offer a distinct contrast in texture, an important garden design element. When the foxgloves fade, their place will be taken by stately lilies, whose sharp, shiny leaves will add foliage texture in early **summer**. The rhododendrons will lose their blossoms, but their glossy leaves will become a perfect backdrop for late-summer blooms in the three-season garden. The tree, adding a vertical element, offers some shade for part of the day—some hours of coolness are essential for both the foxgloves and the rhododendrons. In the **fall**, annuals will provide color until frost, supplemented by lavender and purple chrysanthemums.

Earliest-Blooming Spring Perennials

Spring perennials begin with pale pastel blooms on diminutive plants, followed by a taller group with richer colors. White flowers can be used to set off the pinks, blues, purples, and yellows.

PLANT	FLOWER COLOR	HEIGHT	SCENT	ZONES	LIGHT
Arabis caucasica (wall rock cress)	pink/white	6-12 inches	medium	3-7	full sun
Aurinia saxatilis (basket-of-gold)	yellow	9-12 inches	none	3-7	full sun
Doronicum orientalis (leopard's bane)	yellow	18-24 inches	none	4-7	sun/part shade
Helleborus orientalis (Lenten rose)	purple/pink/cream	15-18 inches	none	4-9	part/full shade
Iberis sempervirens (candytuft)	white	6-12 inches	none	3-9	full sun
Primula (primrose)	pink/red/white/yellow	12-24 inches	medium	3-8	part/full shade
Pulmonaria (lungwort)	blue/pink	12 inches	none	3-7	part/full shade
Sanguinaria canadensis (bloodroot)	white	6-12 inches	none	3-8	part shade
Viola odorata (sweet violet)	deep violet/rose/white	6-8 inches	strong	5-8	part shade

▲ SUMMER

▲ FALL

Taking Care of Spring Perennials

Regardless of how well prepared the soil, perennials in a closely planted three-season garden will need a boost of nutrients to keep them healthy, blooming well, and pest-free during the peak demand time in spring, when they are growing fast. They require three key elements—nitrogen for good growth and healthy green leaves, phosphorous to stimulate flowering, and potassium to encourage strong root systems—as well as smaller amounts of other nutrients such as calcium, iron, magnesium, and sulfur. These substances also stimulate the growth of beneficial soil bacteria and fungi that help to break down organic matter so that a plant can more readily absorb its nutrients.

The simplest way to fertilize is organically, by top-dressing the soil in spring and fall with a 2-inch layer of a nutrient-rich mulch, such as compost. Spread the mulch around the plants but keep it away from plant crowns and stems to prevent rot. For a richer diet, spread a 1-inch layer of well-rotted manure or worm castings, and top that with a layer of shredded bark.

Artificial fertilizers are convenient to use and provide specific nutrients in controlled amounts. Fertilizer with a 10-10-10 nutrient reading is generally the best for flowers. Avoid fertilizers that have a preponderance of one nutrient, such as nitrogen, which encourages lush foliage growth at the expense of sturdiness and flowering.

Encapsulated, slow-release artificial fertilizers are a two-edged sword. They release their contents gradually, ensuring that your plants get a steady dose of nutrients over time and taking some of the guesswork out of a regular feeding regime. But they may continue to deliver certain nutrients to a plant unnecessarily—nitrogen, for example, late in the season, which stimulates tender new growth that can be damaged by cold. Avoid the problem by cutting off the supply of slow-release fertilizer after mid-summer.

Another way to apply fertilizer is to pour a diluted nutrient solution over and around your plants, feeding them through the foliage as well as through the root system. This is a good way to feed container plants and to give small gardens a quick nutrient boost.

You can buy concentrated liquid fertilizer solutions, such as the common organic fertilizer known as fish emulsion. Or you can make a well-balanced liquid food easily, if somewhat messily, by soaking a burlap bag filled with manure in a basin of water. The resulting manure tea can be poured directly onto and around your plants. ∎

A Gallery of Supports

Perennials to Carry Spring into Summer

Aruncus dioicus (goatsbeard)

Campanula portenschlagiana (Dalmatian bellflower)

Dianthus (pink)

Digitalis (foxglove)

Geranium (cranesbill)

Iris sibirica (Siberian iris)

Nepeta mussinii (Persian catmint)

Paeonia (peony)

Thalictrum (meadow rue)

After the initial spurt of spring bloom, it is time to support later-blooming plants. Plan ahead—once a plant looks like it needs support, it's usually too late to provide it effectively. The best-designed supports are those that gently but firmly keep your plants upright as they grow, without being noticeable.

Cages and Hoops
These supports are best for peonies, phlox, and other weak-stemmed plants with heavy flower heads. Place them over the plants when the stems are less than a foot high so that as the stems elongate they will grow through the cage, as shown in the inset. Guide into place any errant stems. Once the plant foliage has thickened, you will not see the support.

A Gallery of Mulches

The right mulch properly applied can reduce weeds, retain moisture, cool the soil, and keep dirt off plants. It also visually ties together all the parts of a bed or border.

Bark and Wood Chips
Re-create a woodland setting for a planting of deciduous trees and shrubs with bark nuggets or wood chips.

Cocoa Hulls
Dark-colored cocoa hulls absorb the sun's heat and provide warmth for heat-loving plants growing in rich soil.

Shredded Bark
Shredded bark mulch is less dense than bark nuggets or wood chips, but breaks down faster and must be replenished more often.

Rock Chips
The ability of stone to absorb and retain heat makes rock chips a great choice around cacti and succulents, and for rock gardens.

Pine Needles
These help maintain the proper soil pH for acid-loving evergreens and conifers, while adding a silky coat of brown color to the border.

Buckwheat Hulls
These provide a neat appearance in a bed of plants requiring organic, rich soil that retains moisture.

Twigs
Bushy twigs make ideal supports for broad, floppy plants such as yarrows and asters. Use finely branched stems pruned from fruit trees or shrubs. In early spring, push the twigs into the ground all around the plant, as shown in the inset, and prop up the floppy stems in a decorative manner as they grow. This technique also works for delicate vines such as sweet pea, shown below.

Stakes and Loops
These are designed to support individual tall stems, such as those of delphiniums, as shown above. Place a stake firmly in the ground next to the stem. Be careful not to damage the root system or pierce the bulb; some gardeners install the stake at planting time to avoid such damage.

Use soft cord or yarn to attach single stems or a small cluster of stems to the stake, as shown in the inset, continuing to tie the stems higher along the stake as they grow. Do not tie too tightly, or a stem may snap in the wind or rain. Plastic-coated metal stakes with a loop at the top are an easy-to-use alternative.

The Ground Covers of Spring

Ground covers unify the lowest layer of the garden with a continuous sweep of flowers or foliage, and they act as a living mulch to keep the soil cool and weed free and retain moisture. They are easy to install and maintain. A large expanse of ground cover is such a strong statement that you could plan a spring color scheme around a single type, such as a lilac-blue carpet of *Vinca* 'Bowles Variety', or a spread of white, pink, or lavender moss pink. Annual edging lobelia, available in violet-blue, rose, and white, makes an excellent flowering ground cover in the spring garden, as it blooms best in cool weather. It goes well with honey-scented *Lobularia maritima* (sweet alyssum), another cool-weather annual ground cover.

Combining Ground Covers with Other Plants

Use ground covers as the bottom tier or "floor" to coordinate and unify flower color in the rest of the garden. For example, plant shade-tolerant *Chrysogonum virginianum* (golden star) or violets beneath small shrubs or trees such as *Salix discolor* (pussy willow), yellow-flowering cornelian cherry, or white double-flowered *Prunus mume* 'Alboplena' (Japanese apricot). In sunny areas, use masses of rosy purple *Aubrietta deltoidea* (rock cress) or *Iberis sempervirens* (candytuft) to edge beds and to complement pink or red tulips, and blue *Brunnera macrophylla* (Siberian bugloss) at the back of a border. Double the amount of bloom in the same space by planting clumps of daffodils, minor bulbs, and species tulips in concert with a low-growing, spring-blooming ground cover such as coppery-leafed *Ajuga* 'Catlin's Giant' (bugleweed), moss pink, or vinca.

Planting and Maintaining Ground Covers

Mass planting ground covers can become expensive, so look for plants sold as inexpensive plugs. A plug is a small, young plant sold in a plastic six- or 12-pack, the way many annuals are sold. Since ground covers grow quickly, you do not need larger plants.

Spacing of the plugs will depend on the ultimate size of the plant and the speed with which you want to cover the ground. The usual planting scheme for plugs is a rough grid; use 18-inch spacing for particularly fast-spreading plants such as bugleweed, *Tiarella cordifolia* 'Slick Rock' (foamflower), and *Lamium maculatum* 'Pink Pewter' (spotted dead nettle). Slower growers like *Epimedium* (barrenwort) are best planted a foot apart. Plant closer together if you want a solid cover in a hurry.

Wherever they meet, lawns and ground covers are inclined to grow together. The simplest way to keep each in its place is

Tip

To save time snipping dead stems and leaves of ground covers like lilyturf, cut or shear the entire plant to the ground. This makes room for new spring growth. In addition, it allows you to enjoy the new flowers undistracted by dead or dying foliage.

to chop into the soil at the boundary with a sharp spade, cutting a wedge that is angled away from the lawn. A border of stones or bricks will hold back all but the most rampant growers. Metal or plastic edging takes up less space and is also a deterrent to aggressively spreading ground covers.

A Dense Ground Cover for Low Maintenance

Densely established ground covers are easy-care plants that keep weeds to a minimum. Cut back and tidy up herbaceous ground covers in the fall or spring much as you would do with perennials in a garden bed. Evergreen ground covers are best left until spring, so that their winter foliage shows to best advantage. Shrubby ground covers will need occasional pruning to rein in exuberant growth or to remove damaged stems. If fall leaves threaten to smother your ground covers, protect them by temporarily roofing them over with a wide swath of plastic bird netting before the leaves drop; when the trees are bare, remove the netting and leaves together. ■

What are good three-season companions for vinca in partial sun?

Try *Dicentra eximia* (wild bleeding heart), *Campanula persicifolia* (peachleaf bellflower), and *Hemerocallis* 'Stella d'Oro' (daylily).

Best Spring-Blooming Ground Covers

Ajuga repens
(bugleweed)

Epimedium grandiflorum
(bishop's hat)

Galium odoratum
(sweet woodruff)

Lamium maculatum
(spotted dead nettle)

Phlox subulata
(moss pink)

Rhododendron pemakoense
(Pemako rhododendron)

Thymus serphyllum
(lemon thyme)

Tiarella cordifolia
(foamflower)

Vinca minor
(common periwinkle)

Color Coordination
Late-blooming single tulips take their place over a mass of low-growing moss pinks, whose starry flowers pick up the tulips' rosy hue in this Pipersville, Pennsylvania, garden. Earlier-blooming purple and lavender pansies pop through the floral carpet.

Spring-Blooming Shrubs and Vines

Shrubs and vines add beauty and structure to the spring garden. The naked branches of some deciduous shrubs give the first sign of seasonal change in late winter, as their buds swell and burst open into silvery pussy willow catkins or dainty white clusters of serviceberry flowers. Without foliage, the spring floral display of shrubs is even more eye-catching. The blossoms of many shrubs and vines, such as *Viburnum* x *carlcephalum* (fragrant viburnum) and *Gelsemium sempervirens* (Carolina jessamine), also add wonderful aroma to the garden, and those with tubular flowers, such as *Weigela*, attract hummingbirds.

Vines carry blooms to an even higher level in the spring garden. They can stand alone on trellises as structural elements, or climb naturally through shrubs and up trees, providing vertical color accents in spaces too tight for shrubs. Spring-blooming vines, in colors from the pastel of wisteria to the vivid red of *Lonicera sempervirens* (trumpet honeysuckle), usually appear at the top of a woody main stem, forming a crown of flowers that can tumble over a shrub or cascade across an arbor.

Shrubs are natural companions to the spring bulbs, annuals, and perennials that spread at their feet, filling out the middle level in the garden—from 3 to 15 feet. Their intermediary presence allows you to use them to set the spring color theme, or as companions to more prominent plants. The chart at right can help you plan effective combinations.

Shrubs and Vines in the Three-Season Garden

Shade-tolerant shrubs such as *Calycanthus* (Carolina allspice) and rhododendron are particularly lovely when planted beneath tall canopy trees, where their presence helps to visually pull the garden into a comfortable scale. Tall shrubs such as *Chionanthus* (fringe tree) and *Enkianthus* also combine with smaller flowering shrub specimens like *Spiraea* and *Daphne*, which in turn can be underplanted with ground covers.

Vines growing up and through shrubs and trees will embellish existing flowering combinations or carry a later-blooming shrub or tree through to its flowering time. For instance, try growing early-blooming white *Clematis montana* (anemone clematis) up into the branches of a summer-blooming *Koelreuteria* (golden-rain tree). ■

Tropical Delight
The purple blossoms of Japanese wisteria raise the color stakes to new heights against cymbidium orchids and the lone orange flower of the aloe in spring in this southern California garden.

Spring-Blooming Shrubs and Vines

Shrubs can be used as accents for both flowers and foliage, but a single species will also serve as a hedge or a flowering backdrop for other flowers. In the small garden, you can use a space-saving vine for background interest.

DECIDUOUS SHRUBS	BLOOM TIME	FLOWER COLOR	HEIGHT	ZONES
Aesculus parviflora (buckeye)	late	white	8-12 feet	3-7
Aronia (chokeberry)	mid-season	red/white	1½-12 feet	4-9
Calycanthus floridus (Carolina allspice)	mid-season	red	6-9 feet	4-9
Chaenomeles japonica (lesser flowering quince)	mid-season	pink/red/white	1-3 feet	4-8
Chionanthus virginicus (old-man's-beard)	late	white	12-30 feet	3-9
Corylopsis (winter hazel)	early	yellow	4-15 feet	5-8
Deutzia (deutzia)	late	white/yellow	2-5 feet	4-8
Enkianthus campanulatus (enkianthus)	mid-season	pink/red	6-30 feet	4-8
Forsythia (forsythia)	early	yellow	1-10 feet	5-8
Fothergilla gardenii (witch alder)	mid-season	white	2-3 feet	4-8
Philadelphus (mock orange)	late	white	4-9 feet	4-8
Prinsepia sinensis (cherry prinsepia)	early	pale yellow	to 10 feet	3-7
Prunus tomentosa (Nanking cherry)	early	white	6-10 feet	3-9
Rhododendron (rhododendron, azalea)	early to late	variable	1-30 feet	4-9
Spiraea (spirea)	early and late	white	3-5 feet	3-8
Styrax (snowbell)	late	white	to 30 feet	5-8
Syringa meyeri (lilac)	mid-season	purple	4-8 feet	3-8
Viburnum (viburnum)	early to mid-season	white	6-20 feet	4-8
Weigela florida (weigela)	mid-season	pink/red/white	4-9 feet	4-9

DECIDUOUS VINES	BLOOM TIME	FLOWER COLOR	HEIGHT	ZONES
Clematis montana (anemone clematis)	early to mid-season	pink/white	to 20 feet	5-8
Lonicera sempervirens (trumpet honeysuckle)	mid-season	orange	to 20 feet	4-9
Wisteria (wisteria)	mid-season	blue/white	10-50 feet	4-9

EVERGREEN SHRUBS	BLOOM TIME	FLOWER COLOR	HEIGHT	ZONES
Camellia (camellia)	early to mid-season	pink/red/white	6-25 feet	6-10
Daphne (daphne)	early to mid-season	pink/white	3-5 feet	4-9
Kalmia latifolia (mountain laurel)	late	pink/white	2-15 feet	4-9
Leucothoe fontanesiana (drooping leucothoe)	late	white	2-6 feet	4-8
Pieris japonica (lily-of-the-valley bush)	early	pink/white	2-12 feet	4-8
Raphiolepis indica (Indian hawthorn)	early	pink/white	3-6 feet	8-10

EVERGREEN VINES	BLOOM TIME	FLOWER COLOR	HEIGHT	ZONES
Bignonia capreolata (cross vine)	late	orange/red	30-50 feet	6-9
Gelsemium sempervirens (Carolina jessamine)	early to mid-season	yellow	to 20 feet	6-9

The Trees of Spring

The early-spring garden boasts the largest and most diverse selection of flowering trees of any season. Early-flowering trees bring the garden's canopy into glorious color. Like spring-blooming shrubs, many trees bloom before their own leaves emerge, so the flowers show to full advantage on bare stems, and the trees seem cloaked with blooms.

The smaller flowering trees, such as dogwoods and redbuds, form a layer known as the understory to the taller shade tree canopy. Because these understory trees are leafless early in the season, they not only display their own blossoms gloriously, but also allow ample sun to reach spring-flowering bulbs and perennials beneath them. As the season progresses and they leaf

out, the shade they cast creates a cool, moist microclimate that tempers the heat in the rest of the garden and shelters shade-loving plants of summer.

Selecting the Right Tree

When you are choosing spring-flowering trees, think about their overall effect on the garden. A tree should have a deep-growing root system that will not compete with the roots of smaller, frailer plants. Its leaf canopy should not be so thick that its shade will prevent the plants under it from blooming. Note also what it will do the rest of the year. A flowering tree may produce fleshy fruit or messy seedpods that will prove more of a nuisance than its two weeks of flowers are worth,

Selected Spring-Flowering Trees

DECIDUOUS	BLOOM TIME	FLOWER COLOR	FALL COLOR	FRUIT COLOR
Aesculus pavia (red buckeye)	late	red	orange/yellow/red	brown
Amelanchier x *grandiflora* (serviceberry)	mid-season	white	orange-red	purple-red
Asimina triloba (pawpaw)	mid-season	purple	yellow	brown-yellow
Cercis canadensis (redbud)	early	pink-purple	yellow	inconspicuous
Cladrastis lutea (yellowwood)	late	white	yellow	inconspicuous
Cornus (dogwood)	early	pink/white	purple/red	red
Crataegus (hawthorn)	mid-season/late	white/pink	purple/red	red
Davidia involucrata (dove tree)	late	white	none	inconspicuous
Halesia carolina (Carolina silverbell)	early	pink/white	yellow	green
Magnolia (magnolia)	early/mid-season	pink/purple/white	yellow	red
Malus (crab apple)	mid-season	pink/white	red/yellow	red/yellow
Prunus (cherry)	early	pink/white	red/yellow	black/red
Sorbus alnifolia (Korean mountain ash)	mid-season	white	red/yellow	orange/red
Styrax japonicus (Japanese snowbell)	late	white	none	inconspicuous
Syringa reticulata (Japanese tree lilac)	late	white	greenish yellow	inconspicuous
Viburnum prunifolium (black haw)	late	white	red	blue-black
EVERGREEN				
Acacia (acacia)	early	yellow	none	tan
Arbutus unedo (strawberry tree)	early	white	none	orange-red
Magnolia grandiflora (southern magnolia)	late	white	none	red
Rhododendron arboreum (tree rhododendron)	late	scarlet	none	inconspicuous

should you place it so that it overhangs a patio or a driveway.

Because a flowering tree is large and permanent compared to most other garden plants, its attributes can easily dominate other aspects of the garden. The color of its copious flowers in spring may virtually dictate the color theme of the spring garden around it. Later, its foliage texture, fall leaf color, and ornamental fruit will have something to say about the color themes of those seasons. So when you choose a spring-blooming tree, be sure you are familiar with its form in winter, when it is devoid of leaves, the texture of those leaves once they emerge, their fall color, and what ornamental fruit it produces, if any .

Most spring-flowering trees bloom in pastel shades of pink

or yellow, or in white. These hues call for a cool color theme in the garden. For a pink composition you could, for example, underplant a pink 'San Jose' magnolia with 'Pink Paradise' daffodils. Or you could create a white theme, with a white-flowered *Halesia carolina* (silverbell) over a carpet of pastel blue or pink Virginia bluebells, or combine a colorful grove of white-flowered *Sorbus* (mountain ash) and pink redbuds with an underplanting of shell-pink azaleas and clusters of 'Imperial Antique Pink' pansies in a mix of soft watercolor shades. Or use the pure snowy whiteness of a *Malus* 'Fuji' (crab apple) as a cool counterpoint to sweeps of red, orange, and nearly-black tulips, fronted by vivid 'Spanish Sun' pansies and orange 'Gold Dust' Exbury azaleas. ∎

Pruning an Ornamental Fruit Tree

Flower bud formation results from a delicate balance of carbohydrates and nitrogen. Leaves need light to make carbohydrates, which is why flowers abound at the ends of branches but are sparse near the center of the tree. Pruning limbs from the tree's center admits light to this area, allowing more flower buds to form. Maintain the health of the tree by removing any damaged, diseased, or weak branches. Limbs that cross other limbs, or ones that compromise the appearance of the tree also should be removed. Ornamental fruit trees that have not been pruned for many years may need 30 to 50 percent of their branches removed to return them to health. Once corrective pruning has been done, the same tree can be maintained by removing 5 to 10 percent of its limbs annually.

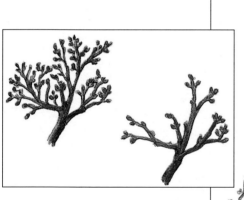

Flower Buds
Ornamental fruit trees such as this crabapple that have not been pruned properly can produce too many flower buds. The resulting crowded display of blossoms stresses the tree, reducing flowering in subsequent years. In late winter thin these crowded terminal branches by 30 to 50 percent. This will ensure a lovely display of flowers that does not stress the tree.

Watersprouts
Watersprouts are fast-growing non-flowering shoots that deplete a tree's reserve of nutrients. Remove one-third of these shoots each year when the tree is dormant to maintain its vigor throughout the year.

Garden Pointers

Winter weeds, which germinate in fall and grow through winter, can compete with newly planted perennial and annual seedlings, as well as self-sown annuals. To control weeds, pull them on a warm day in early spring, before they have set seed for next year's crop.

To protect plants from spring cold snaps, put off cleaning up the garden and removing winter mulch until after the danger of freezing weather has passed.

Harden off seedlings gradually before transplanting, to reduce stress and improve their performance. Set them in a protected spot outdoors for increasing amounts of time each day for a week, then plant in the garden.

Don't work the soil until it is dry enough to crumble; working wet spring soil will compact it, destroying tilth.

The Chores of Spring

Bulbs

◆ Top-dress bulb plantings with compost or a balanced fertilizer before they start to emerge from the ground.

◆ Deadhead bulbs as flowers fade, but let the foliage ripen. Cut back spent tulip flowers to the first stem leaf.

◆ Order summer bulbs or pick them up at the nursery. Plant lily bulbs as soon as they arrive.

◆ Plant summer bulbs in late spring. Hold tender species, such as caladiums, until the soil has warmed and the danger of frost has passed.

Perennials

◆ Remove winter mulch or evergreen boughs.

◆ Pull any winter weeds or any perennial weeds missed in the fall.

◆ Cut down all herbaceous plants left standing over the winter.

◆ Top-dress beds with compost, well-rotted manure, or shredded leaves after the soil warms up. Add fertilizers according to soil-test recommendations.

◆ Put supports in place before plants grow too tall (see pages 46-47).

◆ Remove leaves of spring-flowering plants as they yellow.

◆ Divide summer- and fall-blooming plants (see pages 43-44).

Annuals

◆ Plant hardy annuals such as pansies in mid-spring, when frosts are easing.

◆ Plant tender annuals such as impatiens and petunias after danger of frost has passed and the soil has warmed.

◆ After seedlings have been planted outside, sterilize seed flats with a 9:1 solution of water and bleach, then store.

Ground Covers

◆ Shear winter-burned ground covers to the ground before growth begins (see page 48).

◆ Cut turf and ornamental grasses to 3 or 4 inches.

◆ Top-dress beds with compost or rotted manure (see pages 46-47).

◆ Shear early bloomers, such as candytuft, after flowering to promote reblooming (see page 48).

Pruning Wisteria

Before the plants flower in spring remove suckers and unwanted branches from main stem with a pair of sharp pruning shears (right). One month after flowering, prune lateral branches to three plump buds near the stem or at the base of a strong branch (far right).

Young wisteria plants should be pruned to a single whip, which is then trained around a strong support. When the vine reaches the top of the support it can be pruned as described at left.

Shrubs and Vines

- In late winter, before growth begins, thin crowded branches and remove several of the oldest stems on late-blooming shrubs for healthy growth.
- Renewal-prune shrubs in late winter, before growth begins.
- In late winter or early spring, prune clematises that bloom in summer on new wood , including *C.* x *jackmanii* and its cultivars.
- Prune roses in late winter or very early spring, before the buds break.
- Remove dead wood on vines.
- Top-dress shrubs with mulch.
- Prune one-third of the oldest stems of early-flowering shrubs in late spring, immediately after they finish blooming (see list at right).

Trees

- Prune out dead wood in early spring (see page 53).
- Prune to control size and enhance shape immediately after the blooms wither.

First Flowers of Spring

Some of the earliest heralds of the coming gardening season include:

Anemone nemorosa
(wood anemone)

Chionodoxa
(glory-of-the-snow)

Crocus vernus ▲
(Dutch crocus)

Eranthis hyemalis
(winter aconite)

Forsythia (forsythia)

Galanthus (snowdrop)

Helleborus niger
(Christmas rose)

Iris reticulata (reticulated iris)

Shrubs to Prune after Blooming

Spring-blooming shrubs that form flower buds on the previous season's growth should be pruned immediately after they flower to promote healthy summer growth and plenty of blooms the next year. Rejuvenate older plants by cutting out both the large-caliber and spindly branches to encourage strong shoots.

Daphne (daphne)
Zones 4-10

Deutzia (deutzia)
Zones 4-8

Erica (heath)
Zones 4-8

Forsythia (forsythia)
Zones 5-9

Jasminum (jasmine)
Zones 6-10

Kerria japonica
(Japanese rose)
Zones 4-9

Kolkwitzia amabilis
(beautybush)
Zones 4-8

Lonicera
(honeysuckle)
Zones 4-9

Philadelphus
(mock orange)
Zones 4-8

Spiraea (spirea)
Zones 3-8

Syringa (lilac)
Zones 3-7

Viburnum
(viburnum)
Zones 3-8

Weigela (weigela)
Zones 4-8

Daphne

Deutzia

Spiraea

Syringa

Viburnum

Plant Wake-up

1 Carefully remove protective mulch; avoid damaging new stems. Top-dress with granular fertilizer, sprinkling pellets in a circle 6 inches from base of plant.

2 Prune winterkill (deadwood) back to green wood.

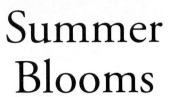

Summer Blooms

Summer is a time of bounty, when flowering bulbs, perennials, roses, shrubs, and trees fill the air with fragrance and the garden with beauty. As the season progresses, gentle pastel color schemes give way to strong yellows, oranges, and reds, and blues, purples, silvers, and white provide a cooling effect. Rain can come with drenching swiftness or not at all, and plants must be protected from both extremes with staking, mulches and regular watering. When the sun is at its hottest, outdoor living moves to the shade. That's when the cool, shady garden—or a miniature oasis created with the studied planting of a dwarf tree or a grouping of large shrubs—has its greatest appeal.

A Riot of Color

The varying reds and pinks of poppies, double-flowered stock, and gladiolus give this Brentwood, California, garden plenty of punch. Cool contrast is supplied by the tall delphiniums and the blue, funnel-shaped flowers of the ground morning glory.

Summer Perennials

Perennials enliven the summer garden despite the vagaries of heat, drought, and downpours. Most summer perennials tend to have a longer season of bloom than their short-lived counterparts of spring. Some bloom for a month or more, and many, including purple coneflower, black-eyed Susan, coreopsis cultivars such as 'Early Sunrise' and 'Goldfink', sage, and many of the hardy geraniums, are in flower for almost the entire season.

Still, a gap may often appear in the perennial show as summer's full heat bears down. Your garden in mid- and late summer can be bare of flowers, especially in the South. The plants listed at left can help fill this gap; they work hard to carry the summer garden through the season.

Perennials to Take Summer into Autumn

Boltonia asteroides (boltonia)

Ceratostigma plumbaginoides (dwarf plumbago)

Chelone (turtlehead)

Eupatorium maculatum (Joe-Pye weed)

Helenium autumnale (sneezeweed)

Lobelia cardinalis (cardinal flower)

Phygelius capensis (cape fuchsia)

Physostegia virginiana (obedience)

Salvia (sage)

Sanguisorba canadensis (Canadian burnet)

A Calendar of Flowers

Whether summertime in your area is long or short, characteristic perennial blooms mark its flow. You will know that the season has arrived when the last of the bearded irises fade and the first of the delphiniums, *Campanula* (bellflower), yarrow, and lavender begin to bloom. Characteristic signs of summer occur when trees, such as golden-rain tree, and roses open their blossoms. Old-fashioned summer shrubs such as *Kolkwitzia amabilis* (beautybush) and *Cotinus* (smoketree) add a tier of blossoms between the trees and the perennials around them.

The early-summer phase reaches its peak when a profusion of intense colors breaks out, supplied by such spectacular perennials as red 'Fire King' yarrow, pink *Saponaria ocymoides* (soapwort), deep purple 'Black Knight' delphinium, and purple and blue veronicas. But subtle shades abound as well. Pastel pink phlox, buttery 'Moonbeam' coreopsis, sky-blue veronica and *Centaurea*, and a rainbow of yarrows parade across the garden border. They blend with the brighter hues of the ruffled trumpets of Asiatic and, later, Oriental lilies, and annuals such as nasturtiums, *Nicotiana* (flowering tobacco), and verbenas.

By mid-summer much of the garden

is ablaze with the yellows and golds of summer representatives of the sunflower family, such as *Helianthus* x *multiflorus* (sunflower), *Heliopsis* (false sunflower), black-eyed Susan, and coreopsis. Play these yellows against rich scarlet *Hemerocallis* 'James Marsh' and 'Scarlet Apache' and *Hibiscus* 'Disco Belle' (mallow) hybrids in lustrous reds and pinks.

Cool down the combination with phlox, especially the mildew-resistant cultivars *P. paniculata* 'David' (summer perennial phlox) and *P. carolina* 'Miss Lingard' (thick-leaf phlox). Not only will these add lovely color, but they will also ensure that the garden is alive with beautiful butterflies. As summer fades into autumn, the sedums take over, accompanied by a commotion of goldenrods *(Solidago)* and asters of

The Ever-Blooming Garden

The Fourth of July is heralded in this Pennsylvania garden by the brilliant colors of *Kniphofia* 'Royal Standard' (red-hot poker), with *Chrysanthemum leucanthemum* (oxeye daisy) and bright blue salvia and campanula. The **summer** garden also has elegant foxgloves in the rear, saucy orange poppies, and, for a slightly later bloom, a graceful pink 'Anthony Waterer' spirea to back up the display of summer flowers. Some of the plants, such as campanula and *Boltonia* bridge the seasons to ensure that the garden has no intermission time. **Springtime** in this planting would have witnesseed the purple lilac blooms casting their scent over the garden, while 'Apricot Beauty' and 'Yellow Present' tulips sent up tall orange and yellow blooms. Forget-me-nots would have picked up the blue of the spring sky while various traditional daffodils played their spring role. When summer moves toward **fall,** the deep purple-blue of *Aconitum* (monkshood) will provide a long span of color, along with pink *Boltonia*, deep purple asters, and scarlet sneezeweed.

varying heights, and a glorious stand of blooming and ripening ornamental grasses, which add motion as well as texture.

Perennials for Garden Styles

The style of your garden can dictate which summer perennials you choose from the vast array available. Cottage gardens are particularly blessed with the availability of a large group of old-fashioned summer bloomers. No cottage garden would be complete without such favorites as *Lupinus* (lupine), black-eyed Susans and daisies, delphiniums, and chrysanthemums. Newer cottage garden plants include *Perovskia atriplicifolia* (Russian sage) and *Coreopsis rosea* (rose coreopsis).

Native-plant enthusiasts can look for plants that originated in their own regions to create a sense of environmental harmony as well as to reduce their garden's maintenance requirements. In the East, try such regional natives as scarlet *Monarda didyma* (bee balm), creamy *Allium tricoccum* (wild leek), white *Chelone glabra* (turtlehead), and *Lobelia siphilitica* (great blue lobelia). In the Midwest, focus on prairie plants, such as *Helianthus maximiliani* (Maximilian sunflower) and *Liatris* (gay feather).

In the Southeast, your choices might include *Iris fulva* (copper iris) and *Campanula divaricata* (southern harebell). Southwestern gardeners can plant orange-and-red *Sphaeralcea parvifolia* (globe mallow), *Gaillardia pulchella* (Indian blanket), deep pink *Allium falcifolium* (sickle-leaf onion), and the marigold relative *Tagetes lemmoni*. In the Northwest, try bright red *Mimulus* (monkey flower), purplish pink *Allium validum* (swamp onion), or *Dicentra formosa* (western bleeding heart).

Some summer-blooming perennials are native all across the United States: *Allium cernuum* (nodding onion) produces white to pink blooms in dangling clusters; *Asclepias* (milkweed) blooms range from orange to rose to purple; *Helenium autumnale* (common sneezeweed) has a yellow, daisylike flower, as does *Rudbeckia* (coneflower); *Smilacina* (false Solomon's-seal) produces white flowers. ■

▲ SPRING

▲ FALL

Tender Perennials

The wonder of tender perennials is their durability and their constant flowering. Because they come from frost-free zones, tender perennials such as impatiens, *Begonia* x. *semperflorens-cultorum* (wax begonia), *Pelargonium* (bedding or zonal geranium), *Fuchsia,* and *Scaevola* do not exhibit the seasonal bloom cycles of temperate plants. This heritage makes them ideal for a three-season garden, because they provide heat resistance, vigor, and uninterrupted season-long bloom in the face of summer heat.

Tender perennials such as the cultivars of *Datura* (angel's-trumpet) offer exotic molded forms associated with the tropics. They have large, down-facing, flared flowers with intoxicating fragrance, and grow so fast in a single season that they can take the role of shrubs in the summer garden. Try soft apricot *Datura* 'Grand Marnier' with lavender-blue annuals such as 'Blue Ribbon' and 'Blue Mink' ageratum, perennial 'Monch' aster, and another tender perennial, *Heliotropium arborescens* 'Marine' (heliotrope), with rich deep purple flower heads. Or contrast the pristine white trumpets of *Datura suaveolens* with zingy red 'Amy' tuberous begonias at their feet. ∎

Overwintering Tender Perennials

Tender perennials can be brought indoors when the growing season ends. With sufficient warmth, light, and moisture, they will continue to grow, ready to be planted outside again in the spring. The new growth produced during the winter also can provide cuttings for starting new plants.

1 When frost threatens, dig up the plant with enough soil to keep most of the roots intact. Check the plant carefully for insects and disease before bringing it into the house.

2 Pot the plant, using a container larger than the rootball to allow for growth. Use potting soil to fill in around the roots. Water the plant well, and keep the soil moist until the plant has had time to establish itself in the new pot.

3 The plant will grow best in a sunny area, with temperatures between 60° and 70° F. Provide adequate moisture through regular watering and occasional misting. During the short days of winter, the plant may stretch toward a light source. Cutting or pinching off the new growth will help maintain a compact form.

Perennials That Endure Sultry Days

Astilbe chinensis (Chinese astilbe)

Coreopsis (tickseed)

Echinacea (purple coneflower)

Echinops ritro (small globe thistle)

Eupatorium maculatum (Joe-Pye weed)

Hemerocallis (daylily)

Liatris (gay-feather)

Monarda didyma (bee balm)

Perovskia atriplicifolia (Russian sage)

Platycodon grandiflorus (balloon flower)

Rudbeckia hirta (black-eyed Susan)

Sedum (stonecrop)

Sidalcea malviflora (checkerbloom)

Silphium perfoliatum (cup plant)

Verbena (vervain)

Veronica (speedwell)

Refreshing Summer Flowers
The lantana in this Del Mar, California, garden is at home in the heat of summer, its bright flowers staying perky through even the worst of the dog days.

Annuals and Biennials

Because perennial flowers often tend to become relatively few and far between in mid-summer, when early bloomers have faded and the flowers of autumn are still lying low, easy-growing annuals and biennials have a key role to play in the three-season garden. They transplant without difficulty, slipping between perennials or bulbs, and they bloom prolifically from summer through fall until frost. They also offer an extraordinary diversity of plant and flower forms, from low carpets of sapphire edging lobelia to bushy *Mirabilis longiflora* (four-o'clock) to towering 9-foot sunflowers and hollyhocks *(Alcea)*. Many have shallow, fibrous roots that can be planted directly over dormant spring bulbs.

Annuals in the Summer Garden

When choosing annuals for your summer garden, there is no good reason to confine yourself to the familiar bed of marigolds or petunias, though these two stalwart plants deserve a place in your planting plan. For example, try 'Lemon Gem' signet marigolds *(Tagetes tenuifolia)* for their fernlike, fragrant foliage and tiny, clear yellow flowers that are not only pretty but are tasty in salads. Or look for tough 'Purple Wave' petunias—a show-stopping variety that brightens the garden and does good service as a ground cover as well.

Experiment also with more unusual annuals. *Nicotiana* 'Fragrant Cloud' is a stately cultivar of flowering tobacco that looks lovely next to perennial *Scabiosa caucasica* (pincushion flower). A white tea rose, bare and twiggy at its base, can be beautified with a skirt of *Nigella damascena* (love-in-a-mist), with pink or sky-blue flowers that intensify in color as they age.

Most summer annuals are medium to tall plants, although plant breeders have developed dwarf varieties of marigolds, flowering tobacco, and wax begonias that can create a low mass of color for edging the front of a bed and for planting over small, dormant spring bulbs. Trailing petunias, nasturtiums, and sweet peas are also good for this purpose, as well as for growing in pots mounted on pedestals in the garden to add a higher layer of color.

Taller annuals also bring long-lasting color to the higher reaches of your bed or border. Their roots take up little space, so you can position them between perennials that are past their season. When Siberian irises have gone by in early summer, plant some graceful, ferny *Cosmos* 'Sensation Mix' or 'Sea Shell' in their midst, color-matched with *Cleome* (spider flower) and *Lavatera trimestris* 'Silver Cup' (tree mallow). This combination will carry the garden until frost.

Dependable Biennials

Biennials are similar to annuals, except that they take two

Vertical Blooms
These upright stalks of zinnias and sunflowers in Brentwood, California, create a multilayered display of dazzling summer color.

growing seasons to produce flowers. The first year, biennials form a rosette of leaves and then go dormant in autumn, much as a perennial does. The following season, in spring or summer, the plant flowers, sets seed, and dies.

Gardens planted in the cottage style often contain summer-blooming biennials. Foxgloves begin flowering in late spring, and carry the garden into summer. For the middle of the border, *Campanula medium* (Canterbury bells) grows 2 to 4 feet tall and has white, blue, lavender, or rose bell-shaped flowers; *Alcea rosea* (hollyhock) rises up to a spectacular 9 feet tall and blooms all summer in shades of white, rose, yellow, pink, red, and a nearly black cultivar called 'Nigra'. *Lunaria* (money plant) does double duty: An everlasting, it blooms in pinkish purple or white, and then develops interesting flat, coin-shaped seed pods, which can be dried and used in arrangements.

If you plant biennials successively year after year, you can expect your garden to have plants in each of the two stages of growth every year. Many will also reseed on their own, helping the process along. The blooms that appear annually will pop up in continually varying locations, lending fluidity and interest to your garden design.

Buying and Planting Annuals and Biennials

Both annuals and biennials can be purchased either to be grown from seed or as young plants in cell packs, often in bud or in bloom. Nursery-grown plants are convenient and give you a jump on the season, but growing your own plants from seed is less expensive and offers you a broader selection. Annuals grow rapidly from seed, but need sun and space to mature. If you don't have room to start them in the garden, sow them indoors under lights, timing them according to the instructions on the packet. ∎

Tip

To introduce some immediate color in a perennial border left empty by early summer bloomers like bleeding hearts, fill bare spots with containers of annuals and biennials in full bloom. Choose low-maintenance petunias and geraniums for sun, impatiens for shade.

Caring for Annuals and Tender Perennials

Summer maintenance of the annuals, biennials, and tender perennials in your garden should be relatively easy. They are forgiving plants that endure the season's intense heat, all the while producing blooms and healthy foliage—provided you have given them a good start in rich soil, the light and water they need, and accommodating neighbors. Nipping off their spent flowers keeps them blooming longer, as shown below. The list at right identifies some of the most reliable of this group of plants.

Giving Your Plants Room to Grow

Whether you are starting your annuals from seed or planting them from a cell pack, they will be small when they are getting their start, and in this tender state could easily be shouldered aside by stout, fast-growing perennials and weeds. Pay special attention to the spacing indicated on the seed packet or to the information on the plant label giving your plant's eventual size. Skimping on growing space when the plants are first making their way could result in spindly specimens that are vulnerable to diseases. Combine plants of complementary form to make sure there is room for all—a tall, airy *Verbena bonariensis* (vervain), for example, next to mounding dwarf signet marigolds and sprawling *Silene coeli-rosa* (catchfly).

Keep the way clear for emerging plants as they grow by snipping faded leaves from spring bulbs as soon as they have ripened and withered, and by removing weeds promptly. Restrain the stems of encroaching perennials with wire loops or supports consisting of short, twiggy branches, or cut back a few stems. As perennials like yarrow or phlox finish blooming, cut back the flower stalks.

Biennials such as foxgloves, *Verbascum* (mullein), and Canterbury bells surge in their second year from tidy rosettes to elongated, leafy flower stems. Be sure to provide them the room they need.

Meeting Your Plants' Water Needs

Keeping your plants' moisture at the right levels during the summer can be a real challenge. Too much water may suffocate plant roots; too little could cause foliage to dehydrate, destroying cell tissues. Annuals in crowded conditions, or in containers, are especially vulnerable, and can become weakened and susceptible to disease.

Proper soil preparation and a thick mulch layer can help to optimize the distribution of moisture in the ground. In sandy soil, water drains away too quickly; in clay soil, it stays at or just below the surface, promoting root rot. Loamy soil is ideal: Wa-

How to Deadhead

Deadheading, the removal of spent blossoms to encourage the formation of additional flowers, is quick and easy. Old flower heads of annuals, such as petunias and marigolds, can be removed by pinching between the thumb and forefinger.

Removing old flowers redirects the plant's energy from the developing seedheads to the buds, leaves, and roots. New shoots will sprout from the one or two buds nearest the cut, producing bushier growth and more flowers later in the season.

ter percolates down deeply, promoting the growth of deep-reaching, healthy root systems, yet the soil retains enough moisture to keep the plant supplied. Dig in compost or leaf mold to achieve the right mix, and cover the surrounding soil with the appropriate mulch (see page 47).

Water the plants infrequently but well. When the soil be-comes dry to a depth of 1 to 2 inches, apply enough water to moisten the soil deeply—about 1 inch of water. Use soaker hoses or sprinklers for large areas, a watering can or a hose spray attachment for containers. Water in the early morning if possible, both to lessen evaporation and to allow foliage to dry out, reducing the risk of fungal diseases. ■

Annuals, Biennials, and Tender Perennials

The list of annuals, biennials, and tender perennials that bloom during the summer is long and varied. This chart presents a representative selection of versatile, hard-working plants in a variety of flower-head types, growth habits, colors, heights, and leaf textures. They are adaptable to a wide range of climate, soil, and light conditions.

ANNUALS	FLOWER COLOR	HEIGHT	LEAF TEXTURE	LIGHT
Abelmoschus moschatus (musk mallow)	yellow	4-6 feet	coarse	full sun
Amaranthus caudatus (love-lies-bleeding)	green	3-5 feet	medium	full sun
Ammi majus (bishop's flower)	white	2-3 feet	fine	full sun/partial shade
Browallia speciosa (bush violet)	blue/white	12-15 inches	medium	partial to full shade
Gomphrena globosa (globe amaranth)	pink/red/white	12-18 inches	medium	full sun
Impatiens (impatiens)	orange/pink/red/white	12-18 inches	medium	partial to full shade
Lavatera trimestris (tree mallow)	pink/white	2-6 feet	coarse	full sun
Lobularia maritima (sweet alyssum)	white/pink/purple	4-12 inches	fine	full sun/partial shade
Mimulus (monkey flower)	orange/red/yellow	10-12 inches	medium	partial to full shade
Nicotiana alata (flowering tobacco)	pink/red/white	2-5 feet	medium	full sun/partial shade
Nigella damascena (love-in-a-mist)	blue/pink/white	18-24 inches	fine	full sun
Portulaca grandiflora (moss rose)	orange/pink/red/white	4-6 inches	fine	full sun
Torenia fournieri (bluewings)	purple	8-12 inches	medium	full sun/partial shade
Tropaeolum majus (nasturtium)	orange/red/yellow	10 inches	coarse	full sun
BIENNIALS				
Alcea rosea (hollyhock)	yellow/white/red	2-8 feet	coarse	full sun
Digitalis purpurea (foxglove)	pink/white	3-4 feet	medium	full sun/partial shade
Eustoma grandiflorum (prairie gentian)	pink/purple/white	2-3 feet	medium	full sun/partial shade
Moluccella laevis (bells-of-Ireland)	green	2-3 feet	medium	full sun
TENDER PERENNIALS				
Argemone munita (white prickly poppy)	white	1-3 feet	coarse	full sun
Datura inoxia (angel's-trumpet)	pink/white	3 feet	coarse	full sun/light shade
Dyssodia tenuiloba (Dahlberg daisy)	orange/red/yellow	4-12 inches	fine	full sun
Heliotropium arborescens (heliotrope)	purple/white	2-3 feet	med./coarse	full sun/partial shade
Mirabilis jalapa (four-o'clock)	pink/red/yellow	2-3 feet	medium	full sun/partial shade
Oxypetalum caeruleum (blue milkweed)	blue	3 feet	medium	full sun

Bulb Flowers of Summer

While tulips and the other spring-flowering bulbs are fading, their summer cousins take the stage. Bulbs such as lily, dahlia, gladiolus, crinum, calla, and agapanthus fill garden beds with exotic flowers of unusual form and vivid color. Unlike spring bulbs, fading foliage is not a problem with these plants, as most retain their leaves until blackened by frost.

Many summer bulbs can also fit into tight spaces, enriching already luxuriant plantings of other flowers. Tuck *Lycoris* (spider lily), hot-colored *Crocosmia* (montbretia), and others among existing flowers in the garden bed, crowding them for maximum effect. They look best when they have billowy, small-flowered perennials such as *Gypsophila* (baby's-breath) nestled around their stems. Some, such as *Lycoris squamigera* (magic lily), have bare, leafless flower stems in summer, and benefit from an underplanting of lower-growing perennials such as lily-of-the-valley or hostas.

Flowering Bulbs in the Summer Garden

Versatile Asiatic and Oriental hybrid lilies add large, colorful flowers at a good height during the transition period between the spring colors of tulips and irises and the summer flush of sages and sunflowers. The extravagant blossoms of sunny yellow 'Connecticut Yankee' and other Asiatic hybrids look best contrasted with summer perennials of a finer texture, such as Russian sage, or with spiky flower forms like those of *Veronica* (speedwell) and the dramatic purple *Salvia* 'Mainacht'. Oriental lilies and many kinds of dahlias, especially those with small flowers, help make the transition from summer to fall. Dahlias' long-lasting blooms, from daisy-sized to dinner plate, are a significant presence until frost, so allow them more room in the summer garden than other bulbs, and mark them on your fall plan, too.

Stately Color
The brilliant blue of lily-of-the-Nile regally supports the front of this California garden, set off by silvery green artemisia, pink spirea, and a Japanese maple.

The swordlike vertical leaves of gladiolus are notoriously difficult to incorporate comfortably into a garden design, but their gorgeous, colorful flowers make it worth a try. Work with a single hue, avoiding the hodgepodge of a mixed-color gladiolus planting. Create a free-form but densely spaced clump of two dozen or more so they don't stand like lone soldiers, and place them with a mid-height perennial or annual of similar color. Tuck new groups of gladiolus corms among previously planted ones every few weeks until mid-summer to extend their bloom until frost. Remove blooms as they fade.

For an adventurous color scheme of blue, lavender-purple, and chartreuse, mix an oddball green gladiolus cultivar such as 'St. Patrick's' or 'Green Spire' with *Veronica latifolia* 'Crater Lake Blue' (Hungarian speedwell) and *V. longifolia* 'Foerster's Blue' (longleaf speedwell), chartreuse *Alchemilla* (lady's mantle), and annual lime-green 'Envy' zinnia and *Moluccella laevis* (bells-of-Ireland). Balance the height of the gladiolus with summer-blooming shrubs such as *Caryopteris* 'Heavenly Blue' (bluebeard). *Gladiolus nanus* (dwarf gladiolus) is hardy to Zone

4, and at 1 to 2 feet tall, is easier to blend into the summer garden. The flowers open in early summer in pink, salmon, cerise, and white on loose, graceful stems.

The architectural form of the large leaves and the bold, hummingbird-attracting flowers of canna give the summer garden a tropical air. Like many summer-flowering bulbs—tuberous begonias, agapanthus, and *Hymenocallis* (spider lily), for example—cannas are a tropical genus whose plants are perennial south of Zone 8 but will not survive winter in northern zones. Grow them in pots or dig them after frost begins, and overwinter them in a cool basement.

Planting and Caring for Summer Bulbs

Buy summer bulbs early in spring, as soon as they appear on the shelves, because they tend to dry out. They are often sold in plastic bags filled with slightly damp peat moss, both to retain moisture and to prevent damage to the brittle bulbs. The tubers and tuberous roots are particularly vulnerable to drying, because they are thin-skinned. Select only those that are plump and fresh and have no gouges, bruises, or decay, and plant them as soon as possible. If you must delay planting, store them in barely damp peat moss in the refrigerator.

Most summer bulbs need rich, moist soil to grow to their fullest. Amend the soil with compost and aged manure to ensure adequate nutrition and to improve the soil structure. Many, such as *Zantedeschia* (calla lily), *Alstroemeria* (Peruvian lily), and canna, come from regions of winter drought and summer rains, and they thrive in moist, sometimes wet, but well-drained soil in full sun. They do well in marshy areas or next to a pond, or you can plant them in pots if your garden tends to dry out in summer, but make sure you keep the potting mix moist.

Planting depths vary depending on the bulb. Generally, tubers are planted at or just below the soil line. True bulbs are set one to two times as deep as the height of the bulb. Crinums are an exception. They are planted with the neck of the bulb above the soil line.

As with spring bulbs, you should deadhead summer-flowering bulbs as their flowers wither to encourage them to make more blooms. Some of these plants, such as dahlias, produce so many blooms that their weight topples them over. Be sure to stake them carefully as they grow, and pinch out the buds that form between the main stem and the side leaves, so that only two or three buds are left at the tops of the stems. ∎

Stalwart Summer-Flowering Bulbs

Allium aflatunense (Persian onion)

Anemone tomentosa (hairy anemone)

Canna x *generalis* (canna)

Crinum x *powellii* (Powell's swamp lily)

Crocosmia hybrids (montbretia)

Dahlia x *hybrida* (dahlia)

Lilium Oriental, Asiatic, and Trumpet Hybrids (lily)

Tricyrtis hirta (hairy toad lily)

Mass-Planting Hardy Lilies

You can plant summer-blooming lily bulbs as soon as you have them in hand in spring, provided the ground has warmed up. Inspect them for signs of damage or discoloration that may indicate rot. Don't delay planting, or the bulbs may dry out.

To make a massed display of lilies, dig a hole 1 foot deep and broad enough to space your bulbs 8 inches apart. For example, a hole 2 feet across will accommodate 4 to 8 bulbs. Loosen the soil at the bottom and around the edges, and dig in a layer of compost to build up the planting bed. In light, sandy soils, set the tops of the bulbs 6 to 8 inches below the surface; in heavy clay soils, 4 to 6 inches down.

2 Place the bulbs at the proper intervals, setting them so that the pointed ends point up. Handle them with care, as lily bulbs lack the papery tunic that protects bulbs such as daffodils and tulips. Then refill the hole with a mixture of compost and soil. Cover with a layer of mulch and mark the spot with a plant label.

Ground Covers and Grasses

Summer-blooming ground covers do double duty. They work as a living mulch, keeping the soil cool and moist and suppressing weeds. As part of the garden design, they also provide continuous sweeps of color when in bloom and, later, calm swaths of foliage that unify the garden.

In the summer garden, ornamental grasses may do the same work as ground covers, or they may stand alone as focal points or textural accents. In bloom, they put forth an astonishing range of color displays. Most, furthermore, are decorative all year because of their enduring foliage, which adds architectural presence and a sense of movement to the garden.

Summer's Verdant Carpet

For maximum color, look for ground covers with a long season of bloom. They exist in all categories, from annuals to low-growing shrubs. Among the annuals, try *Petunia integrifolia*, with small flowers in a magenta pink that leaves an indelible effect. *P.* 'Purple Wave' is a petunia hybrid whose flowers last all summer. Another all-summer annual bloomer is *Verbena* 'Homestead Purple', which flowers nonstop and spreads fast.

Hostas are ground-covering perennials of enormous variety, any of which could be blooming from spring through fall. Try summer-blooming *H. lancifolia,* with narrow, dark green leaves and lilac flowers, or *H. plantaginea* 'Aphrodite', with bright green leaves and fragrant double white flowers. In late summer, *H. sieboldiana* 'Elegans' sends up stems of tubular white flowers above its foot-wide blue-green leaves.

Grasses: Beauty in Motion

Ornamental grasses bring the garden to life as their delicate or strappy leaves and plumy blooms move with every shift of the breeze. Flowers are an important aspect of grasses, but plant form is just as important. Because grasses have such distinct, eye-catching shapes, they make strong accent plants for creating a sense of rhythm in the garden.

Grasses that spread by running roots, such as gardener's garters *(Phalaris arundinacea* var. *picta),* can quickly grow out into a lovely and useful ground cover—or an invasive weed. Where you want grasses to stay under control, plant clump-forming types such as *Miscanthus* (eulalia) or *Festuca* 'Kentucky Blue'.

Tip

Pink primrose is ideal for underplanting roses, phlox, and other perennials, but its quickly colonizing roots are a threat to other plants. Keep this ground cover in its place with a metal or plastic barrier around the planting. Leave a 2-inch lip exposed so the plants can't creep over. Even with such measures, you'll need to watch for seedlings and escapees.

No Room for Weeds

For the first few years after you plant your ground cover, you'll see a lot of weeds on the site. They gain entry as you work the soil, add compost, and, of necessity, leave bare soil between young plants. Mulching newly planted ground cover with grass clippings, shredded bark, or chopped leaves can help reduce the weed infestation during those early years. Once the ground cover plants gain vigor and begin to spread and fill in, the number of weeds will tail off.

An established three-season garden is so chock-full of plants that not much light is available to let weeds germinate and grow. The most bothersome weeds, such as lamb's-quarters, pigweed, plantain, and crabgrass, can't get a healthy start in such crowded conditions, and so are not a major problem. Pull weeds as soon as you notice them, and toss them onto the compost pile. If particularly tenacious weeds sprout through a ground cover, hold down the ground cover with one hand while you pull the weed; then, if the soil was dislodged, push the ground cover firmly against it to tamp it down.

Cool- and Warm-Season Grasses

Cool-season grasses such as *Calamagrostis* 'Karl Foerster' bloom in early summer, along with the main flush of perennials. The gun-metal color of low-growing blue fescue can intensify the rosy blooms of heather planted in combination with it. Plant prairie grasses such as big bluestem *(Andropogon gerardii)* and Indian grass *(Sorghastrum nutans),* which will mellow into ripeness as the flowers bloom.

Late summer is when grasses come alive, as graceful companions to the finale of the summer bloomers. Warm-season grasses, including the popular *Miscanthus* cultivars, push up silky flowers from late summer into fall. Look for *M. sinensis* 'Purpurascens' (Chinese silver grass), whose inflorescences go beautifully with large-flowered, blush pink 'Silver Years' dahlias. Striped green-and-white grasses such as *M.* 'Variegatus' add a cool tone to color schemes with pink, red, and white flowers, but if your garden is composed of yellows and blues, try yellow-variegated 'Goldfeder' instead.

Tall perennials planted among grasses create a prairie look in mid-summer. Among these are *Aster tataricus* (Tartarian aster), with violet-purple flowers 8 feet high, *Coreopsis tripteris* (Atlantic coreopsis), the tallest of that genus at 7 feet, and *Rudbeckia maxima* (great coneflower), as tall as a sunflower. ■

Easy Landscape Maintenance
The ground floor in this Greenwood, South Carolina, landscape is covered with the summer-flowering grasses Pennisetum villosum and Vinca 'Little Bright Eyes', which require little care and offer a unique textural contrast.

Summer-Flowering Ground Covers

The plants listed here—either sun loving or shade tolerant—not only brighten the summertime garden with their blooms, but also have visual appeal and utility during the other two growing seasons. Lavender, dead nettle, and hosta, for instance, grace the three-season garden with exceptional foliage, which can unify the planting or serve as a flattering backdrop for other flowering specimens. *Laminum maculatum* 'White Nancy', for example, offers pure white flowers among its silvery leaves for several weeks but is just as effective out of bloom.

▲ *Sangina subulata* (Irish moss)

Sun loving	Shade tolerant
Cerastium tomentosum (snow-in-summer)	*Campanula poscharskyana* (bellflower)
Coronilla varia (crown vetch)	*Dianthus gratianopolitanus* (cheddar pink)
Cytisus decumbens (prostrate broom)	*Geranium sanguineum* var. *striatum* (geranium)
Gypsophila repens 'Rosea' (creeping gypsophila)	*Hemerocallis fulva* 'Europa' (tawny daylily)
Hypericum calycinum (creeping St.-Johns-wort)	*Hosta* (hosta)
Lavandula angustifolia (English lavender)	*Lamium maculatum* (spotted dead nettle)
Sagina subulata (Irish moss)	*Liriope* (lilyturf)
Thymus serpyllum (lemon thyme)	*Potentilla fruticosa* (bush cinquefoil)
	Sedum (stonecrop)

Roses

oses are wonderfully romantic for the summer garden, but they're also very practical. As useful as any perennial for their flowers, they offer a bonus of height and structure. Their fragrance is welcome, and their foliage and bright fruit keep the plants interesting when they're not in bloom. Roses are natural partners to lavender, catmint, or white Shasta daisies, and the perfect complement to clematis.

If you choose disease-resistant plants, your roses will be as easy to care for as any other plants in your three-season garden. Excellent choices for warding off disease include the David Austin series of "English roses," which have the blooms and fragrance of antique roses; modern hybrids such as 'Country Dancer', a loosely ruffled deep pink; and old reliables such as the silvery pink *Rosa rugosa* 'Frau Dagmar Hartopp' and the blush pink climber 'New Dawn'.

Roses in the Summer Garden

The most important criterion for roses in a three-season garden is lengthy or repeated bloom. Many varieties, such as the cupped, pink 'Mary Rose', the 2-foot-tall 'Morden Blush', and the vigorous 'Abraham Darby', a rich apricot good for warming up blue and purple color schemes, offer extended bloom that carries the garden through the whole season. Clear golden yellow 'Graham Thomas' and old-fashioned pink 'Queen of Denmark' are repeat bloomers: The main flush of bloom lasts a few weeks, then new blossoms occur on and off until frost.

Many of the most appealing older and "antique" varieties, such as pink 'Louise Odier', with its intoxicating scent, have only a single flush of bloom, which limits their usefulness in the three-season garden. Because they are large plants, they're hard to camouflage with other flowers. If you want to include these roses, plant clematis on a tower or trellis nearby, and direct a trailing stem or two of the vine over the rosebush. (Don't smother the rose; sunlight keeps it healthy.) Fabulous almost-blue 'Perle d'Azur' clematis is a wonderful complement to roses of any color, and it stays in bloom from early summer through fall. The rugosa roses, including deep crimson 'Rotes Meer' and classic white 'Blanc Double de Coubert' are also one-time bloomers, but their wrinkled, glossy foliage and abundant, showy hips are additional assets in the garden. ■

Cascades of Roses

The arching stems of antique roses grace the fence and gazebo in this Ashton, Maryland, garden, filling the spring air with their intoxicating fragrance.

Roses for Every Garden

CLIMBERS/RAMBLERS	FRAGRANCE	FLOWER	COLOR	REBLOOMING	ZONES
'Constance Spry'	intense	double	pink	none	4-10
'Don Juan'	medium	double	burgundy red	light	6-9
'Golden Showers'	light	semi-double	clear yellow	good	6-9
'New Dawn'	medium	semi-double	pearl	good	5-9
'Rhonda'	light	double	coral	excellent	5-9
HYBRID TEAS					
'Bride's Dream'	light	double	lavender-pink	light	5-9
'Mister Lincoln'	intense	double	crimson	light	5-9
'Paradise'	medium	double	lavender edged with red	good	5-10
'Pascali'	light	double	pure white	light	5-9
'Peace'	medium	double	yellow edged with pink	good	5-9
MINIATURES					
'Cinderella'	medium	double	shell pink	ever-blooming	5-9
'Green Ice'	light	double	soft green fading to white	ever-blooming	5-9
'Plum Dandy'	medium	double	mauve	ever-blooming	5-10
'Rise 'n' Shine'	medium	double	canary yellow	ever-blooming	5-9
'Starina'	light	double	vermilion red	ever-blooming	5-9
SHRUBS					
'Carefree Beauty'	light	semi-double	rose	good	4-9
'Frau Karl Druschki'	none	double	snow white	good	4-9
'Golden Wings'	light	single	creamy yellow	ever-blooming	4-9
'The Fairy'	light	double	pink	ever-blooming	4-9
'Will Scarlet'	medium	semi-double	red	good	5-10
SPECIES					
Rosa glauca	light	single	pink	none	2-8
Rosa hugonis	none	single	lemon yellow	none	4-8
Rosa moschata	medium	single	white	none	6-9
Rosa moyesii	none	single	bright red	none	5-8
ENGLISH					
'Graham Thomas'	very intense	double	sun yellow	light	5-9
'Mary Rose'	medium	double	clear pink	good	5-9
'Shropshire Lass'	very intense	single	blush white	light	5-9
'Wife of Bath'	medium	double	antique pink	good	5-9

Shrubs and Small Trees in Summer

Shrubs and trees are essential components of the summer garden. Their mass anchors the landscape, providing permanent height as the lower-growing, herbaceous layers of the garden work their way upward. The shade these woody stalwarts provide tempers the bright heat of summer, creating cool, restful oases. And their shadows trace out contrasting patterns of light and darkness over the ground.

Summer-blooming shrubs and trees grace the landscape in a rainbow of colors. Like perennials, many summer-flowering woody plants bloom for an extended period, providing vibrant color to the middle and upper stories of the garden. In a summer garden of cool colors, try the tiered effect of *Viburnum plicatum* var. *tomentosum* 'Summer Snowflake' (doublefile viburnum) with blue and white delphiniums, white *Dianthus deltoides* 'Albus' and 'Musgrave's White' (pink), and yarrows such as the rich gold *Achillea* 'Gold Plate' or lemony 'Moonshine'. The viburnum's long, spreading branches will be lined with lacy white flower clusters that keep opening all summer.

For a completely different look, try *Cotinus coggygria* (smoketree), a small shrub or tree that transforms into a haze of soft, pinkish bloom in early summer. Dramatic *C.* 'Royal Purple' has dark purple-red matte foliage that makes it an excellent foil for lively red, orange-red, and yellow flowers such as yarrows, *Lobelia cardinalis* (cardinal flower), coreopsis, double-flowered zinnias, and dahlias. If you can plant a golden-rain tree nearby without casting shade on the flowering part of the garden, its graceful pendant sprays of minuscule yellow flowers will serve as a high-level accent in mid-summer, and its incandescent golden-orange fall foliage will contrast well with the deep tones of the smoketree.

For all their attributes, shrubs and flowering trees take up a lot of space. If you have only a small garden or you wish to bring bloom to a tight area, espalier, the art of training shrubs and trees against a vertical surface, can add height to the garden without taking up ground space. Try splaying a shrub against a wall, pinning its branches in arcs from its center, and cutting back growth that projects away from the wall. For training a tree in the shape of a candelabra, see page 73. ■

Three-Season Verticality
A pear tree being wall-trained on this small midwestern patio (above) shows how vertical elements can contribute striking contrast to the three-season garden. The tree's branches in springtime are clothed with white blossoms, and in summer its green foliage acts as a backdrop to the colorful plants beneath it. In fall the fruit dangles prettily against the brick.

Training a Candelabra Espalier

Stretch two strong horizontal wires 2 feet apart between sturdy poles set 8 to 15 feet apart, or attach the wires to a wall or fence. Link the wires vertically with a centrally placed leader wire and a training wire on either side near the poles. In early spring, plant a young ornamental fruit sapling bearing a few flexible stems in front of the central wire. Tie the sapling's leader to the central wire as shown, using gardening twine or twist ties.

2 **To begin training the plant for the espalier,** trim all side shoots off the leader except for two opposite shoots that align approximately with the lowest lateral wire. As these shoots grow, train them horizontally by bending and tying them to the lateral wire, as shown. When the shoots reach the two vertical training wires, bend each shoot gently upward and tie it to a vertical wire. If a shoot has become stiff, wrap it with heavy wire and flex the wire-wrapped stem gradually over time till it accepts the bending.

3 **As the plant grows,** add a third horizontal wire and two more vertical wires, as shown. When the central leader reaches the second horizontal wire, clip it at that level just above two opposite buds to force the development of new side shoots. Train these shoots horizontally and then vertically. To retain the candelabra shape and encourage the growth of flowering spurs, in midsummer cut back mature side shoots on the trained branches to just above the three leaves nearest the base of each shoot. In fall, cut back the secondary growth on these shoots to one bud. Check the ties periodically and loosen them as necessary.

Quiet Summer Days
Graceful plumes of gooseneck loosestrife wash over sapphire clusters of 'Nikko Blue' hydrangea in this Southport, Connecticut, mid-summer garden.

Vines and Climbers

Luxuriant foliage and exotic flowers are the hallmarks of summer-blooming annual and perennial vines. Vines allow you to add tiers of color above and behind perennial borders, setting the garden ablaze with colors that stand up to the brightest July sun. Erect a trellis for vines or simply train them up a bamboo support in a bed or over non-flowering shrubs.

Flowering vines scramble in all directions in summer, dangling blossoms at every level of the garden for the benefit of people and wildlife alike. Hummingbirds are particularly fond of vines with tubular flowers: *Campsis radicans* (trumpet creeper), *Lonicera* spp. (honeysuckle), and *Ipomoea quamoclit* (cypress vine) are guaranteed to attract any hummer in the area. Butterflies prefer smaller, clustered flowers, such as *Polygonum aubertii* (silver lace vine).

Vines High and Low

Woody perennial vines, such as wisteria and clematis, generally grow to greater heights than do herbaceous annual types, such as purple-stemmed, lavender-flowered *Dolichos lablab* (hyacinth bean), which only climbs to 15 feet, compared to wisteria's lofty 50 feet. You can combine woody and herbaceous types to achieve rapid coverage of a wall or fence. For example, plant fast-growing annuals like night-blooming *Ipomoea alba* (moonflower) and 'Heavenly Blue' morning glories in combination with a vigorous perennial like silver lace vine against a weathered board fence.

Not every garden has a picturesque wall or fence to serve as a stage and support for vines and climbing shrubs. A trellis at the back of a narrow border is a good way to add vertical interest without occupying too much ground space. Train a white climbing rose such as *Rosa bracteata* up the support and interweave its canes with a long-blooming, light pink 'Hagley Hybrid' clematis, for example.

You also can allow vines of delicate habit, such as *Cardiospermum halicacbum* (balloon vine), cypress vine, or *Asarina* spp. (twining snapdragon) to creep about at will. They will insinuate themselves among the other plants, and the places where they bloom are often a delightful surprise. Tall pink-and-rose 'Sensation' cosmos, for example, may be decorated with the tiny white flower clusters and dangling, inflated, lime-green puffs of a balloon vine. Deep purple twining snapdrag-

Warm-Hued Creepers
In an Ashton, Maryland, summertime garden, intertwining blooms of Clematis x jackmanii and roses yield a colorful display of purple and red.

ons may scale the tall, bare stems of verbenas to provide a complementary color combination.

Vegetable-bearing vines, in addition to providing items for the dinner table, can be decorative in the summer garden; they are fast-growing and bear lovely large flowers. Cover a fence with *Lagenaria siceraria* (birdhouse gourd) and you'll enjoy pristine, ruffled white blossoms all summer, as well as a bonus crop of gourds big enough to make birdhouses. Pumpkins, squash, and melons also make decorative vines.

The foliage of many vines enhances their drama and utility in the garden. The deep lobes of *Tropaelolum peregrinum* (ca-nary creeper) and *Passiflora* spp. (passionflower), and the soft, ferny foliage of cypress vine add textural interest. Allow the sweet potato cultivar *Ipomoea batatas* 'Blackie' to sprawl at the front of the bed, where its bold black leaves will act as the perfect foil for hot-colored annuals and perennials. Large-leaved vines also are good for softening or hiding gas lines, meters, utility poles, air conditioners, and other eyesores. Annuals such as moonflower, hyacinth bean, and *Phaseolus coccineus* (scarlet runner bean) make convenient temporary screens, trained on a string trellis, to obscure unattractive views or to block hot summer sun from a porch. ∎

Annual, Biennial, and Perennial Vines for Summer Bloom

HERBACEOUS	FLOWER COLOR	HEIGHT	TEXTURE	ZONES
Adlumia fungosa (mountain-fringe)	lilac/pink	12 feet	fine	biennial
Antigonon leptopus (coral vine)	pink	40 feet	medium	10
Ipomoea alba (moonflower)	white	15 feet	coarse	8-10
Ipomoea x multifida (cardinal climber)	red	4 feet	fine	annual
Lathyrus latifolius (perennial pea)	rose	6 feet	medium	5-9
Lathyrus odoratus (sweet pea)	blue/white/pink	8 feet	medium	annual
Passiflora caerulea (blue passionflower)	blue/white	12 feet	coarse	7-10
Passiflora incarnata (wild passionflower)	purple/white	12 feet	coarse	6-10
Polygonum aubertii (silver lace vine)	white	35 feet	medium	4-7
Thunbergia alata (black-eyed Susan vine)	orange	6 feet	medium	10
Tropaeolum majus (nasturtium)	orange/red/yellow	6 feet	coarse	annual
WOODY				
Akebia quinata (five-leaf akebia)	purple	40 feet	medium	4-8
Bougainvillea spectabilis (bougainvillea)	red	30 feet	medium	10
Campsis radicans (trumpet creeper)	orange/red	40 feet	medium	4-9
Clematis armandii (Armand clematis)	white	16 feet	medium	7-10
Clematis x jackmanii (Jackman clematis)	pink/purple/white	18 feet	medium	3-9
Clerodendrum thomsoniae (bleeding glory-bower)	red-and-white	10 feet	medium	6-9
Clytostoma callistegioides (Argentine trumpet vine)	pink	20 feet	medium	10
Cobaea scandens (cup-and-saucer vine)	purple	40 feet	medium	9-10
Decumaria barbara (climbing hydrangea)	white	35 feet	medium	7-10
Hydrangea anomala ssp. *petiolaris* (climbing hydrangea)	white	70 feet	coarse	4-7
Jasminum polyanthum (jasmine)	white	35 feet	fine	8-10
Mandevilla laxa (Chilean jasmine)	pink/white	18 feet	coarse	9-10
Schizophragma hydrangeoides (Japanese hydrangea vine)	white	40 feet	coarse	5-9
Trachelospermum jasminoides (star jasmine)	white	12 feet	medium	8-9

Garden Pointers

Check plants regularly for garden pests such as aphids and mites, especially among roses. Knock them off leaves and stems with a strong spray of water from a hose. Repeat every few days until populations are greatly reduced.

Pick off leaves infected by diseases such as powdery mildew to control their spread. Prune away infected stems and bloom clusters as well. Discard or burn diseased plant parts; do not put them in your compost pile.

Refresh the mulch in beds and borders to keep the soil cool and retain essential moisture. Keep mulch away from plant stems to prevent them from rotting.

Cultivate the garden with a hand-held Dutch hook weeder or a scuffle hoe to safely remove weeds without damaging the roots of desired plants.

The Chores of Summer

Perennials

◆ Raise support hoops on plants as they grow. Stake plants before they are tall enough to droop or break.

◆ For repeat bloom, deadhead or shear plants such as hardy geraniums and catmint.

◆ To keep plants from setting seed, remove spent blossoms and cut back bloom stalks as the flowers fade. Allow plants with decorative seedheads to go to seed.

Tender Perennials

◆ Set out tender perennials in early summer, after the last danger of frost has passed. Add a balanced fertilizer to the soil before planting.

◆ Cut back large salvias and other plants to control their size, to keep them full-looking, and to promote continued bloom.

Annuals and Biennials

◆ Add a balanced fertilizer to the soil before planting tender annuals.

In late summer, top-dress them with a high-phosphate fertilizer or a layer of well-rotted manure.

◆ Deadhead annuals regularly to keep them blooming.

◆ Shear heat-intolerant annuals such as lobelia to encourage reblooming in fall.

◆ Fertilize containers regularly to ensure uninterrupted bloom. Pay close attention to moisture levels.

Bulbs

◆ Deadhead late tulips, lilies, and tender bulbs.

◆ Remove spring bulb foliage after it has turned completely yellow.

◆ Order spring-blooming bulbs early for late-summer and fall planting to ensure having a good selection.

◆ Lift hardy bulbs for dividing before the foliage disappears. Store in a cool, dry place for replanting in fall.

Locating Pests

Many garden pests like to hide. Here are some places to check:

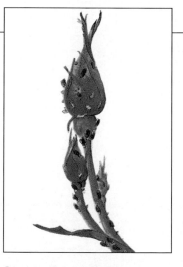

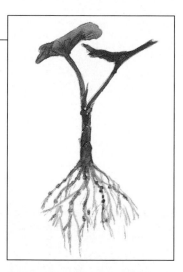

The undersides of leaves, where pests hide from predators. Look for leafhoppers, aphids, scales, and mites. Control with a spray of water or by releasing ladybugs in the garden.

Stems, from the tips of branches to the base of plants. Watch for scales, aphids, carpenter ants, and borers. Remove and burn infested stems.

Plant roots, for mealybugs, root aphids, and root knot nematodes. Destroy heavily infested plants. To control nematodes, plant marigolds and dig them into the soil in fall.

Grasses and Ground Covers

♦ Shear certain ground covers to promote reblooming (see page 48).

Roses

♦ Check for pests such as aphids, and diseases such as black spot. Apply controls as soon as pests are noticed.

♦ Train new climbers and ramblers on their supports when new canes reach one foot tall.

♦ Do not apply nitrogen fertilizer after late summer.

Wall Shrubs and Espalier

♦ Prune and train stems while they are young and flexible (see page 73).

Vines and Climbers

♦ Prune herbaceous clematises after they have flowered.

♦ Prune wisteria and other vines to three or four nodes after flowers fade.

Drought-Resistant Summer Perennials

Achillea (yarrow) ▲

Anthemis tinctoria (golden marguerite)

Euphorbia cyparissius (cypress spurge)

Gaillardia (blanketflower)

Gypsophila paniculata (baby's breath)

Liatris (gayfeather)

Yucca (yucca)

Pruning to Encourage Rebloom

Pruning in summer involves cutting back some perennials to encourage rebloom and trimming annuals to promote more abundant flowering. Cut perennials back to the base of the flower cluster. New shoots will arise from the stems, producing a second bloom later in the season. For annuals, pinch or remove the dead blossoms to stimulate additional flowering.

Achillea millefolium (yarrow) Zones 4-8

Ageratum houstonianum (ageratum) annual

Aster ssp. (aster) Zones 3-9

Callistephus chinensis (China aster) annual

Dicentra

Coreopsis grandiflora (tickseed) Zones 4-9

Delphinium (larkspur) Zones 4-8

Dicentra eximia (wild bleeding heart) Zones 5-9

Petunia

Perlargonium x *hortorum* (zonal geranium) Zones 9-10

Petunia (petunia) annual

Phlox (phlox) Zones 4-8

Phlox

Platicodon grandiflorus (balloon flower) Zones 4-9

Tagetes (marigold) annual

Building a String Teepee

I **A string teepee is easy** to build, and displays summer-to-fall blooms of annual vines to good effect. Install a post so that it stands 6 feet high and screw in a hook near the top. Drive 5 to 10 tent stakes into the ground spaced evenly in a circle or semicircle around the post, 4 to 6 feet from it.

2 **Tie a string securely** from each stake to the hook. Set plants at the bottom of each stake and train them up the strings.

The Fall Garden

The return of cool weather and low humidity brings renewed vigor to summer-weary plants, and sparks a tumult of autumn bloom. Lovely, strong hues take over the scene, establishing a new range of color themes for the season based on blazing golds, sun-kissed yellows, sky blues, and royal purples, which dominate the garden as the growing year plays out its last act. Fall is a time for tidying up the excesses of summer and preparing the garden to come to a rest. But all is not work. Take the time to revel in a many-faceted color show—not only the brilliantly blooming plants, but also the bright berries, the swaying flowerheads of grasses backlit by the sun, the fiery colors of changing foliage—all revealed in their most flattering form by the unfiltered sunlight of fall. Though flowers in this season now must share the limelight with these new sources of color, the three-season garden concedes nothing in splendor in its rush to the finish line.

The Flowers of Fall

Spidery cleome in the background and pink and yellow roses and dahlias pick up the frosted autumn tints of blue Lyme grass along the path in this New England garden.

Perennials of Autumn

With summer advancing into autumn, late-season perennials such as pink *Physostegia virginiana* (obedient plant), white *Chelone glabra* (turtlehead), and golden *Helianthus* x *multiflorus* (sunflower) carry the garden seamlessly forward. A variety of asters, mostly in shades of lavender-blue and pink, and floriferous pink, rose, and white *Anemone* x *hybrida* (Japanese anemone) join to keep the garden in bloom until frost. Hardy chrysanthemums, which you can drop into place for instant effect, add rich tones.

The foliage of bygone perennial flowers of earlier seasons is integral to the autumn garden, establishing a palette of strong colors and shapes. The deeply cut leaves of hardy geraniums turn scarlet and burgundy as the days shorten. Silvery lamb's ears and artemisias capture and reflect the sunlight. The plumes of ornamental grasses rise in abundant sweeps, glistening silver or flushed with rose before their seedheads form. The orchidlike flowers of toad lily add an exotic air from late summer into fall, while the tall spikes of *Cimicifuga simplex* (Kamchatka bugbane) fill the breeze with their intoxicating scent.

Fall perennials produce not only flowers and foliage, but also berries in white, red, blue, purple, and black. For example, *Actaea rubra* (red baneberry), *A. pachypoda* (white baneberry), and blue-black *Polygonatum* (Solomon's seal) berries stand out brilliantly. The black pincushion seedheads of coneflowers are a strong structural foil to a pink cloud of blooming Japanese anemone, which themselves develop fluffy powder-puff seedheads. The seedheads of Siberian iris and other perennials are

Frost-Tolerant Perennials

Although many perennials flower in autumn, few have blooms tough enough to make it past the first freezes of the season. The perennials listed here have dense, woody stems and compact, daisylike flower heads that enable them to survive some frost with surprising hardiness, giving you extended bloom time.

▼ *Aster novae-angliae* 'Alma Potschke' (New England Aster)

Aster lateriflorus (aster)
Aster novae-angliae (New England aster)
Chrysanthemum x *morifolium* (florist's chrysanthemum)
Chrysanthemum nipponicum (Nippon chrysanthemum)
Chrysanthemum x *zawadskii* (chrysanthemum)
Helianthus angustifolius (swamp sunflower)
Helianthus maximiliani (Maximilian sunflower)
Solidago canadensis (Canada goldenrod)

The Ever-Blooming Garden

The mind tends to paint **fall** in reds, oranges, and golds, lit by slanting sun and a sudden clarity in the air. This garden lets the feeling of summer linger, even as fall begins to add a deeper tone. Cactus dahlias, pink with creamy centers, create a summery foreground to the deep purple spires of salvia and the final bloom of bright yellow *Crotalaria spectabilis* (rattlebox). The *Berberis* (barberry) bushes at the back are arriving at their best season, turning fiery orange and dangling bright red berries. Pink *Penstemon hirsutus* 'Roseus' (beardtongue) contrasts with the flowing stalks of eulalia to create another seasonal bridge. In **spring**, both the barberry and the perennial grasses would have provided a fresh green contrast to bright purple pansy faces and clumps of *Primula japonica* (Japanese primrose). **Summer** brought the blooms of low-growing, lilac *Iris germanica* (German iris) and petunias to the foreground. Spikes of sky-blue speedwell at right and yellow rattlebox at left framed the dahlias that would then carry this North Carolina garden into fall.

decorative in fall, especially when contrasted against masses of delicately textured flowers, such as white, asterlike boltonia.

Plotting the Autumn Perennials

Most perennials of this season bloom in cool shades of blue, lavender-blue, or pink, making a stimulating contrast with the warm fall color scheme, driven by the flaming foliage of trees, shrubs, and ripening grasses.

Because foliage dominates the fall scene, it makes sense to orient a fall garden plan to a key woody plant. Start, for example, with the yellow autumn foliage of a *Hamamelis* (witch hazel), the burgundy fall leaves of *Cotinus* 'Royal Purple', or the showy orange, yellow, and red of *Fothergilla*. Cool these colors down with the soothing lavender-blue flowers of a knee-high planting of asters next to the shrubs. Or match the brilliance of fall foliage with deep-hued 'Purple Dome' aster, vivid rose pink 'Alma Potschke' aster, and deep pink *Sedum* 'Autumn Joy'. Mix asters and mums with *Miscanthus* cultivars, which produce tufted or tassled flower heads and make a gorgeous backdrop. ■

Tip

If you need to move a valued but delicate perennial because it doesn't work visually in its present location, don't just dig it up and then try to figure out where to put it. Experiment first with a few flowers cut from the plant. Place the cut blossoms in a vase, and move the vase to different spots in the garden where you think the plant might fit in. Evaluate each new position from every angle; when you're sure you've found the right spot, carefully dig the plant with a trowel and replant it.

▲ SPRING

▲ SUMMER

Maintaining Fall Perennials

When the final blooming season gets underway, take the time to groom the garden. Begin with the big items. Cut down large and medium-sized plants that are going dormant, such as phlox and peonies. Thin out the foliage of plants with decorative seedheads, such as mallows and *Agastache foeniculum* (anise hyssop), so that spikes and pods are more visible. Shear back plants that are flopping over onto their smaller neighbors, or those like catmint that will bloom anew as the weather cools, as shown on the facing page. Deadhead pinks, soapworts, and bluebells to keep them blooming well.

As you stop to deadhead a spent phlox or prune away a runaway *Monarda*, pull any weeds you see. Lay down a fresh layer of compost, shredded bark, or other mulch so that fall bloomers have a good-looking background and emerging weeds will be smothered. If rain has been scarce, water the garden, soaking the soil deeply around any shrubs or small trees that were planted in the past year or two.

Now is also the time to divide and increase your stock of perennials, as shown on the facing page. You might relocate the offspring of a particularly vigorous favorite to other parts of the garden, making visual links from place to place. Remember, too, to share your plant bounty with friends.

Preparing for Winter

When nights get cold and hard frosts begin, the gardening season starts to close down. The last of the late asters, the plumes of ornamental grasses, a host of seedheads, and some berries will be all that is left. Cut back irises and yarrows, and remove annuals. If any plants were attacked by pests or diseases during the growing season, discard the remains instead of composting them.

Early Fall Color

Boltonia, goldenrod, and New England asters, all early-fall perennials, stand out against a lush green backround in this Northeast garden. They are a harbinger of the coming vibrant colors of fall.

Preserve the decorative seedheads of Joe-Pye weeds, black-eyed Susans, purple coneflowers, astilbes, and other perennials that may strike your fancy to add interesting textures and forms to the bare winter landscape. Leave ornamental grasses standing as well. In addition to being beautiful, these plants provide seeds and shelter for birds and other wildlife.

In northern zones, a fresh winter mulch will help protect plants from severe cold and drying winds. Add a deep layer of straw or other light mulch after the ground freezes hard to keep the soil uniformly cold, thus moderating the usual winter cycle of freezing and thawing that can heave shallow-rooted perennials like *Pulmonaria* clear out of the ground. Recycle your Christmas tree by laying its cut boughs over clump-forming perennials. In milder climates, renew the mulch layer for a different reason—to keep the garden neat. ∎

Shearing Back for a Second Flowering

Not all plants are destined for mere moments of glory. Clumpy, mounding perennials such as catmint, geranium, coreopsis, and candytuft bloom for weeks on end. As a result of so much flowering, they tend to look leggy and unkempt by mid-summer. When flowering trails off, it's time to shear them. Using a sharp pruner or shears, chop them back by half. As new buds emerge on the lower stems, they will produce compact, bushy growth and a fresh crop of blooms.

Dividing Overgrown Perennials

Sooner or later, plants grow large enough to need dividing. Some, such as *Monarda*, grow so quickly they can be divided every other year. A plant is ready for division when it has outgrown its allotted space, or when it has depleted the soil around it and the plant be- gins to loose vigor: Blooming trails off, and the clumps often begin to die out in the center. Begin by watering plants thoroughly the night before you divide them. If the soil is already moist, however, no additional water is necessary.

1 Lift the plant carefully from the soil with a spade or garden fork by digging all around the plant to loosen it completely. To remove only a small division for propagation without disturbing the rest of the clump, dig away the soil from only one side of the clump.

2 Gently separate the discrete crowns of the plant with your fingers to see where the best lines of division are. Pull the crowns apart. If the divisions are hard to detect, flush the soil away with a spray from a garden hose, and cut the crowns apart with a sharp knife or shears. Leave sufficient roots to enable the plant to re-establish quickly. Discard any weak or inferior pieces.

3 Replant the healthy divisions into well-amended soil, and water well.

Annuals and Biennials in Fall

With autumn's arrival, annuals such as cosmos and sage have grown large and full. Some have bloomed since late summer, but their flowering will actually now increase. Other annuals, such as pot marigolds, sweet alyssum, and petunias respond to the cooler weather with a burst of fresh growth. Together with geraniums, ageratums, and impatiens, these consistent bloomers will carry the garden into frosty weather.

Fall annuals blend seamlessly with perennials and shrubs. At the front of the border, blue ageratum, snowy alyssum, and *Sanvitalia procumbens* (creeping zinnia) form lush edges. Pink and yellow verbenas spread in waves, filling spaces left open by dormant summer bulbs. The feathery plumes of *Celosia cristata* (cockscomb), snapdragons' characteristic flowers, and cheery sunflowers add spectacular color contrast against fall's flowering mainstays, the deep-hued asters and bright mums.

To keep annuals at their best, cut back rangy plants like petunias and *Lantana* (shrub verbena) that have more stalks and leaves than flowers. Shear back lobelias, verbenas, and *Diascia* by one third or more to stimulate a flush of fresh growth. And pinch back zonal geraniums to encourage the growth of flowering side shoots. ■

Pinching Back Annuals for an Attractive Display

With a little encouragement, annuals like zonal geraniums will bloom throughout the frost-free months. To keep new flowers coming, first pinch back the growing tips when the plant is young. Slide your thumb and forefinger down the stem until you reach a well-developed leaf. Pinch the stem just above the leaf, using

your nails as shown, or cut it with scissors. Secondary flowering shoots will develop at the leaf axils. Make the plant even bushier by pinching the tips of these new shoots after they have developed a few leaves.

My baskets and containers of annuals seem to peter out by the end of summer. How can I keep them blooming through fall?

Fertilize. Use a balanced, water-soluble fertilizer mixed according to label directions for weekly or biweekly feeding, or a time-released granular fertilizer good for the whole season.

Annuals and Tender Perennials to Brighten the Fall Scene

As summer's flowers fade, sturdy annuals get a new lease on life, and tender perennials such as verbenas help fill the spaces created by fading summer flowers. Here are just a few of the many plants that will put verve into the garden and complete the bridge to first frost. Some will even endure a number of icy mornings before they succumb to winter.

Antirrhinum (snapdragon)	*Lobelia erinus* (edging lobelia)
Argemone mexicana (Mexican poppy)	*Lobularia maritima* (sweet alyssum)
Brachycome iberidifolia (Swan River daisy)	*Matthiola* (stock)
Dyssodia tenuiloba (Dahlberg daisy)	*Nicotiana alata* (flowering tobacco)
Gentianopsis crinita (fringed gentian)	*Petunia* (petunia)
Gaura (gaura)	*Satureja montana* (winter savory)
	Tagetes (marigold)
	Zinnia (zinnia)

◀ *Frost makes the blooms on stock plants glisten in this Illinois garden.*

Using Annuals for Bold Blocks of Color
In fall, mass-planted tall yellow zinnias and delicate 'Lemon Gem' marigolds give definition to this Portland, Oregon, mixed border (left) dominated by azaleas.

Autumn Bulbs

The careful planning that goes into planting spring-blooming bulbs is often forgotten when it comes to their fall-blooming counterparts. These lesser-known flowers can spark the garden with fresh color just as most of it is declining into winter. Some straddle summer and fall, such as tender dahlias in their myriad forms and colors, tuberous begonias, spider lilies in red or yellow, and red *Amaryllis belladonna* (belladonna lily). In most regions these will need special care to preserve them from year to year.

Others can endure the coldest winters and, like *Crocus sativus* (saffron crocus), bloom just before winter settles in to stay. Many have the unusual tendency to send up their foliage early in spring, where it remains until mid-summer, and then yellows and fades before their flowers alone appear in the fall. Buy any of these bulbs as early as possible in summer, and plant them immediately to give them a good start.

The Tender Bulbs

Dahlias and *Polianthes tuberosa* (tuberose) are frost-tender, as are gladioli, cannas, and vibrant red *Lycoris radiata* (spider lily). They must be lifted out of the ground after the first frost and overwintered indoors, as shown on page 87, to protect them from the cold.

North of Zone 8, treat *Polianthes* and other tender bulbs as container plants. Tuberose flowers will appear in the fall; after they fade, store the pot indoors over winter. When new foliage emerges in spring, move the pot into the sun, and feed and water the plant well. Or plant the pot in the ground and use the tufted, strappy foliage in your spring garden scene, as a green foil for other flowers and to fill bare spaces.

Hardy Bulbs in the Fall Garden

Fall-blooming hardy bulbs tend to be diminutive and intensely colored. These include an array of hardy cyclamens with exquisitely delicate flowers, such as rose-red *C. hederifolium* and pink *C. cilicium*, with slightly twisted petals.

Several crocuses and crocuslike bulbs bloom throughout the fall. Bulbs known as autumn crocus belong, in fact, to the genus *Colchicum* and they bloom in a range of colors, such as white *C. autumnale*, pale lilac-purple *C. cilicicum*, yellow *C. luteum*, and double-flowered *C.* 'Water Lily'. These bulbs are among the fall bloomers that send up spring foliage. Many fall-blooming crocuses appear at the end of the season, displaying lavender, purple, or white flowers. *Sternbergia lutea*, sometimes called winter daffodil, has shimmering, waxy yellow, goblet-shaped flowers. ∎

Hardy Bulbs Add Late-Season Color
Lavender-colored colchicum flowers have been interplanted with impatiens, which mask their bare stems in late fall in this three-season Eugene, Oregon, garden.

Lifting and Storing Tender Gladioli

Hybrid gladioli are tropical corms that must be dug from the garden in areas north of Zone 8 and stored indoors over winter. Wait until the leaves have turned brown, but before the first hard frost, before digging. This is also a good time to check the health of these plants, and to divide the bulbs for propagation. Be sure to separate and label bulbs as you dig them, as they are impossible to identify by sight. The process applies to all bulbs, including tubers like dahlias and begonias, and true bulbs like belladonna lilies.

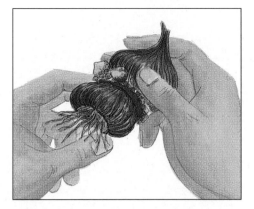

1 Use a spade or garden fork to lift the plant in a clump. Shake and wash all the soil from the roots, cut the plant down to 2 inches from the top of the corm, and air-dry it in the sun for several hours. Over the summer, the original corm will have withered and a new corm will have formed atop it.

2 To separate the old corm from the new one, hold them gently and twist them apart. Remove, as well, the small cormels that formed around the old corm, and discard the old corm. Keep only the corms and cormels that are firm and whole, and label them immediately.

3 Place the corms on a screen to dry in the sun for a week or so. Then store them in paper bags in a cool, dark, dry place until it's time to replant them in the spring. The cormels can be planted as well, and should flower in two or three years.

Hardy Autumn Bulbs

Include these bulbs and their cousins in your fall garden for a surprise burst of color at the end of the season. They are perfect as underplantings, and they'll also add a special touch to borders and rock gardens.

PLANT	HEIGHT	COLOR	ZONES	NOTES
Colchicum (autumn crocus)				
C. autumnale	4-6 inches	rosy purple	5-8	plant in well-drained, moist soil in partial shade
C. 'The Giant'	10-12 inches	lavender	5-8	large blooms
C. 'Waterlily'	8-10 inches	lilac-pink	5-8	double flowers
Crocus (crocus)				
C. medius	10 inches	purple	6-7	plant in full sun
C. sativus (saffron crocus)	3-6 inches	lilac to purple	5-8	stamens are source of saffron
C. serotinus ssp. *clusii*	3-4 inches	pale lilac and purple	5-8	foliage is sparse in fall
Cyclamen (Persian violet)				
C. cilicium (Sicily cyclamen)	3-4 inches	pink	5-8	needs winter protection in Zones 5-6
C. hederifolium (baby cyclamen)	3-6 inches	pink, red, white	4-8	plant in summer in light shade
Sternbergia (winter daffodil)				
S. lutea	6-8 inches	bright yellow	6-9	needs winter protection in Zones 6-7

Shrubs and Vines

Although the majority of shrubs bloom in spring and summer, a fair number, including butterfly bush, *Caryopteris incana* (common bluebeard), and hydrangea, produce flowers into the cooler months of autumn. The exquisite *Camellia sasanqua* and the ribbony *Hamamelis virginiana* (common witch hazel) save their displays until the last days of the season.

Vines augment the fall display with foliage and flowers alike, whether they are weaving through shrubs, festooning a fence, or scaling a trellis. Such annual vines as scarlet runner bean, hy-

acinth bean, and morning glory, including the ethereal 'Heavenly Blue', get off to a slow start in the early summer, are well established by fall, and bloom in autumn splendor. They are joined by the sweet-scented, creamy-white blooms of *Clematis paniculata* (autumn clematis).

In addition to the striking flowers of some shrubs, fall is, of course, the prime season for colorful foliage and fruits of shrubs, vines, and trees, which carry the garden well into winter. The brilliant yellows, flaming oranges, glowing reds, and rich burgundies of these plants in autumn work as starting

Autumn's Best-Fruiting Shrubs and Vines

In addition to their colorful fall foliage, the plants listed here produce bright berries in myriad hues, including white, pink, red, red-orange, yellow, blue, purple, and black. Once their leaves fall, the deciduous species garland the garden with their fruit and supply visiting birds, squirrels, and other wildlife with food throughout the winter.

◀ *The fruit of a flowering dogwood becomes a highlight in this Silver Spring, Maryland, garden, contrasting with the blue-green junipers in the front.*

Aronia (chokeberry)

Callicarpa (beautyberry)

Celastrus scandens (American bittersweet)

Cornus (dogwood)

Cotoneaster spp. (cotoneaster)

Euonymus (spindle tree)

Ilex (holly)

Mahonia (Oregon grape)

Malus (crab apple)

Parthenocissus quinquefolia (Virginia creeper)

Rosa spp. (wild rose)

Sorbus (mountain ash)

Symphoricarpos (snowberry)

Viburnum (virburnum)

Vitis (grape)

points for gorgeous combinations with fall-flowering perennials, annuals, and grasses.

Plant low-growing lilac-purple autumn crocuses under the butter-yellow leaves of *Lindera benzoin* (common spicebush) or the red-berried branches of *Ilex verticillata* (common winterberry). A graceful fountain of tawny *Pennisetum* grass in front of the *Ilex* will set off the bright holly fruit. Or use groups of bronze and coral mums, mingled with blue-lavender fall asters and pink dahlias or a low, ever-blooming rose like 'The Fairy'. Punctuate with a background clump of tall *Miscanthus* 'Morning Light', and contrast the grass with ground-hugging heather, whose foliage intensifies in color during the season.

The beauty of shrubs does not end with the dropping of the last leaf. Berries persist well into winter on the branches of numerous shrubs. They dangle like jewels from ice-encrusted stems, tempting hungry birds. Holly berries are among the longest-lasting fall fruit, as they do not become edible until after a few hard frosts have softened them. Tall and mid-height grasses, which include most of the *Miscanthus* cultivars, are beautiful with hawthorns and crabapples, presenting a golden contrast to their bright red or yellow fruit. ∎

Fall Splendor
Miscanthus softens the effect of brilliant goldenrod, purple New England asters, and bright fruits on a winterberry shrub in this Nashville, Tennessee, garden.

Garden  Pointers

A winter mulch is important for protecting plants from freeze-and-thaw cycles, but do not apply it until after the ground freezes. A mulch laid down earlier may keep the soil too warm to allow plants to become completely dormant. Mulching after the ground has frozen also ensures that mice and other rodent pests will have found places other than the garden to nest for the winter. For an easy winter mulch, chop leaves by running a lawn mower over them. Don't use whole leaves, as they tend to mat down and could cause rot over winter.

Stop pruning and deadheading plants five to six weeks before the first fall frost so that new growth engendered by the cutting will have time to harden off.

The Chores of Fall

Perennials
◆ Divide spring-blooming perennials (see page 83).
◆ Plant new perennials as soon as you have them.
◆ Cut back phlox, peonies, daylilies, and other plants that will not be left standing over the winter.
◆ Apply winter mulch once the ground has frozen.

Annuals and Biennials
◆ Fertilize container-grown annuals and tender perennials to keep them blooming until frost.
◆ Plant hardy annuals and biennials such as pansies and foxgloves.
◆ After frost, pull dead annuals and put them in the compost pile.

Bulbs
◆ Plant spring bulbs after the soil cools. To hasten root formation, soak bulbs for 12 hours before planting, especially if planting late. Add a specially formulated bulb fertilizer or a 9-9-6 fertilizer to the bottom of the hole at the rate recommended on the package if the soil is poor.
◆ Dig tender bulbs and prepare them for winter storage (see page 87).
◆ Cut back lilies to ground level.

Shrubs and Vines
◆ Wrap evergreen shrubs with burlap for winter protection, or spray the leaves with an antidessicant.
◆ In cold climates, cut roses back to 1 to 2 feet and mound soil, mulch, or leaves over the canes up to 1 foot high.

Using Water to Protect Plants from Frost Damage

Commercial nurseries shield their plants from frigid temperatures by spraying them with water just before a light freeze. When the water freezes, it releases heat that helps preserve leaves and stems. For low-growing plants (far left), run a sprinkler or mister over them when the temperature is below freezing. Tall plants (left) may break under the weight of ice, so instead of watering the foliage, soak the ground a few hours before frost occurs. The freezing water will release protective heat into the air around the plants.

Fall-Blooming Shrubs and Vines

Camellia sasanqua (sasanqua camellia)

Clematis virginiana (virgin's bower)

Hamamelis virginiana (common witch hazel)

Lonicera sempervirens ▶ (trumpet honeysuckle)

Phaseolus coccineus (scarlet runner bean)

Thunbergia alata (black-eyed Susan vine)

Seed Saving

Gather seeds in fall to store through winter and sow in spring.

| **After a flower fades,** it takes several weeks for the fertilized seed to mature. Usually the capsule will begin to change from green to yellowish brown when the seed is ripe. Before the capsule splits open, cover it with a plastic bag and secure the base with a twist tie. When the capsule splits the seed can be collected.

2 **With sharp scissors or pruning shears** cut the stem below the twist tie and gently shake seeds into bag. If necessary, open the bag slightly and split the capsule with your fingers to release seeds. Separate the seeds from the chaff. Store large seeds, such as those of daylilies, in paper bags filled with fresh sawdust. Store smaller seeds, such as poppy seeds, in sealed paper envelopes. Place the containers in the refrigerator for 8 to 12 weeks to simulate a winter cold spell before sowing.

Plants to Prune When Dormant

The best time to prune shrubs that flower in summer and then fruit in fall is after the growing season is over and the plants have gone dormant. Remove damaged stems and branches. Cut weak growth and limbs that detract from the plant's symmetry. Prune suckers at the base of the tree or shrub.

Callicarpa japonica (beautyberry) Zones 5-8

Calluna vulgaris (heather) Zones 4-6

Cytisus (broom) Zones 5-8

Fatsia japonica (Japanese fatsia) Zones 8-10

Franklinia alatamaha (Franklin tree) Zones 5-8

Hamamelis (witch hazel) Zones 3-8

Hibiscus syriacus (althaea) Zones 5-8

Hydrangea (hydrangea) Zones 4-9

Hypericum (St.-John's-wort) Zones 3-8

Lagerstroemia indica (crape myrtle) Zones 7-9

Potentilla (cinquefoil) Zones 2-7

Symphoricarpos (snowberry) Zones 3-7

Vitex (chaste tree) Zones 6-10

Hibiscus

Hydrangea

Hypericum

Vitex

Color Guide to Herbaceous Plants

Organized by plant type, this chart provides information needed to select species and varieties that will thrive in the particular conditions of your garden. For additional information on each plant, refer to the encyclopedia that begins on page 98.

Color	Plant	Zones	Dry	Well-drained	Moist	Full Sun	Partial Shade	Shade	Spring	Summer	Fall	Winter	Under 1 ft.	1-3 ft.	Over 3 ft.	Form	Foliage	Fragrance	Flowers	Fruit/seeds	Winter Interest
WHITE	Anaphalis margaritacea	3-9	✔	✔		✔	✔			✔	✔			✔			✔	✔	✔		
WHITE	Anemone sylvestris	4-8	✔	✔		✔			✔	✔				✔			✔		✔	✔	✔
WHITE	Argemone munita [3]	7-10		✔		✔	✔		✔					✔				✔	✔		
WHITE	Aruncus dioicus	4-9	✔	✔		✔			✔	✔	✔			✔			✔		✔		
WHITE	Boltonia asteroides 'Snowbank'	4-8		✔	✔		✔			✔	✔				✔		✔		✔		
WHITE	Cerastium tomentosum	4-7	✔	✔	✔	✔				✔	✔			✔				✔			
WHITE	Chrysanthemum x superbum	4-8	✔	✔		✔				✔	✔		✔					✔			
WHITE	Galanthus elwesii	3-8		✔		✔				✔	✔		✔				✔		✔		
WHITE	Gaura lindheimeri	4-9		✔	✔	✔	✔	✔	✔				✔						✔		
WHITE	Lobularia maritima [3]	9-10		✔		✔			✔				✔	✔	✔	✔		✔			
WHITE	Narcissus poeticus 'Actea'	3-10		✔		✔	✔		✔	✔	✔		✔					✔			
WHITE	Physostegia virginiana 'Summer Snow'	4-8		✔		✔	✔			✔			✔	✔				✔	✔		
WHITE	Sanguisorba canadensis	3-8		✔		✔	✔			✔				✔			✔		✔		
WHITE	Satureja montana 'Prostrate White' [3]	4-10		✔	✔	✔	✔			✔	✔				✔		✔				
WHITE	Thalictrum aquilegifolium 'White Cloud'	5-9	✔	✔		✔				✔	✔		✔				✔	✔	✔		
WHITE	Tiarella cordifolia	3-9		✔	✔		✔	✔	✔	✔					✔		✔		✔		
WHITE	Tricytris hirta	7-8		✔	✔		✔	✔	✔	✔			✔				✔	✔	✔		✔
YELLOW	Alchemilla mollis	4-8		✔	✔		✔	✔		✔	✔		✔				✔		✔		
YELLOW	Allium moly	3-10		✔	✔	✔	✔		✔	✔				✔			✔		✔		
YELLOW	Aurinia saxatilis	4-10		✔	✔	✔	✔		✔					✔					✔		
YELLOW	Coreopsis lanceolata	3-9	✔	✔		✔				✔			✔				✔		✔		
YELLOW	Cosmos sulphureus 'Goldcrest' [1]		✔	✔		✔				✔	✔			✔			✔		✔		
YELLOW	Doronicum cordatum 'Madame Mason'	4-8	✔	✔		✔	✔			✔	✔			✔			✔				
YELLOW	Erythronium americanum	3-9			✔	✔	✔		✔					✔			✔		✔		
YELLOW	Hypericum prolificum	3-8		✔	✔	✔	✔	✔					✔				✔		✔		
YELLOW	Phygelius aequalis 'Yellow Trumpet' [3]	8-10	✔	✔		✔	✔			✔				✔	✔		✔		✔	✔	✔
YELLOW	Silphium perfoliatum	3-9		✔		✔	✔			✔	✔				✔				✔		
YELLOW	Zizia aurea	4-8		✔		✔	✔			✔	✔			✔			✔		✔		

[1] Tender annual [2] Half-hardy annual [3] Tender perennial or bulb—grown as an annual in colder zones

	Plant	Zones	SOIL			LIGHT			BLOOM SEASON				PLANT HEIGHT			NOTED FOR					
			Dry	Well-drained	Moist	Full Sun	Partial Shade	Shade	Spring	Summer	Fall	Winter	Under 3 ft.	1-3 ft.	Over 3 ft.	Form	Foliage	Fragrance	Flowers	Fruit/seeds	Winter Interest
ORANGE	Hemerocallis fulva	3-10		✔	✔	✔	✔		✔	✔				✔			✔		✔		
ORANGE	Rudbeckia fulgida 'Goldsturm'	4-9		✔	✔	✔	✔			✔			✔		✔	✔	✔		✔		
ORANGE	Viola cornuta 'Chantreyland'	5-8		✔	✔	✔	✔		✔	✔			✔					✔	✔		
RED	Aquilegia x hybrida 'Crimson Star'	3-9		✔		✔	✔			✔	✔			✔					✔		
RED	Canna x generalis 'Dazzler' [3]	9-10		✔	✔	✔	✔		✔					✔			✔		✔		
RED	Crinum moorei [3]	7-10		✔	✔	✔				✔	✔				✔		✔		✔		
RED	Dahlia x hybrida 'Teds's Choice' [3]	9-10		✔	✔	✔	✔			✔					✔	✔	✔	✔	✔		
RED	Helleborus orientalis 'Queen of the Night'	4-9		✔	✔	✔				✔	✔		✔						✔		
RED	Kniphofia uvaria 'Coral Sea'	6-9		✔	✔		✔	✔	✔				✔				✔		✔		✔
RED	Lobelia cardinalis	3-10		✔	✔	✔				✔	✔		✔	✔			✔		✔		
RED	Monarda didyma	4-9			✔	✔	✔	✔	✔	✔	✔		✔	✔					✔		
PINK	Achillea millefolium 'Cerise Queen'	3-8	✔	✔		✔	✔			✔	✔		✔				✔	✔	✔		
PINK	Astible chinensis 'Pumila'	3-8		✔	✔	✔	✔		✔	✔			✔	✔			✔	✔	✔		
PINK	Bergenia cordifolia	3-9		✔	✔	✔	✔		✔				✔				✔		✔		
PINK	Calamintha grandiflora 'Variegata'	5-9		✔	✔		✔		✔					✔			✔				✔
PINK	Chelone lyonii	3-9		✔		✔				✔				✔			✔	✔	✔		
PINK	Colchicum speciosum 'Waterlily'	4-9		✔	✔	✔	✔		✔					✔					✔		
PINK	Dicentra spectabilis	4-8		✔	✔	✔	✔				✔		✔						✔		
PINK	Epimedium grandiflorum 'Rose Queen'	4-8		✔	✔		✔	✔	✔	✔				✔			✔		✔		
PINK	Filipendula rubra	3-8		✔	✔		✔	✔	✔				✔				✔		✔		✔
PINK	Galega officinalis 'Carnea'	4-10		✔	✔	✔	✔			✔					✔	✔	✔		✔		
PINK	Paeonia lactiflora 'Bowl of Beauty'	3-8		✔		✔	✔			✔			✔				✔		✔		
PINK	Phlox paniculata 'Bright Eyes'	3-8		✔	✔	✔	✔		✔	✔			✔				✔	✔	✔		
PINK	Sedum x 'Autumn Joy'	3-10		✔		✔				✔	✔		✔					✔			
PINK	Zinnia elegans [1]			✔		✔	✔		✔	✔			✔				✔		✔	✔	✔
PURPLE	Allium christophii	4-8		✔		✔			✔	✔			✔						✔		
PURPLE	Clematis x jackmanii	3-8		✔	✔	✔	✔		✔				✔						✔		
PURPLE	Echinacea purpurea	5-8		✔	✔	✔	✔		✔	✔	✔				✔	✔	✔		✔		
PURPLE	Eupatorium maculatum	3-6		✔		✔	✔			✔	✔		✔	✔					✔		
PURPLE	Galega orientalis	6-10		✔	✔	✔	✔			✔	✔		✔	✔			✔		✔		
PURPLE	Lavandula angustifolia 'Hidcote'	5-10		✔		✔	✔			✔			✔				✔		✔		
PURPLE	Liatris spicata 'Kobold'	3-10		✔		✔	✔		✔				✔				✔	✔	✔		

[1] Tender annual   [2] Half-hardy annual   [3] Tender perennial or bulb—grown as an annual in colder zones

	Plant	ZONES	Dry	Well-drained	Moist	Full Sun	Partial shade	Shade	Spring	Summer	Fall	Winter	Under 1 ft.	1-3 ft.	Over 3 ft.	Form	Foliage	Fragrance	Flowers	Fruit/seeds	Winter Interest
PURPLE	Salvia x sylvestris 'Mainacht'	5-8		✔		✔	✔			✔	✔			✔	✔	✔			✔		
	Verbena rigida	6-10		✔		✔				✔	✔			✔			✔	✔	✔		
	Viola cornuta	5-8		✔	✔	✔	✔		✔	✔			✔						✔		
BLUE	Aster x frikartii 'Monch'	5-8		✔	✔	✔				✔	✔			✔					✔		
	Brunnera macrophylla	4-8		✔	✔	✔	✔		✔					✔			✔		✔		
	Campanula lactiflora	5-7		✔		✔	✔			✔					✔				✔		
	Campanula rotundifolia	3-7		✔	✔	✔	✔			✔			✔						✔		
	Ceratostigma plumbaginoides	5-10		✔		✔	✔			✔	✔		✔				✔		✔		✔
	Echinops ritro	3-8		✔	✔	✔				✔				✔	✔	✔			✔		
	Gentiana acaulis	4-8		✔	✔	✔	✔		✔				✔						✔		
	Geranium x 'Johnson's Blue'	5-8		✔		✔	✔		✔	✔				✔			✔		✔		
	Iris sibirica 'Super Ego'	3-10	✔	✔	✔	✔	✔		✔					✔	✔	✔			✔		
	Mertensia virginica	3-8		✔	✔	✔	✔	✔	✔					✔			✔		✔		
	Nepeta x faassenii 'Six Hills Giant'	4-9		✔		✔				✔				✔			✔	✔	✔		
	Perovskia atriplicifolia 'Blue Spire'	5-8		✔		✔				✔	✔			✔	✔	✔	✔	✔	✔		
	Pulmonaria saccharata 'Mrs. Moon'	3-8		✔	✔		✔	✔	✔				✔	✔			✔		✔		
	Veronica 'Crater Lake Blue'	5-7		✔		✔	✔		✔	✔				✔			✔		✔		
MULTICOLOR	Anemone pulsatilla	5-8		✔		✔			✔					✔			✔		✔	✔	
	Antirrhinum majus [3]	8-10		✔		✔	✔		✔	✔	✔			✔					✔		
	Brachycome iberidifolia [1]			✔		✔				✔	✔		✔	✔					✔		
	Chrysanthemum coccineum	3-7		✔			✔		✔	✔				✔			✔		✔		
	Crocosmia x crocosmiiflora [3]	7-9		✔	✔	✔				✔	✔			✔	✔				✔		
	Dianthus barbatus	4-9		✔	✔	✔	✔		✔	✔				✔					✔		
	Digitalis purpurea var. gloxiniiflora	3-9		✔	✔		✔			✔					✔	✔			✔		
	Dyssodia tenuiloba [3]	9-10	✔	✔		✔				✔	✔		✔				✔	✔	✔		
	Geranium sylvaticum	5-9		✔	✔	✔	✔		✔	✔				✔					✔		
	Helenium autumnale	3-10		✔	✔	✔				✔	✔			✔	✔				✔		
	Lilium Hybrids	3-9		✔	✔	✔	✔		✔	✔				✔	✔				✔		
	Nicotiana alata [3]	7-10		✔	✔	✔	✔		✔	✔	✔			✔	✔			✔	✔		
	Petunia x hybrida [2]			✔		✔				✔	✔		✔						✔		
	Tulipa Hybrids	3-8		✔		✔	✔		✔	✔			✔	✔					✔		

[1] Tender annual   [2] Half-hardy annual   [3] Tender perennial or bulb—grown as an annual in colder zones

Guide to Woody Plants

Organized by plant type, this chart provides information needed to select species and varieties that will thrive in the particular conditions of your garden. For additional information on each plant, refer to the encyclopedia that begins on page 98.

	ZONES	SOIL			LIGHT			BLOOM SEASON			PLANT HEIGHT				NOTED FOR					
		Dry	Well-drained	Moist	Full Sun	Partial Shade	Shade	Spring	Summer	Fall	3-6 ft.	6-10 ft.	10-30 ft.	Over 30 ft.	Form	Foliage	Fragrance	Flowers	Fruit/seeds	Winter Interest
DECIDUOUS SHRUBS																				
Amelanchier alnifolia	4-9		✓	✓	✓	✓		✓			✓	✓	✓		✓	✓	✓	✓	✓	✓
Buddleia davidii	5-9		✓		✓				✓	✓	✓	✓				✓	✓	✓	✓	
Calycanthus floridus	4-10		✓	✓	✓	✓		✓	✓			✓				✓	✓	✓		
Clethra almifloia	3-9			✓	✓	✓	✓		✓			✓				✓	✓	✓		
Cornus mas	4-8		✓	✓	✓	✓		✓					✓		✓	✓		✓	✓	✓
Cornus sericea	2-8		✓	✓	✓	✓		✓				✓			✓	✓		✓	✓	✓
Hydrangea macrophylla	6-9		✓	✓	✓	✓	✓		✓		✓					✓		✓		✓
Hydrangea quercifolia	5-9		✓	✓	✓	✓	✓		✓		✓					✓		✓		✓
Spiraea japonica	4-8		✓		✓	✓		✓	✓		✓						✓			
Spiraea x vanhouttei	4-8		✓		✓	✓		✓				✓					✓			
Syringa meyeri	3-8		✓	✓	✓			✓			✓	✓					✓	✓		
Syringa vulgaris	3-7		✓	✓	✓			✓				✓	✓			✓	✓	✓		
Viburnum acerifolium	3-8	✓	✓		✓	✓		✓			✓					✓		✓	✓	
Viburnum dentatum	2-8		✓	✓	✓	✓		✓				✓	✓			✓		✓	✓	
Viburnum plicatum var. tomentosum	5-8		✓	✓	✓	✓		✓				✓			✓	✓		✓	✓	
Viburnum trilobum	2-7		✓	✓	✓	✓		✓				✓				✓		✓	✓	✓
Vitex agnus-castus var. latifolia	6-9		✓	✓	✓				✓	✓		✓	✓				✓	✓		
DECIDUOUS TREES																				
Amelanchier arborea	4-9		✓	✓	✓	✓		✓					✓		✓	✓		✓	✓	✓
Amelanchier canadensis	3-7		✓	✓	✓	✓		✓					✓		✓	✓		✓	✓	✓
Cornus florida	5-9		✓	✓	✓	✓		✓				✓	✓		✓	✓		✓	✓	✓
Cornus Kousa	5-9		✓	✓	✓	✓			✓				✓			✓		✓	✓	✓
Magnolia grandiflora	7-9		✓	✓	✓	✓		✓						✓	✓	✓	✓	✓	✓	
Magnolia x soulangiana	4-9		✓	✓	✓	✓		✓					✓		✓	✓		✓	✓	
Magnolia stellata	5-9		✓	✓	✓	✓		✓					✓		✓	✓	✓	✓	✓	✓
Malus coronaria	2-8		✓	✓	✓			✓					✓		✓	✓		✓	✓	
Malus floribunda	5-8		✓	✓	✓			✓					✓		✓	✓		✓	✓	
Stewartia malacodendron	7-9		✓	✓	✓	✓			✓				✓			✓		✓		✓
Stewartia pseudocamellia	5-7		✓	✓	✓	✓			✓					✓		✓		✓		✓

A Zone Map of the U.S. and Canada

A plant's winter hardiness and tolerance of summer heat are critical in deciding whether it is suitable for your garden. The map below divides the United States and Canada into 11 climatic zones based on average minimum temperatures, as compiled by the U.S. Department of Agriculture. Find your zone and check the zone information in the plant selection guide *(pages 92-95)* or the encyclopedia *(pages 98-151)* to help you choose the plants most likely to flourish in your climate.

Zone 1: Below -50° F

Zone 2: -50° to -40°

Zone 3: -40° to -30°

Zone 4: -30° to -20°

Zone 5: -20° to -10°

Zone 6: -10° to 0°

Zone 7: 0° to 10°

Zone 8: 10° to 20°

Zone 9: 20° to 30°

Zone 10: 30° to 40°

Zone 11: Above 40°

Cross-Reference Guide to Plant Names

Annual phlox—*Phlox drummondii*

Arrowwood—*Viburnum dentatum*

Autumn crocus—*Colchicum autumnale*

Balloon flower—*Platycodon grandiflorus*

Basket-of-gold—*Aurinia saxatilis*

Bee balm—*Monarda didyma*

Bellflower—*Campanula*

Bergenia—*Bergenia grandiflorum*

Bishop's hat—*Epimedium*

Black-eyed Susan—*Rudbeckia hirta*

Bleeding heart—*Dicentra spectabilis*

Bluebells—*Mertensia*

Blue phlox—*Phlox divarticata*

Boltonia—*Boltonia*

Boneset—*Eupatorium perfoliatum*

Brunnera—*Brunnera*

Bunchberry—*Cornus canadensis*

Burnet—*Sanguisorba*

Butterfly bush—*Buddleia*

Calamint—*Calamintha*

Canna—*Canna*

Cape fuchsia—*Phygelius capensis*

Cardinal flower—*Lobelia cardinalis*

Catmint—*Nepeta*

Chaste tree—*Vitex angus-castus*

Christmas rose—*Helleborus niger*

Columbine—*Aquilegia*

Compass plant—*Silphium laciniatum*

Coneflower—*Rudbeckia*

Crab apple—*Malus*

Cranberry bush—*Viburnum trilobum*

Creeping St.-John's-wort—*Hypericum calycinum*

Cross vine—*Bignonia capreolata*

Daffodil—*Narcissus*

Dahlberg daisy—*Dyssodia tenuiloba*

Daylily—*Hemerocallis*

Dogwood—*Cornus*

Dutchman's-breeches—*Dicentra cucullaria*

English lavender—*Lavandula angustifolia*

Everlasting—*Anaphalis*

False spirea—*Astilbe x arendsii*

Florida swamp lily—*Crinum americanum*

Flowering dogwood tree—*Cornus florida*

Flowering tobacco—*Nicotiana alata*

Foamflower—*Tiarella cordifolia*

Foxglove—*Digitalis*

French lavender—*Lavandula dentata*

Gay-feather—*Liatris*

Geranium—*Pelargonium*

Giant allium—*Allium christophii*

Giant snowdrop—*Galanthus elwesii*

Globe thistle—*Echinops*

Goat's rue—*Galega officinalis*

Goatsbeard—*Aruncus dioicus*

Golden alexanders—*Zizia aurea*

Great blue lobelia—*Lobelia siphilitica*

Great globe thistle—*Echinops sphaerocephalus*

Japanese anemone—*Anemone x hybrida*

Japanese stewartia—*Stewartia pseudocamellia*

Joe-Pye weed—*Eupatorium maculatum*

Johnny-jump-up—*Viola tricolor*

Knautia—*Knautia macedonica*

Lady's-mantle—*Alchemilla*

Lavender—*Lavandula*

Leadwort—*Ceratostigma plumbaginoides*

Lenten rose—*Helleborus orientalis*

Leopard's-bane—*Doronicum*

Lilac—*Syringa*

Lungwort—*Pulmonaria*

Meadow rue—*Thalictrum*

Meadowsweet—*Filipendula*

Mexican poppy—*Argemone mexicana*

Montbretia—*Crocosmia*

Obedience plant—*Physostegia virginiana*

Pansy—*Viola x wittrockiana*

Peony—*Paeonia*

Pink—*Dianthus*

Prickly poppy—*Argemone*

Purple coneflower—*Echinacea*

Red-hot poker—*Kniphofia uvaria*

Russian sage—*Perovskia atriplicifolia*

Sage—*Salvia*

Serviceberry—*Amelanchier*

Shadblow serviceberry—*Amelanchier canadensis*

Siberian bugloss—*Brunnera macrophylla*

Snapdragon—*Antirrhinum majus*

Sneezeweed—*Helenium autumnale*

Snow-in-summer—*Cerastium tomentosum*

Snowdrop—*Galanthus*

Speedwell—*Veronica*

Squirrel corn—*Dicentra*

canadensis

St.-John's-wort—*Hypericum*

Stewartia—*Stewartia*

Stonecrop—*Sedum*

Summer-sweet—*Clethra alnifolia*

Swan River daisy—*Brachycome iberidifolia*

Sweet alyssum—*Lobularia maritima*

Sweet shrub—*Calycanthus occidentalis*

Sweet William—*Dianthus barbatus*

Tickseed—*Coreopsis*

Toad lily—*Tricyrtis*

Tree peony—*Paeonia suffruticosa*

Trout lily—*Erythronium americanum*

Trumpet flower—*Bignonia*

Tulip—*Tulipa*

Turtlehead—*Chelone glabra*

Vervain—*Verbena*

Violet—*Viola*

Virginia bluebells—*Mertensia virginica*

Wild bergamot—*Monarda fistulosa*

Wild bleeding heart—*Dicentra eximia*

Wild geranium—*Geranium maculatum*

Wild sweet crab apple—*Malus coronaria*

Wild sweet William—*Phlox maculata*

Windflower—*Anemone*

Winter savory—*Satureja montana*

Yarrow—*Achillea*

Yellow flag—*Iris pseudacorus*

Yellow foxglove—*Digitalis grandiflora*

Zinnia—*Zinnia elegans*

Encyclopedia of Plants

The plants described here are listed alphabetically by genus. The genus name is followed by its pronunciation and, in bold type, its common name or names. If you know a plant only by its common name, refer to the cross-reference chart on page 97 or to the index.

A botanical name consists of the genus and a species, both usually printed in italics. Species may have common names, which appear in parentheses, and many species contain one or more cultivars, whose names appear between single quotation marks. An "x" before the name indicates a hybrid.

"Hardiness" refers to the zones described on the USDA Hardiness Zone Map for the United States and Canada (page 96). Plants that are grown outside the zones recommended here may do poorly or fail to survive. For annuals, hardiness refers to their ability to withstand spring frost. Hardy annuals, as small seedlings, can survive all but extreme cold; half-hardy annuals can tolerate a light frost; tender annuals can be started indoors but should not be planted outdoors until all danger of frost has passed.

Flowering times are given for each species to facilitate planning for three seasons of bloom.

"Pro's Picks" are cultivars or hybrids that have proven to be exceptionally prized for their vigor, color, fragrance, form, or other quality.

Achillea (a-kil-EE-a)
YARROW

Hardiness: Zones 3-8
Plant type: perennial
Height: 1 to 4 feet
Interest: flowers, foliage, fragrance
Soil: well-drained, dry
Light: full sun to partial shade

◀ *Achillea filipendulina* 'Gold Plate'

Yarrows make effective border, rock garden, and meadow plants, both for their flat-topped clusters of small, colorful, five-petaled flowers and their attractive, gray-green, aromatic, fernlike foliage. The basal rosette of leaves bolts in summer, producing tall, strong flower stalks. Yarrows make long-lasting cut flowers, and can be dried for use in everlasting flower arrangements.

Growing conditions and maintenance

Yarrows thrive in regular garden soil and are heat and drought tolerant. They are susceptible to powdery mildew in humid conditions, however. They can be grown from seed, cuttings, or by division, with plants frequently flowering the first year. Sow the small seed ⅛ inch deep in sandy soil that is kept moist, but not wet, until seedlings are established. Thin plants to 1½ to 2 feet apart. Mature plants should be divided every 3 to 4 years to encourage vigorous growth and flowering.

Selected species and varieties

A. filipendulina (fern-leaf yarrow, golden yarrow)—robust, 3 to 4 feet tall with large clusters of bright yellow flowers in midsummer, and 10-inch leaves finely divided and hairy; var. **alba** has white flowers; 'Gold Plate' has pewter green leaves and bright yellow flowers.

A. millefolium—1- to 3-foot native or naturalized meadow species with flat-topped clusters of small white flowers from early summer into fall.

★ PRO'S PICK ★

A. millefolium 'Cerise Queen' has bright pink blossoms adorned with pale centers instead of the white flowers of the species. Leaves are aromatic and slightly hairy.

Alchemilla *(al-kem-ILL-a)*
LADY'S-MANTLE

Hardiness: Zones 4-8

Plant type: perennial

Height: 8 to 18 inches

Interest: flowers, foliage

Soil: well-drained, evenly moist, rich in organic matter

Light: full sun to partial shade

◀ *Alchemilla mollis*

Lady's-mantles are old-fashioned plants grown for their distinctive gray-green foliage and attractive sprays of tiny greenish yellow flowers. Their large leaves and wavy, serrated edges make them popular plants for edging and as a filler for borders. Lady's-mantles' low, spreading habit and rapid growth make them excellent seasonal ground covers.

Growing conditions and maintenance

These species grow best where summers are cool and moist; in hot, dry locations, they benefit from the addition of compost and extra water. Cut back brown or tattered foliage, which will quickly regrow. Lady's-mantle can be grown from seed, and established plants often self-sow. Thin seedlings to 1½ feet apart. Once established, these rugged perennials will need to be divided every year or so. Dig up small clumps with a sharp trowel in early spring and transplant to desired locations.

Selected species and varieties

A. alpina (alpine lady's-mantle)—8-inch creeping mounds of small, toothed, dark green leaves with silver undersides and light green flowers in late spring.

A. mollis [also listed as *A. vulgaris*]—robust, spreading clumps of rich, gray-green leaves reaching 18 inches with open sprays of tiny chartreuse flowers from late spring to early summer.

A. pentaphylla—creeping mats of ¾-inch leaves with tiny sprays of greenish flowers in late spring.

A. sericata—clumps of coarsely toothed leaves forming 10-inch mounds of dark green foliage beneath delicate displays of pale yellow flowers in spring.

★ **Point of interest:** *Lady's-mantle foliage is water-repellent and even more attractive when raindrops bead on its dusky leaves after a summer shower.*

Allium *(AL-lee-um)*
ORNAMENTAL ONION, ALLIUM

Hardiness: Zones 3-10

Plant type: perennial

Height: 8 inches to 5 feet

Interest: flowers, foliage, fragrance

Soil: dry to moist, well-drained

Light: full sun to partial shade

◀ *Allium moly*

These relatives of chives, garlic, and edible onions add color and texture to beds, borders, rock gardens, and wildflower meadows. All have small, six-petaled flowers gathered into round or nodding clusters borne atop erect stalks. Flowering seasons vary from spring to late summer. The aromatic, pungent leaves, either cylindrical and hollow or flattened and grasslike, die back to the bulb after flowering.

Growing conditions and maintenance

Plant ornamental onion bulbs at a depth about three times the width of the bulb, with the pointed end up. Space smaller bulbs 4 to 6 inches apart, larger ones about a foot apart. In regions with cold winters, plant bulbs in the fall; in warm regions, they can be planted in either fall or spring. *A. cernuum* needs neutral to alkaline soil that is rich in organic matter, but once established will thrive in moist or dry sites. Taller types such as *A. aflatunense* and *A. sphaerocephalum* benefit from staking, and should be planted in areas away from winds that may break the flower stalks. Since all onions have foliage that dies back after flowering is completed, plant them with perennials or annuals such as daylilies or cockscomb, which will hide their withering leaves. Remove the leaves when they have turned tan, at which time the spent flower stalks also can be cut. Protect the bulbs by mulching in regions colder than Zone 5. Divide bulbs only when flowering decreases. Propagate by seed or by separating and replanting the small bulblets that form at the base of mature bulbs. It takes about 2 years for seedlings or bulblet transplants to reach flowering size. *Continued* ▶

Allium, continued

Selected species and varieties

A. aflatunense (Persian onion)—4-inch purple flowers in late spring on 2- to 4-foot stems; Zones 4-8.

A. cepa—1- to 1½- foot blue-green stems topped with rounded clusters of white or lilac flowers in late spring and early summer; var. **viviparum** produces small bulblets in fruiting clusters atop the stems; Zones 5-10.

A. cernuum (nodding onion)—white or pink ⅓-inch flowers in nodding clusters in summer on 1- to 2-foot stalks; native to meadows in the eastern United States.

A. christophii [also listed as **A. albopilosum**] (giant allium, stars-of-Persia)—1½ to 2 feet with scapes bearing 6- to 8-inch clusters of up to 50 star-shaped, lilac purple flowers in late spring; Zones 4-8.

A. cyaneum—stunning, bright blue nodding flowers on 10-inch stems above dense clumps of grasslike leaves in late summer; Zones 5-8.

A. moly (lily leek, golden onion)—flat clusters of ¾-inch to 1-inch starlike, bright yellow flowers in spring on thin, 1-foot stems above broad, straplike, gray-green leaves; Zones 3-9.

A. neapolitanum (daffodil garlic, Naples garlic)—loose, open, 3-inch clusters of up to 30 fragrant 1-inch white flowers on 12- to 18-inch stems in early spring; Zones 6-9.

A. sphaerocephalum (drumstick chive, roundheaded leek)—densely packed 2-inch oval heads of bell-shaped, deep purple flowers in summer on 2- to 3-foot stalks with hollow, cylindrical leaves up to 24 inches long; Zones 4-8.

Allium sphaerocephalum

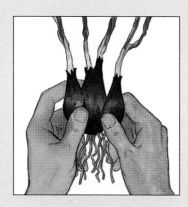

How to: Divide bulbs by digging clumps in summer after the leaves have turned yellow. Using your fingers, gently separate daughter bulbs from the parent bulb, making sure they come away with a portion of the basal plate attached. Replant the parent bulb about 6 inches deep and the daughter bulbs about 2 inches deep in well-worked soil.

★ **Point of interest:** *Alliums make excellent companion plants because they contain natural substances that repel insects and nematodes harmful to many ornamental plants.*

Amelanchier (am-el-ANG-kee-er)
SERVICEBERRY

◀ *Amelanchier alnifolia*

Hardiness: Zones 4-9

Plant type: large shrub or small tree

Height: 4 to 40 feet

Interest: flowers, foliage, fruit, bark, form, fragrance

Soil: acid, dry to moist, well-drained

Light: full sun to partial shade

These compact shrubs or small trees provide four-season interest and are known by a number of common names, including shadbush, sarviceberry, juneberry, and serviceberry. Their 1- to 2-inch white flowers are among the earliest to appear in the spring, covering the tips of the graceful branches with showy, slightly pendulous clusters. Flowers are soon followed by gray-green leaves that turn medium green in summer and brilliant shades of yellow, apricot, bronze, or red in fall. All species produce tasty red-purple fruit that matures in late spring or early summer and attracts many kinds of birds. The dark purple, berrylike fruit of *A. arborea* ripens in June and is the main ingredient of serviceberry pie, a southern delicacy reminiscent of blueberry pie. The ripe berries of *A. alnifolia* were added to buffalo meat by the Plains Indians to make pemmican, a winter staple. Serviceberry plants often have multiple stems with smooth, silvery gray bark streaked with darker gray. They can be used as specimen trees, in shrub borders, at woodland edges, or for naturalizing. They are especially effective along the shore of a stream or pond, where their seasonal accents can be reflected in the water.

Growing conditions and maintenance

Serviceberries thrive in slightly acid soil that is rich in organic matter. *A. canadensis* adapts to wet conditions, particularly in sandy soil. Multiple-stemmed species can be pruned into single stems or limbed into a small clump if desired. Propagate species from seed chilled for 3 to 4 months at 40° F, and cultivars from softwood cuttings taken in late spring.

Selected species and varieties

A. alnifolia—multibranched shrub to 20 feet tall with small, toothed, bright green leaves, and clusters of thin-petaled, lightly fragrant flowers in spring.

A. arborea—15- to 25-foot multibranched shrub or small tree with pendulous clusters of dainty white flowers in spring and tasty purplish black fruit in summer.

A. asiatica (Asian serviceberry)—15- to 40-foot tree with fragrant flowers in midspring, a

Continued ▶

Amelanchier, *continued*

long flowering period, and deep red buds in winter; Zones 5-8.

A. canadensis (shadblow serviceberry)—large shrub or small tree native to Atlantic coastal bogs and swamps, growing slowly to 20 feet with erect clusters of white flowers and 2-inch silvery leaves that emerge in spring, turn green in summer, and yellow-gold in fall.

Amelanchier canadensis

A. x grandiflora (apple serviceberry)—multistemmed shrub or small tree to 30 feet tall with white spring flowers in 4- to 6-inch pendulous clusters, gray fissured bark with a reddish cast, and bright orange-red leaves that accent the purple fruit in fall; 'Cumulus' is noted for its fluffy white flowers and oval form; 'Rubescens' has purplish pink buds that open to reveal blush-colored flowers.

A. laevis (Allegheny serviceberry)—multistemmed small tree about 20 feet tall, similar to **A. arborea,** with 4-inch-long fleecy white flowering panicles in early spring, bronzy new foliage, and sweet black fruit in early summer.

A. stolonifera (running serviceberry)—small, thicket-forming shrub 4 to 6 feet tall spreading by stolons, with white spring flowers producing purple-black fruit in mid-summer; Zones 4-8.

How to: Propagate by cutting the root connection between a basal shoot and the parent in late summer and then transplanting the shoot in early spring before it flowers.

Anaphalis (an-AFF-al-is)
EVERLASTING

◀ *Anaphalis margaritacea*

Hardiness: Zones 3-9
Plant type: perennial
Height: 1 to 3 feet
Interest: flowers, foliage
Soil: well-drained
Light: full sun

Everlastings are vigorous, woolly plants that add contrast to borders and rock gardens from summer through fall. Narrow, elongated white leaves clasp the stems. The small, tight, globular summer flowers often are cut before they are fully open, to be dried and used in flower arrangements. In addition to their ornamental qualities, everlastings repel some insects harmful to garden plants and also attract butterflies.

Growing conditions and maintenance

Everlastings do well in nutrient-poor sandy soil. They need no additional fertilizers and, once established, are quite drought resistant. They spread freely by underground stems called rhizomes, and form large clumps in just a few years. Separate rhizomes in early spring and plant ½ inch deep. Or propagate from fresh seed sown in the fall, planting ⅛ inch deep, or start in flats and transplant seedlings 18 inches apart.

Selected species and varieties

A. margaritacea (pearly everlasting, silverleaf)—native to the North Temperate Region, including North America, ¼- to ½-inch pearly white flower heads with burnt yellow centers appear in late summer on 8- to 24-inch stems, and narrow, 4- to 8-inch green leaves often so densely covered with hairs that they appear to have a silvery cast.

A. triplinervis—3- to 8-inch woolly, narrowly oblong leaves, each with three to five prominent veins, on 8- to 30-inch stems bearing large numbers of ½- to ¾-inch white, fluffy flower heads from summer through fall; var. **monocephala** has leaves more egg-shaped and flowers in summer; Zones 3-8.

★ **Point of interest:** *Male and female flowers of everlasting are borne on separate plants but there is little difference in the overall appearance of the flowers other than the yellow anthers present in male flowers.*

Anemone *(a-NEM-o-nee)*
ANEMONE, WINDFLOWER

◀ *Anemone nemorosa*

Hardiness: Zones 2-9

Plant type: perennial

Height: 3 inches to 4 feet

Interest: flowers, foliage, fragrance, fruit

Soil: moist, well-drained

Light: full sun to partial shade

These members of the buttercup family have open-faced flowers with single or double rows of colorful, showy sepals rather than petals. Thin, pliant stems support the 1- to 3-inch flowers in shades of white, pink, red, and blue. Anemones bloom from spring through fall, depending on the species. Some species, such as *A. pulsatilla*, have attractive plumed fruit. When the plant is not in flower, its mounds of finely cut leaves provide delicate foliage textures for borders, edges, or backgrounds. Windflowers are stunning in mixed plantings and lend charm to rock gardens and along woodland paths.

Growing conditions and maintenance

Anemones grow well in humus-rich soil that is moist during the growing season but dry when plants are dormant in winter. *A. pulsatilla* needs full sun and neutral to alkaline soil, while other species are not as selective about soil conditions and grow in full sun or partial shade. Plant anemones in groups for best effect, spacing the smaller varieties 1 foot apart and larger varieties 2 feet apart. *A. x hybrida* needs protection from wind and hot sun, especially during the first two years after initial planting. Divide *A. hupehensis* and *A. x hybrida* in spring, and *A. sylvestris* and *A. canadensis* in late fall. Plant divisions just below the soil surface.

How to: *A. canadensis* spreads quickly, but can be restrained by planting it in open-bottom containers. Cut a 5-gallon plastic bucket in half and bury the top half so its rim is just below the soil surface. Divide plants every three years to maintain their vigor.

Selected species and varieties

A. alpina [also listed as ***Pulsatilla alpina***] (Alpine windflower)—airy clusters of fernlike foliage beneath 18-inch stems ornamented with large white flowers from spring through summer; var. ***sulphurea*** has yellow flowers; Zones 6-8.

A. blanda (Grecian windflower, Greek anemone)—2-inch-wide pastel blue, pink, or white daisylike flowers from early to midspring on 4- to 8-inch stems with divided leaves that die back after blooming season; excellent for rock gardens or naturalizing under deciduous trees; 'Atrocaerulea' has dark blue flowers; 'Rosea' has pink flowers; Zones 6-8.

Anemone blanda

A. canadensis (meadow anemone, Canada anemone)—1½-inch white flowers often tinged with light green in late spring to early summer on 2- to 2½-foot stems above rosettes of maple-shaped leaves; Zones 2-6.

A. hupehensis (Japanese anemone)—2- to 3-inch white flowers tinged with pink on 1- to 3-foot stems from late summer through early fall; 'September Charm' bears loads of single, soft pink blossoms; var. ***japonica*** has deep violet-pink blossoms; 'Praecox' has rich pink flowers with dark rose edges in mid-summer.

A. x hybrida (Japanese anemone)—2- to 3-inch white, pink, rose, or crimson flowers in late summer through early fall on 2½- to 4-foot stems adorned with dark green foliage; 'Honorine Jobert' has single white flowers with yellow centers from late summer to fall; 'Lesseri' bears crimson flowers in summer; 'Pamina', semidouble antique rose flowers in fall; 'Rosea Superba', deep rose flowers; Zones 6-8.

A. nemorosa (European wood anemone)—1-inch white flowers tinged with pink or purple and yellow centers appearing in early to mid-spring on 6- to 10-inch stems; excellent for rock gardens or woodland naturalizing; Zones 4-8.

A. pulsatilla [also listed as ***Pulsatilla amoena***] (pasqueflower)— 2-inch blue, purple, white, or bicolored flowers atop 2-foot stems that appear before the soft, hairy, deeply lobed leaves in early spring; Zones 5-8.

A. sylvestris (snowdrop anemone)—solitary, fragrant 2-inch midspring flowers on 1- to 1½-foot stems above tufts of light green foliage; Zones 4-8.

Anemone sylvestris

A. tomentosa (hairy anemone)—2- to 3-inch pastel pink flowers on 4-foot stems above dense, deeply lobed leaves in mid- to late summer; Zones 3-9.

Antirrhinum *(an-tir-RYE-num)*
SNAPDRAGON

Hardiness: Zones 8-10

Plant type: tender perennial often grown as an annual

Height: 6 inches to 4 feet

Interest: flowers

Soil: well-drained, fertile

Light: full sun to light shade

◄ *Antirrhinum majus* 'Sonnet'

Snapdragons are longtime garden favorites esteemed for their stately appearance and vivid colors. Modern snapdragons are among the most versatile of plants, ranging in height from robust 4-foot giants perfect for the back of the border to 6-inch dwarfs that lend vibrance to rock gardens and edgings. The long-lasting spring-to-summer flowers range in color from the traditional magenta or white to flashy orange, red, pink, and chromium yellow. The pouched, 1½-inch flowers have a two-lobed upper lip and a three-lobed lower lip. Flowers are clustered at the top of the smooth stems, which bear numerous 3-inch-long, deep green, lance-shaped leaves. Snapdragons make superb cut flowers.

Growing conditions and maintenance

Snapdragons flower most abundantly in evenly moist soil with full sun, yet even in partial shade the display is dazzling. They should have afternoon shade in regions where summers are hot. Sow seed indoors 8 to 10 weeks before transplanting in late spring. Do not cover seed with soil, as they need light to germinate. Space dwarf varieties 6 inches apart and taller ones about 18 inches apart. Pinch young plants to encourage a more bushy form and greater flower production. The blooming season can be prolonged by removing withering flowers before they set seed.

Selected species and varieties

A. majus—prolific bloomer in a wide spectrum of colors; 'Coronette' grows to 3 feet with conical flower clusters in a range of intense colors; 'His Excellency' grows 12 to 24 inches tall with bright scarlet flowers; 'Sonnet' is early flowering with well-formed clusters of white, yellow, crimson, copper, orange, bronze, or carmine flowers on 20-inch stems; 'Tahiti' is a dwarf with rose, white, red, or yellow blossoms on compact 7-inch stems; 'Trumpet Serenade' is 6 to 12 inches tall with bicolored, funnel-shaped flowers in pastel golds and oranges.

Aquilegia *(ak-wil-EE-jee-a)*
COLUMBINE

Hardiness: Zones 3-9

Plant type: perennial

Height: 8 inches to 3 feet

Interest: flowers, foliage

Soil: moist, well-drained

Light: full sun to full shade

◄ *Aquilegia canadensis*

Columbines have complex erect or nodding flowers with reflexed spurs at the base of brightly colored petals, and rounded, lacy, blue-green foliage that adds a soft accent to the garden. American columbine is native to the tall-grass prairies of the Midwest and deciduous woodlands of the East. It is an excellent addition to the wildflower garden or naturalized in meadows, while the large-flowered hybrids are used most effectively in beds, borders, and rock gardens.

Growing conditions and maintenance

Columbines thrive in organic-rich soil with even moisture. *A.* x *hybrida* tolerates light shade, and the native North American species does well in deep shade. The hybrids often are short-lived, but indigenous species self-sow prolifically. Propagate native columbines by sowing the small seed indoors in late winter. Do not cover seed, as they need light to germinate properly. Leaf miners sometimes do cosmetic damage to the foliage in summer.

Selected species and varieties

A. canadensis (American columbine)—graceful, 2-foot stems bearing dainty, nodding crimson and yellow blossoms from spring to mid-summer.

A. x *hybrida* (hybrid columbine)—large, 3-inch spring-blooming flowers on 3-foot stems; 'Dragonfly Hybrids' are 12 inches tall and range in color from red, yellow, or blue to various bicolors; 'Long-spurred Hybrids' grow to 2 feet with the same range of colors; 'McKana Giant Hybrids' have oversized flowers borne on 30-inch stems.

★ PRO'S PICK ★

A. x *hybrida* 'Crimson Star' has 1½-inch flowers with red spurs, white central petal tips, and a projecting shower of elegant golden stamens.

Argemone   (ar-JEM-o-nee)
PRICKLY POPPY

◄ *Argemone munita*

Hardiness: Zones 7-10

Plant type: annual, biennial, tender perennial grown as an annual

Height: 2 to 4 feet

Interest: flowers, foliage

Soil: dry, well-drained

Light: full sun

The light blue-green, crinkled, spiny foliage and large flowers of prickly poppies make a bold statement in the garden. The flowers come in shades of white, yellow, and orange, and have four to six petals with a unique crepe-paper texture that surround a mass of yellow stamens. The fruit of prickly poppies is composed of small, spiny capsules filled with tiny seeds. The size of this plant makes it useful for the back of borders and beds.

Growing conditions and maintenance

Some prickly poppies can be grown as perennials in Zone 10; north of this region treat them as annuals grown from seed. Start prickly poppies indoors in late winter and transplant after danger of frost has passed, spacing plants 1 to 2 feet apart.

Selected species and varieties

A. grandiflora (showy prickly poppy)—annual or short-lived perennial with 2-inch bright yellow or white summer flowers atop 2- to 3-foot stems, and sparsely spined blue-green foliage veined with white; Zones 8-10.

A. mexicana (Mexican poppy)—annual with 1- to 2-foot spiny stems bearing 2- to 2½-inch yellow, golden, or orange flowers in summer above green leaves often spotted with white; Zones 8-10.

A. munita (white prickly poppy)—annual or perennial to 3 feet tall with many 2- to 5-inch showy white summer flowers surrounding yellow stamens and a purple stigma.

A. platyceras (crested poppy)—annual with very spiny, lobed leaves clasping a robust 2- to 4-foot stem bearing white, purple, or pale yellow 4- to 5-inch summer flowers; Zones 8-10.

A. polyanthemos (white prickly poppy)—annual or biennial with 2- to 3-foot stems and 2½- to 4-inch white flowers in summer; Zones 8-10.

Aruncus   (a-RUNK-us)
GOATSBEARD

◄ *Aruncus dioicus*

Hardiness: Zones 3-7

Plant type: perennial

Height: 1 to 6 feet

Interest: flowers, foliage

Soil: rich, well-drained, moist

Light: partial shade

Goatsbeards bear dramatic 6- to 10-inch plumes of minute, cream-colored flowers on 1- to 6-foot stems from midspring to early summer. After the flowers fade, the tall mounds of deep-green compound leaves provide a stately background for later-blooming plants. Goatsbeards are native to deciduous woodlands of the eastern and central United States and western Europe. The dwarf varieties often are mistaken for astilbes.

Growing conditions and maintenance

Goatsbeards benefit from yearly additions of compost. They can be grown in full sun where summers are cool and the soil remains moist. Space plants 4 to 5 feet apart, and propagate by seed or from early spring division of young plants.

Selected species and varieties

A. dioicus [also listed as ***A. sylvester*** or ***Spiraea aruncus***]—pinnately compound leaves bearing 20 or more 1- to 2½-inch dark green doubly-toothed oval leaflets, and stems forming mounds up to 6 feet high with 4- to 16-inch-wide flower clusters borne at the tips of shoots and branches; 'Kneiffii' grows to about 3 feet high and has more finely divided foliage, giving it a more delicate appearance.

A. sinensis—similar to ***A. dioicus*** but flowering a few weeks later, and with more coarsely toothed, deep green leaves that are overlain with light brown.

★ **Point of interest:** *Goatsbeard's flowers are especially attractive to honeybees.*

Aster (AS-ter)
ASTER

Hardiness: Zones 3-8

Plant type: perennial

Height: 1 to 5 feet

Interest: flowers

Soil: moist, well-drained, fertile

Light: full sun

◀ *Aster novae-angliae*

Asters have daisylike flowers composed of narrow white, blue, violet, red, or pink ray petals that surround a bright yellow central disk. Most species flower in late summer and fall, but some, such as *A. alpinus*, display their cheerful bouquets in late spring. Asters are excellent plants for borders and rock gardens. *A. novae-angliae* is especially effective when naturalized in meadows or wildflower gardens.

Growing conditions and maintenance

Space dwarfs 1 foot apart and taller plants 2 to 3 feet apart. Many asters produce heavy flower heads, so it is best to stake the plants when they reach a height of 2 feet. Remove withered blossoms to prolong the flowering season. In Zones 3 to 5, protect *A.* x *frikartii* with mulch during the winter. Propagate by stem cuttings taken in spring and early summer, or by division in early spring. All asters except hybrids can be propagated by seed.

Selected species and varieties

A. alpinus (Alpine aster)—low-growing, 6- to 10-inch clumps with 1- to 3-inch violet-blue flowers with yellow centers; 'Happy End' has pink flowers; Zones 4-7.

A. x *frikartii* (Frikart's aster)—2 to 3 feet tall with fragrant 2½-inch lavender-blue flowers with yellow centers; Zones 5-8.

A. novae-angliae (New England aster)—3 to 5 feet with 4- to 5-inch lance-shaped leaves and 2-inch violet-purple flowers appearing in early fall; 'Harrington's Pink' has soft pink flowers; Zones 3-7.

> ### ★ PRO'S PICK ★
> *A.* x *frikartii* 'Mönch' has hyacinth blue flowers from midsummer through mid-fall.
>
>

Astilbe (a-STIL-bee)
ASTILBE

Hardiness: Zones 3-9

Plant type: perennial

Height: 8 inches to 4 feet

Interest: flowers, foliage

Soil: moist, well-drained, fertile

Light: partial shade to full sun

◀ *Astilbe x arendsii* 'Rheinland'

The feathery plumes held above mounds of graceful, deep green to bronze fernlike foliage make astilbe an ideal filler in shady borders, or for use as a background accent, woodland edging, or near water elements in the landscape. The 1- to 4-foot stalks bear thousands of tiny five-petaled flowers that resemble white, pink, lavender, or red clouds when massed in the garden.

Growing conditions and maintenance

Plant astilbes 1½ to 2 feet apart in moist soil, preferably in a cool, shady location. Water well and mulch if in full sun or average soil. Propagate by division every 3 to 4 years in spring or early summer. Feed plants each spring with a high-phosphorus fertilizer, and provide extra water during hot, dry periods.

Selected species and varieties

A. x *arendsii* (false spirea)—2 to 4 feet with loose panicles of pink, white, red, or lavender flowers in summer; 'Fanal' combines rich bronze foliage with deep red flowers; 'Rheinland' has clear pink flowers on sturdy 2-foot stems; Zones 4-9.

A. chinensis (Chinese astilbe)—8 inches to 4 feet with white, rose-tinged, or purple flowers; 'Finale', bright pink flowers; var. *davidii* has light purple-pink flowers on 4-foot stems; 'Intermezzo' has salmon pink flowers in late summer; Zones 3-8.

A. x *rosea* (rose astilbe)—compact form with 1½- to 2½-foot stems and feathery, deeply cut foliage beneath pink summer flowers; 'Peach Blossom' has light salmon flowers.

> ### ★ PRO'S PICK ★
> *A. chinensis* 'Pumila' has a dwarf habit with tight spires of mauve-pink flowers in late summer on 8-inch stems, and is a good ground cover.
>
>

Aurinia (o-RIN-ee-a)
BASKET-OF-GOLD

Hardiness: Zones 3-10

Plant type: perennial

Height: 6 to 12 inches

Interest: flowers, foliage

Soil: dry, well-drained

Light: full sun

◀ *Aurinia saxatilis*

The masses of tiny yellow flowers in early to midspring on compact mats of silvery gray foliage make basket-of-gold an excellent plant for rock gardens, for borders, or for cascading over rocks and walls. The tiny four-petaled flowers look like golden versions of their close relative sweet alyssum (*Lobularia maritima*), but have longer leaves that are cleft in three.

Growing conditions and maintenance

Basket-of-gold has been a popular plant for generations, in part because it thrives in a wide variety of conditions. It will spread quickly and produce a profusion of flowers. After early spring flowering, shear the top of the plant back by one-third to encourage rebloom. Remove old plants that have become woody. Propagate by division in early spring or sow seed (except double-flowered varieties) in summer for bloom the following year. Do not cover seed, as light stimulates germination. Space plants 9 to 12 inches apart.

Selected species and varieties

A. petraea—clusters of bright yellow flowers and whitish, spatula-shaped leaves on 12-inch woody stems; Zones 7-10.

A. saxatilis [also listed as *Alyssum saxatile*]—mounds of 10-inch stems bearing 3-inch lance-shaped leaves covered with smooth, silvery hairs, and dense clusters of yellow flowers; 'Citrina' has pale yellow flowers; 'Plena' has deep yellow double flowers; Zones 3-7.

★ PRO'S PICK ★

A. saxatilis 'Sunny Border' maintains the cascading habit of the species and adds a bold yellow color to the flowers.

Bergenia (ber-JEN-ee-a)
BERGENIA

Hardiness: Zones 3-9

Plant type: perennial

Height: 1 to 1½ feet

Interest: flowers, foliage

Soil: well-drained, moist

Light: partial shade

◀ *Bergenia cordifolia*

Bergenias are noted for their large, showy rosettes of bold, leathery leaves and 3- to 6-inch spikes of white, pink, or lavender-rose flowers in spring. In warmer climates the leaves are evergreen, while in the North they turn a dusky burgundy or bronze in the fall. Use bergenias in rock gardens, in beds and borders, as edging, or as a ground cover.

Growing conditions and maintenance

Bergenias are very tolerant of cold, heat and moist soil. A site that remains wet in winter may cause the roots to rot. Space plants 1 foot apart. They will spread quickly by rhizomes to form a thick ground cover. Propagate by sowing seed in spring, or by division after flowering. Divide every 3 to 4 years to promote vigorous growth and flowering.

Selected species and varieties

B. ciliata (winter begonia)—lightly fragrant white flowers tinged with rose in early spring above glossy, deep green leaves that turn reddish bronze in cold weather; Zones 7-9.

B. cordifolia [formerly listed as *Saxifraga cordifolia*] (heartleaf bergenia, pig squeak)—clumps of 8- to 10-inch leaves with wavy edges and heart-lobed bases, and clusters of 1-inch pink flowers atop 10- to 18-inch stalks in early spring; 'Alba' has white flowers; 'Purpurea' has purple flowers.

B. crassifolia (leather bergenia)—leaves more rounded than *B. cordifolia*, and lavender-pink flowers held high above bright green foliage.

B. stracheyi (Strachey bergenia)—similar to *B. cordifolia* but with unwavy foliage and edges fringed with hairs, and white flowers in late winter or early spring turning pink-tinged, pink, or yellowish; Zones 6-9.

Bignonia (big-NO-nee-a)
CROSS VINE

Hardiness: Zones 6-9

Plant type: woody vine

Height: 30 to 50 feet

Interest: flowers, foliage

Soil: moist, well-drained

Light: full sun to shade

◀ *Bignonia capreolata*

A rapidly growing plant, cross vine is graced in the spring with clusters of large, trumpet-shaped flowers that are dark orange on the outside and yellow-orange on the inside. In summer, this Southeast native produces slender, 4- to 6-inch flattened fruit that turns from green to brown. Cross vine's attractive, 2- to 6-inch dark green compound leaves are borne in pairs along with clasping tendrils by which the vine attaches itself to trees, fences, trellises, or buildings. Where winters are mild, the foliage turns reddish purple in the fall and remains on the vine.

Growing conditions and maintenance

Cross vine tolerates shade but produces the greatest abundance of flowers and leaves when grown in full sun. A rugged plant, it thrives in all but excessively wet or dry soil. In Zone 6 cross vine dies back to the ground each winter, but sends up vigorous new shoots in spring. Propagate by seed or cuttings.

Selected species and varieties

B. capreolata (cross vine, trumpet flower)—30 to 50 feet with lustrous, thinly spaced, dark green, semievergreen to evergreen leaves that turn reddish purple in cold weather, and brownish orange or brownish red to orange and orange-red lightly mocha-scented flowers 2 inches long and 1½ inches wide in clusters of two to five; 'Atrosanguinea' [also classified as *B. capreolata* var. *atrosanguinea*] has more narrow, dark purple-red flowers tinted with brown or sometimes orange-red, and longer, narrower leaves than the species.

★ **Point of interest:** *Cross vines attract hummingbirds; they can be used as ground covers or as climbing vines.*

Boltonia (bowl-TO-nee-a)
BOLTONIA

Hardiness: Zones 4-8

Plant type: perennial

Height: 3 to 5 feet

Interest: flowers

Soil: dry to moist, well-drained

Light: full sun

◀ *Boltonia asteroides var. latisquama*

Clouds of asterlike flowers atop the tall, branching stems of boltonia add an airy accent to island beds, borders, and meadows from mid-summer through early fall. Boltonia's gray-green, willowlike, 5-inch leaves contrast with its white, pink, or lavender flowers. The plants are native to the eastern and midwestern United States, where they grow in gravelly, sandy soil.

Growing conditions and maintenance

Space taller varieties 3 to 5 feet apart, and smaller varieties 1 to 2 feet apart. Propagate species by seed or division, and cultivars by division in early spring or late fall. Pinch tops in late spring to encourage bushy, compact growth. The tallest varieties may need staking.

Selected species and varieties

B. asteroides (white boltonia)—3 to 5 feet tall with 1-inch daisy-like flowers; var. *latisquama* (violet boltonia) has 1½-inch purple to pink flowers; 'Nana' bears white flowers on 1- to 2-foot stems; 'Pink Beauty' has pale pink blossoms in late summer on 4- to 5-foot stems and delicate, dusky green, mildew-resistant foliage.

B. incisa—open mounds of 4-inch dark green, lance-shaped leaves with whitish undersides, and 4-foot stems decorated with purple to pale lavender flowers.

★ PRO'S PICK ★

B. asteroides 'Snowbank' has drifts of pure white flowers in early fall on compact 3- to 4-foot stems, and small blue-green leaves.

Brachycome (bra-KIK-o-me)
SWAN RIVER DAISY

Hardiness: Zones 8-10

Plant type: annual or tender perennial grown as an annual

Height: 9 to 14 inches

Interest: flowers

Soil: moist, well-drained, fertile

Light: full sun

◀ *Brachycome iberidifolia*

Swan River daisy produces mounds of well-branched, feathery foliage covered throughout the summer with an abundance of small, vibrant, daisylike flowers. These plants are native to Australia and New Guinea, and thrive in containers and hanging baskets. They also can be used in beds and borders, where they add colorful accents. In the Deep South they can be used in rock gardens, beds and borders, where they will be at home for many years.

Growing conditions and maintenance

Propagate Swan River daisies from seed started indoors 5 to 6 weeks prior to the last killing frost, or sow ¼ inch deep after the soil has warmed and danger of frost has passed. Thin seedlings to 6 to 12 inches apart. Keep soil moist, as dry conditions will discourage formation of flower buds.

Selected species and varieties

B. aculeata—18- to 24-inch multibranched stems with 4-inch oblong leaves and white, blue, or lavender flowers.

B. iberidifolia (Swan River daisy)—annual with 12- to 18-inch mounds of highly dissected gray-green leaves and blue, rose, or white flowers.

B. nivalis—8 to 12 inches with fernlike, narrow, 6-inch leaves and white flowers.

B. rigidula—compact, 10- to 15-inch multibranched stems with small, coarsely toothed leaves and blue flowers.

B. scapigera—4- to 6-inch leaves in loose basal rosettes with 12- to 18-inch stems bearing solitary white or pink flowers.

Brunnera (BRUN-er-a)
BRUNNERA

Hardiness: Zones 4-8

Plant type: perennial

Height: 1 to 2 feet

Interest: flowers, foliage

Soil: moist, well-drained

Light: full sun to partial shade

◀ *Brunnera macrophylla*

Brunnera is native to the Caucasus, where its mounds of lightly wrinkled, heart-shaped leaves grow beneath groves of spruce and on grassy hillsides. In early spring the plants produce masses of showy, small blue flowers that resemble forget-me-nots. The foliage enlarges after the plants flower, and remains attractive throughout the fall. These are excellent plants for borders or rock gardens, and put on an unforgettable springtime show when naturalized with forget-me-nots and daffodils in woodland gardens or meadows.

Growing conditions and maintenance

Space plants 1 foot apart and mulch to keep roots cool and soil moist. Fertilize lightly after flowers have faded. Propagate by division in spring or fall, or by transplanting self-sown seedlings. This also rejuvenates older clumps.

Selected species and varieties

B. macrophylla [also listed as **Anchusa myosotidiflora**] (Siberian bugloss)—loosely branched flower clusters on 12- to 18-inch stems above rough-textured clumps of heart-shaped leaves with fuzzy petioles; 'Hadspen Cream' has sky blue flowers and light green leaves edged with white.

★ **Point of interest:** *Brunnera is effective when interplanted with spring bulbs, filling the spaces created as the bulb foliage fades.*

Buddleia (BUD-lee-a)
BUTTERFLY BUSH

Hardiness: Zones 5-9

Plant type: shrub

Height: 4 to 20 feet

Interest: flowers, foliage, fragrance, form

Soil: well-drained, fertile

Light: full sun

◀ *Buddleia alternifolia*

Butterfly bushes have arching stems tipped with long, conical clusters of tiny, exceptionally fragrant summer flowers in shades of white, red, pink, lavender, or purple. Butterflies find the blossoms irresistible, sometimes completely covering the flower heads with their slowly beating wings on warm days. The willow-shaped leaves are dark green above and slightly hairy beneath. These shrubs are superb as specimens or massed as background in a shrub border.

Growing conditions and maintenance

Butterfly bushes are vigorous, pest-free plants. Prune flower heads after blossoms fade to prolong the flowering season. *B. davidii* produces flowers on the current year's growth. Prune in early spring before growth begins. In regions north of Zone 6 it dies back to the roots and resprouts in the spring. *B. alternifolia* produces flowers on the previous year's growth. Prune immediately after flowering in summer.

Selected species and varieties

B. alternifolia (fountain butterfly bush)—8 to 15 feet with 4-inch dull, dark green leaves that are gray on the underside, and long, drooping clusters of soft purple flowers.

B. davidii (summer lilac, orange-eye butterfly bush)—to 10 feet with 10-inch leaves that are white underneath, and 8- to 18-inch clusters of orange-throated flowers in a wide array of colors; var. **magnifica** has dark blue-purple blossoms with a bright orange eye; 'Peace' has ivory flowers.

★ **Point of interest:** *Butterfly bush's fragrant flowers make a lovely and unusual addition to fresh arrangements.*

Calamintha (kal-a-MIN-tha)
CALAMINT

Hardiness: Zones 5-9

Plant type: perennial

Height: 1 to 2 feet

Interest: flowers, foliage, fragrance

Soil: well-drained

Light: full sun

◀ *Calamintha nepeta*

Calamints are members of the mint family. They often are planted at the edge of walkways, where their fragrant foliage emits a pungent, minty aroma when brushed by passers-by. In summer the plants are decorated with clusters of white, pink, or violet flowers that last until fall.

Growing conditions and maintenance

Calamints are heat and drought tolerant. Plant them in the spring, spacing them about 1 foot apart, and mulch. Calamints spread rapidly by underground stolons or self-sown seed. Cut back the foliage after plants have finished flowering in fall, and mulch with pine boughs in areas north of Zone 6.

Selected species and varieties

C. grandiflora [formerly listed as **Satureja grandiflora**] (greater calamint)—12 to 18 inches tall with 2-inch, coarsely toothed oval leaves, and small clusters of 1-inch pink flowers in summer.

C. nepeta [formerly listed as **Satureja calamintha**, and sometimes listed as **C. nepetoides**]—1 to 2 feet tall with hairy, finely toothed leaves and ½-inch white or lilac flowers.

> ★ PRO'S PICK ★
>
> **C. grandiflora** 'Variegata' has the same bright pink flowers as the species but has attractive light green foliage mottled with golden splotches.
>
>

★ **Point of interest:** *Tea made from the leaves and flowers of C. grandiflora is a home remedy for coughs and colds.*

Calycanthus (kal-i-KAN-thus)
SWEET SHRUB

Hardiness: Zones 4-10

Plant type: shrub

Height: 6 to 12 feet

Interest: flowers, fragrance, foliage

Soil: moist, well-drained, acid

Light: full sun to partial shade

◀ *Calycanthus occidentalis*

Native to the United States and China, these shrubs have unusual, segmented flowers with long, ribbonlike petals that have a pleasant fragrance reminiscent of tropical fruit. They are delightful additions to outdoor living areas or to foundation plantings, where the sweet fragrance of the flowers can drift through open windows. Sweet shrubs are medium-sized, with slightly rough, dark green leaves and maroon-red flowers from mid-spring to summer.

Growing conditions and maintenance

Sweet shrub thrives as an understory plant where light shade produces a more treelike form, or in full sun where a bushy habit results. Propagate by dividing and transplanting suckers at the base of stems in fall. Prune after flowering is completed in summer.

Selected species and varieties

C. fertilis (Carolina allspice)—6 to 10 feet tall with 6-inch silvery green leaves and magnolia-like, dark brown fragrant flowers.

C. floridus (sweet shrub, Carolina allspice)—6 to 9 feet tall and up to 12 feet wide with aromatic 2- to 5-inch leaves that turn bronzy yellow in fall, and 2-inch flowers with straplike petals that are usually burgundy-brown; 'Athens' has yellow flowers; 'Urbana' has an exceptionally sweet fragrance.

C. occidentalis—8 to 12 feet tall with 8-inch, slightly hairy, lance-shaped leaves and fragrant cinnamon-rose, narrow-petaled flowers; Zones 8-10.

★ **Point of interest:** *Sweet shrub flowers can be placed in drawers and closets to give clothes a sweet fragrance.*

Campanula (kam-PAN-yew-la)
BELLFLOWER

Hardiness: Zones 3-8

Plant type: perennial

Height: 1 to 4 feet

Interest: flowers, foliage

Soil: moist, well-drained

Light: full sun to partial shade

◀ *Campanula portenschlagiana* 'Resholdt's Variety'

Bellflowers have long been stalwarts of beds, borders, and rock gardens. Their growth forms range from low cushions to tall, upright clumps. The color palette of the tubular or flaring flowers ranges from violet to blue to white. Flowers are borne in clusters or spikes from late spring through summer, with some species lightly reblooming in fall.

Growing conditions and maintenance

In cool-summer regions bellflowers grow best in full sun, but they should be given partial shade in regions with hot summers. Space low-growing bellflowers 12 to 18 inches apart, larger ones 2 feet apart. Propagate by seed or division; divide every 3 to 4 years to maintain vigor.

Selected species and varieties

C. lactiflora (great bellflower)—clusters of 1-inch white or pale blue flowers with 3-inch leaves on 4-foot stems in summer; 'Macrantha' has purplish blue flowers in early summer on 4- to 5-foot stems lined with coarse, toothed leaves; Zones 5-7.

C. persicifolia (peachleaf bellflower)—1-inch nodding, deep blue to white flowers on pliant 2-foot stems in summer and reblooming in fall; 'Grandiflora Alba' has large, pure white flowers; 'Summer Skies' has double white flowers accented with pastel blue.

C. portenschlagiana (Dalmatian bellflower)—loose panicles of purple-blue star-shaped flowers in late spring and early summer above 4- to 8-inch mounds of coarse, kidney-shaped leaves; 'Resholdt's Variety' has large, deep purple flowers on 6-inch stems; Zones 5-7.

C. poscharskyana (Siberian bellflower)—vigorous, creeping, 8- to 12-inch drought-resistant dwarf with 1-inch, light blue flowers decorating mounds of pale green leaves.

C. rotundifolia—(harebell, Scottish bluebell)—profuse clusters of nodding, 1-inch blue-violet flowers in summer on thin, 3- to 12-inch stems; Zones 3-7.

Canna   (CAN-ah)
CANNA

Hardiness: Zones 7-10

Plant type: tender perennial grown as an annual

Height: 2 to 10 feet

Interest: flowers, foliage

Soil: moist to wet, well-drained, fertile

Light: full sun

◄ *Canna x generalis 'The President'*

Cannas are tropical plants with stately spikes of flashy, colorful flowers and bold foliage. They are used as lush summer-to-fall bedding plants. Underground rhizomes produce clumps of 8- to 24-inch-long, glossy deep green leaves on fleshy stems. The impressive 4- to 5-inch flowers have three true petals and several petal-like stamens, and are borne on stiff stems above the foliage.

Growing conditions and maintenance

Grow cannas in warm sites in soil rich in organic matter. North of Zone 8 they can be grown as tender perennials. Cut back tops to 6 inches, lift rhizomes in fall after first killing frost, and store them in barely moist peat moss. Leave rhizomes in ground over winter in Zones 8 to 10, but provide them with protective mulch in Zones 8 and 9. Propagate by dividing rhizomes in spring. Plant after all danger of frost has passed. Some varieties can be grown from seed, but soak seeds in warm water for 2 days to soften their hard coats.

Selected species and varieties

C. x generalis [also listed as **C. x hybrida**]—4- to 6-foot standard varieties, 2- to 3-foot dwarfs, and 7- to 10-foot giants; 'Mohawk' has orange blossoms; 'Panache' is ivory and rose; 'Pfitzer's Primrose Black Knight' has deep blood red flowers; 'The President' has deep green leaves and bright red flowers.

C. flaccida (golden canna)— 3-inch yellow flowers on 5-foot stalks with 2-foot oblong leaves.

> **★ PRO'S PICK ★**
>
> **C. x generalis** 'Dazzler' has brilliant red, large-petaled, or chidlike flowers held 4 feet above its 1-foot bronzy green leaves.
>
>

Cerastium   (ser-RASS-tee-um)
CHICKWEED

Hardiness: Zones 3-7

Plant type: perennial

Height: 6 to 12 inches

Interest: flowers, foliage

Soil: dry, well-drained

Light: full sun

◄ *Cerastium tomentosum*

Chickweeds are robust creeping plants with small, usually silvery green leaves that nearly disappear beneath the mounds of starry white flowers. These vigorous plants make excellent ground covers for dry, sandy sites and can be used as accents near steps and walkways or in rock gardens, although they may crowd other plants.

Growing conditions and maintenance

Propagate by division in fall. Space divided clumps 12 to 18 inches apart. Chickweeds grow well without regular watering or fertilizing. Once established, these plants often naturalize, becoming self-sustaining members of the garden. Divide them regularly to control their spread.

Selected species and varieties

C. alpinum (Alpine chickweed)—tight clusters of small white late spring flowers atop spreading 6-inch mounds of tiny, oval, gray leaves.

C. arvense (starry grasswort)— 1-inch oval leaves beneath 12-inch clusters of star-shaped, white, spring flowers; 'Compactum' has a spreading habit and pure white flowers nestled in a mat of 2- to 3-inch foliage.

C. bierbersteinii—6- to 12-inch mounds of silvery green foliage decorated with masses of ¾-inch pure white star-shaped flowers in late spring; Zones 4-7.

C. tomentosum (snow-in-summer)—6- to 9-inch prostrate stems bearing narrow, 1-inch, lance-shaped, white woolly leaves and ½-inch spring to summer flowers in clusters of three to 15, each with five notched petals; Zones 4-7.

★ Point of interest: *One plant of* **C. tomentosum** *can cover 9 square feet in only a few weeks.*

Ceratostigma (ser-at-o-STIG-ma)
PLUMBAGO, LEADWORT

Hardiness: Zones 5-10

Plant type: perennial

Height: 8 to 12 inches

Interest: flowers, foliage

Soil: well-drained

Light: full sun to partial shade

◀ *Ceratostigma plumbaginoides*

Plumbago's brilliant blue 1-inch-long slightly flattened flowers are borne in profusion on reddish stems from late summer to frost. The plant makes an effective, fast-spreading, semievergreen ground cover or low shrubby perennial. Its glossy green oval leaves turn bronzy red in fall.

Growing conditions and maintenance

Divide plants every 4 years in the spring, spacing them 1 to 2 feet apart in soil amended with peat moss and compost. Mulch young plants in late spring, and water regularly. In Zones 5 and 6, cover with pine boughs in winter. Plumbago benefits from yearly additions of compost and light fertilizing in spring.

How to: Promote vigorous spring growth and summer flowering by removing any visible dead-wood and trimming the top one-third of the plants in early spring before growth begins. This is best done with hedge shears.

Selected species and varieties

C. plumbaginoides (dwarf plumbago)—flat, intensely blue, five-lobed, tubular, ½-inch flowers in dense clusters above tufts of 3-inch-long, glossy, semievergreen leaves on zigzag 8- to 12-inch stems that turn bronzy red in winter in cold regions.

C. willmottianum (Chinese plumbago)—4-foot multibranched woody stems with vibrant blue flowers from late summer to fall, and bright green leaves that turn red in late fall; Zones 8-10.

Chelone (kee-LO-nee)
TURTLEHEAD

Hardiness: Zones 3-9

Plant type: perennial

Height: 1 to 5 feet

Interest: flowers

Soil: moist-to-wet, rich

Light: full sun to partial shade

◀ *Chelone lyonii*

The unique tubular, white, pink, or rose flowers of *Chelone* resemble turtles' heads and have a puckered upper lip and a bearded lower lip. They are borne in a raceme atop straight, smooth, 3- to 5-foot stems with dark green lance-shaped leaves. Turtleheads are native to marshes, stream banks, and moist woodlands of the eastern, southeastern, and western United States. They are ideally suited to bog gardens and wet spots in wildflower gardens and meadows.

Growing conditions and maintenance

Turtleheads can be grown in ordinary garden soil enriched with compost or peat moss. Space plants 8 inches apart and add a layer of mulch in late spring. *C. glabra* benefits from staking or being planted with other tall species that it can use for support. *C. lyonii* is a native of the Southeast and tolerates drier conditions better than other species. Propagate turtleheads by spring division, summer cuttings, or by seed planted in the fall.

How to: Turtlehead seeds require cold treatment of 40° F for 3 to 4 months to germinate. Put fresh seed into a plastic bag along with moist unmilled sphagnum moss, seal, and place in the refrigerator until late winter, when seed can be sown in flats indoors.

Selected species and varieties

C. glabra (white turtlehead)—3 to 5 feet tall with clusters of 1½-inch white to pale pink summer flowers, and 6-inch lance-shaped leaves; Zones 3-8.

C. lyonii (pink turtlehead)—1 to 3 feet tall with 4- to 7-inch dark green oval leaves and 1-inch rose-violet flowers in summer.

Chrysanthemum (kri-SAN-the-mum)
CHRYSANTHEMUM

Hardiness: Zones 3-10

Plant type: perennial

Height: 6 inches to 3 feet

Interest: flowers, foliage, fragrance

Soil: well-drained

Light: full sun to partial shade

◀ *Chrysanthemum zawadskii var. latilobum*

Chrysanthemums bloom from spring through fall in a wide variety of flower forms, from the oxeye daisy of fields and pastures to the button or giant pompon mums. They usually have deep green, deeply lobed leaves that give off a pleasant aroma when bruised. These versatile plants add texture and color to beds, borders, and meadows, and make excellent cut flowers.

Growing conditions and maintenance

Chrysanthemums prefer organic-rich soil and regular additions of fertilizer through early summer. *C. coccineum* grows best in partial shade. In late spring or early summer, pinch the tops of fall-blooming types to increase their flower production. Spring-flowering types can be cut back after flowering to encourage a second bloom. Propagate by division in fall after flowering, or by seed, spacing plants 1 to 2 feet apart. Mulch in regions with cold winters to prevent frost heaving.

Selected species and varieties

C. coccineum [also listed as *Tanacetum coccineum]* (painted daisy, pyrethrum)—wiry, 2 to 3 feet tall with 2- to 3-inch white, pink, red, or lilac flowers, sometimes tipped in yellow, and surrounding yellow centers, from spring to early summer; 'Buckeye' has dark red double flowers; Zones 3-7.

C. leucanthemum [also listed as *Leucanthemum vulgare*] (oxeye daisy)—solitary, 1½-inch white flowers accented with bright yellow centers on 2-foot stems in spring and summer.

C. x morifolium (florist's chrysanthemum)—[also listed as

Dendranthema x grandiflorum]—large flowers from late summer to frost in many forms up to 6 inches across on sturdy 3- to 4-foot stems in all colors but blue; Zones 6-9.

C. x superbum [also listed as *Leucanthemum* x *superbum*] (Shasta daisy)—5- to 6-inch double or single white flowers from summer to frost on strong, 2½-foot stems; Zones 4-8.

C. zawadskii—2-inch white flowers on 18-inch stems; var. *latilobum* has 3-inch single or double white, yellow, red, or purple flowers in late summer.

Clematis (KLEM-a-tis)
CLEMATIS

Hardiness: Zones 3-9

Plant type: woody vine

Height: 6 to 25 feet

Interest: flowers, foliage, seed heads, fragrance

Soil: moist, well-drained

Light: full sun to partial shade

◀ *Clematis x jackmanii 'Gypsy Queen'*

Clematis is a favorite for growing on fences, trellises, or other structures. These vigorous, leafy vines are covered with attractive flowers from late spring to fall depending on the species. Masses of feathery seed heads add attractive accents after the flowers have faded.

Growing conditions and maintenance

Plant clematis 2 to 3 inches deeper than it was growing in its container. Mulch in summer to keep roots cool, and again in late fall to protect from heaving in late winter. Propagate species from cuttings or seed, spacing plants 2 to 4 feet apart.

Selected species and varieties

C. alpina (Alpine clematis)—1½- to 3-inch single, lantern-shaped, mauve or blue flowers in spring on 8-foot vines; Zones 3-7.

C. x jackmanii (Jackman clematis)—4- to 7-inch deep violet flowers on 10-foot robust stems from late spring to frost; many cultivars are available, with flowers in shades of white, red, blue, and purple, some with single flowers, others with double; 'Gypsy Queen' has rich, violet-red flowers; Zones 3-8.

C. montana (anemone clematis)—vigorous species with white, 2-inch four-sepaled rosy red flowers on 4-inch stems in spring.

C. paniculata (sweet autumn clematis)—1- to 4-inch dainty white flowers on 25-foot vines in early fall.

C. texensis (scarlet clematis)—leathery, ¾-inch scarlet flowers in clusters from late spring until frost on 6- to 12-foot stems; Zones 6-9.

★ **Point of interest:** *Clematis flowers consist of four to eight colorful sepals but no petals.*

Clethra (KLETH-ra)
SUMMER-SWEET, CLETHRA

Hardiness: Zones 3-10

Plant type: shrub, small tree

Height: 3 to 25 feet

Interest: flowers, foliage

Soil: moist, acid

Light: full sun to full shade

◀ *Clethra alnifolia*

Summer-sweet's fragrant 4- to 6-inch-long clusters of white or pink flowers appear in late summer. It is found throughout North America, with the most ornamental species native to swamps and wet woodlands of the eastern United States. Summer-sweet is often used as a specimen plant in mixed shrub borders, or naturalized in moist woodland gardens.

Growing conditions and maintenance

Plant summer-sweets in spring in well-worked soil amended with peat moss or compost. Mulch to keep roots cool and to retain moisture. Propagate in spring by transplanting offshoots that appear near the base of the stem.

Selected species and varieties

C. alnifolia (summer-sweet, sweet pepperbush)—3 to 8 feet tall and 4 to 6 feet wide with 4-inch spikes of snowy white, heavily scented flowers in summer and lustrous green leaves that turn gold in fall; 'Pink Spires' has rosy red buds opening to pastel pink flowers; Zones 3-9.

C. arborea (lily-of-the-valley tree)—20 to 25 feet tall with 3- to 4-inch elliptical evergreen leaves and 6-inch softly drooping clusters of fragrant white flowers in late summer and early fall; Zones 9-10.

> ★ **PRO'S PICK** ★
>
> *C. barbinervis* (Japanese clethra) grows to 20 feet tall with 6-inch spikes of lightly fragrant white flowers held away from the 6-inch, coarse-textured leaves that turn sunset red in fall.
>
>

★ **Point of interest:** *C. alnifolia* is also called Indian soap because its flowers produce a sweet lather when rubbed between wet hands. It has traditionally been used by American Indians for summer baths.

Colchicum (KOL-chi-kum)
AUTUMN CROCUS

Hardiness: Zones 4-9

Plant type: bulb

Height: 4 to 12 inches

Interest: flowers

Soil: moist, well-drained, fertile,

Light: full sun to partial shade

◀ *Colchicum speciosum*

Autumn crocus spreads from bulblike corms, each of which produces several leafless stems topped with showy pink, purple, or red flowers. The strap-shaped foliage appears in late winter or early spring, and disappears in late summer a few weeks before the cupped, star-shaped flowers appear. It is excellent for naturalizing or as an addition to borders or rock gardens, and can be forced as a houseplant.

Growing conditions and maintenance

Plant in summer, setting corms 3 to 4 inches deep and 6 to 9 inches apart. *C. autumnale* tolerates light shade. Propagate from cormlets that form at the base of mature corms. If it is naturalized in a meadow or field, be careful not to mow while foliage or flowers remain above ground.

Selected species and varieties

C. autumnale—4-inch white, pink, or purple flowers on 8-inch stems; 'Alboplenum' has pure white double flowers; 'Plenum' has lilac-pink double flowers.

C. speciosum (showy autumn crocus)—4- to 8-inch rose to purple flowers with white throats on 8- to 12-inch stems; 'Atro-rubens' has dark red flowers.

> ★ **PRO'S PICK** ★
>
> *C. speciosum* 'Waterlily' has large, bright pink double-petaled flowers on 10-inch stems, and makes an excellent cut flower.
>
>

Coreopsis *(ko-ree-OP-sis)*
TICKSEED

Hardiness: Zones 3-9

Plant type: annual, perennial

Height: 6 inches to 3 feet

Interest: flowers, foliage

Soil: dry, well-drained

Light: full sun

◀ *Coreopsis rosea*

The colorful, daisylike flowers of tickseeds are displayed over a long season of bloom. Plants have diverse foliage forms ranging from mats or cushions to mounding clumps. They are good choices for edging, for casual borders, or for naturalizing in meadows, and make excellent, long-lasting cut flowers.

Growing conditions and maintenance

Space tickseeds 12 to 18 inches apart. Deadhead withering flowers to prolong bloom. Propagate by seed or spring division, and transplant self-sown seedlings. *C. tinctoria* and *C. verticillata* can be started indoors from seed in late winter.

Selected species and varieties

C. auriculata—strong, 3- to 4-foot stems bearing bright yellow flowers through summer; 'Nana' has clusters of 6-inch stems and sunshine yellow blossoms; Zones 4-9.

C. grandiflora (bigflower coreopsis)—1- to 1½-inch single or double yellow or orange flowers on 1- to 2-foot stems from early to late summer; 'Early Sunrise' has brilliant semidouble blossoms from early summer to frost; 'Robin' has notched yellow petals touched with red on compact 10-inch stems; Zones 4-9.

C. lanceolata (lance-leaved coreopsis)—2½-inch yellow flowers on 1- to 2- foot stems from late spring to summer; 'Flore Pleno' has bright yellow double flowers.

C. rosea (pink coreopsis)— 1-inch pink flowers with yellow centers from summer to fall on 2-foot stems; Zones 4-9.

C. tinctoria (golden coreopsis)—tender annual with showy, 2-inch yellow and burnt red spring to autumn flowers on 1½- to 3-foot stems.

C. verticillata (threadleaf coreopsis)—cushions of lacy, threadlike leaves forming mounds 2 to 3 feet tall with yellow flowers in summer.

★ **Point of interest:** *Tickseeds attract many different species of butterflies to their sweet nectar.*

Cornus *(KOR-nus)*
DOGWOOD

Hardiness: Zones 2-9

Plant type: perennial, shrub, tree

Height: 4 inches to 40 feet

Interest: flowers, foliage, fruit, bark

Soil: moist, well-drained, acid

Light: full sun to partial shade

◀ *Cornus canadensis*

Dogwoods are deciduous flowering woody plants that provide year-round garden interest as specimens, in shrub borders, as backgrounds for beds and borders, or for naturalizing in wetland or woodland settings. Those with attractive winter features, such as the red-barked *C. sericea*, can be located where they can be enjoyed from a favorite sitting area.

Growing conditions and maintenance

Plant dogwoods in spring or fall in soil amended with compost or peat moss. Mulch around the base. *C. sericea* is especially adaptable to damp areas; *C. canadensis* is an excellent woodland ground cover for areas with acid soil. Prune *C. sericea* in late winter to remove older shoots and encourage vigorous spring growth. Propagate by seed or cuttings.

Selected species and varieties

C. canadensis (bunchberry)— ultrahardy, 4- to 8-inch creeping woody perennial with four showy white bracts in late spring and bright red berries in fall; Zones 2-6.

C. florida (flowering dogwood)—20 to 30 feet tall with layered branches bearing 3- to 5-inch creamy white, pink, or red flowery bracts in spring, and bright red berries and foliage in fall; Zones 5-9.

C. kousa (Japanese dogwood)— 20 to 25 feet tall with a bushy, rounded habit bearing 3- to 5-inch creamy white flowery bracts touched with pink in late spring, and bright red fruit and foliage in fall; Zones 5-9.

C. mas (cornelian cherry)— 10- to 25-foot small tree or large shrub with a 15- to 20-foot-wide habit, exfoliating gray and brown bark, bright yellow flowers in very early spring, and red fruit in late summer; Zones 4-8.

C. sericea [also listed as *C. stolonifera*] (red-osier dogwood)—7- to 9-foot shrub with 10-foot spread and multiple bright red stems, and modest white flowers in late spring followed by white fruit; 'Flaviramea' has yellow stems; Zones 2-8.

Cosmos   (KOS-mos)
COSMOS

Hardiness: Zones 9-10

Plant type: annual, tender perennial grown as an annual

Height: 10 inches to 6 feet

Interest: flowers

Soil: dry, well-drained

Light: full sun to light shade

◄ *Cosmos bipinnatus 'Sonata'*

Cosmos display 2- to 4-inch daisylike flowers from summer through frost on loose clumps of slender, pliant stems. The colorful flowers accent graceful masses of feathery-textured foliage. The smaller varieties can be used as edging plants or fillers in borders; taller ones are effective as backdrops or transition plants.

Growing conditions and maintenance

Cosmos produce abundant flowers in poor soil. Taller varieties may need staking, and should be planted in sites protected from summer winds. They are easily propagated from seed sown ¼ inch deep after all danger of frost has passed. Plant seedlings 12 to 18 inches apart.

Selected species and varieties

C. bipinnatus—annual with 4- to 6-foot stems bearing 3- to 4-inch pink, white, or red flowers from summer to frost with yellow centers; 'Daydream' has bright pink flowers with dark red centers; 'Sonata' has pink, white, or red blossoms on 2-foot stems.

C. diversifolius (black cosmos)—tender perennial with velvety, 3-inch rose pink to lilac flowers from summer to frost on 10- to 16-inch stems.

C. sulphureus (yellow cosmos)—annual bearing 2- to 3-inch yellow, orange, gold, or red flowers in early summer on 3- to 6-foot stems.

> ★ **PRO'S PICK** ★
>
> **C. sulphureus** 'Goldcrest' has a sturdy, compact form with bright golden flowers, and is more robust and wind resistant than other species.
>
>

Crinum   (KREE-num)
SPIDER LILY

Hardiness: Zones 7-10

Plant type: bulb

Height: 2 to 4 feet

Interest: flowers, fragrance, foliage

Soil: moist, well-drained, fertile

Light: full sun to partial shade

◄ *Crinum x powellii 'Roseum'*

Whorls of white or pink lilylike flowers with a spicy fragrance and a long season of bloom are the most striking feature of this member of the amaryllis family. Spider lily blossoms are funnel-shaped with petals that are either thick, ridged, and reflexed, or delicate, narrow, and spiderlike. Long, lance-shaped leaves emerge from large bulbs with necks up to 1 foot long. Spider lilies bloom best when crowded together, and provide attractive accents in mixed borders. They also are effective when naturalized in wet gardens in regions with warm winters.

Growing conditions and maintenance

In Zones 7 and 8 plant bulbs 2 to 3 feet apart with about one-third of their necks above ground in locations where they can be left undisturbed. Mulch with pine boughs in fall. Farther north, plant bulbs in tubs and overwinter indoors. Propagate by seed or from offsets that form at the base of mature bulbs.

Selected species and varieties

C. americanum (Florida swamp lily)—southern native with up to six white flower funnels on 2-foot stems appearing in late spring or early summer before its 4-foot-long cornlike leaves emerge; 'Miss Elsie' has white flowers with a tawny exterior.

C. moorei (Cape Coast lily, long-neck swamp lily)—10 to 20 rosy red flowers on 4-foot stalks above 3-foot evergreen leaves in summer; 'Roseum' has pink flowers.

C. x powellii (Powell's swamp lily)—3 to 4 feet tall with pink or white flowers in fall; 'Album' has six to eight icy white flowers on strong, 2-foot stalks; 'Roseum' has pastel pink blossoms.

★ **Point of interest:** *Spider lily seeds sometimes sprout while still inside the green capsule fruit. The partially germinated seeds can be planted ⅓ inch deep in potting mix, but be careful not to break the tiny white roots.*

Crocosmia *(kro-KOS-mee-a)*
MONTBRETIA

Hardiness: Zones 5-9

Plant type: bulb

Height: 2 to 4 feet

Interest: flowers, foliage

Soil: moist, well-drained

Light: full sun

◀ *Crocosmia 'Lucifer'*

Montbretias produce dozens of small, vibrantly colored flowers in summer that seem to float above masses of long, sword-shaped leaves. They make excellent container plants in northern regions, and naturalize where winters are mild. Montbretias are excellent for sunny borders and streambanks.

Growing conditions and maintenance

Plant montbretia corms in spring, setting them 3 to 5 inches deep and 6 to 8 inches apart. Protect from frost with mulch applied in early winter, or lift corms in fall and store at 50°F for spring planting. Propagate montbretias by replanting small cormels that develop at the base of mature corms, or from seed as soon as it ripens in the fall. It takes 3 to 4 years to produce flowers from seed or cormels.

Selected species and varieties

C. aurea—erect, 2- to 3-foot sprays bearing pendant clusters of 2-inch bell-shaped, orange-yellow or golden flowers and 2- to 3-foot narrow leaves; Zones 7-9.

C. x crocosmiiflora—horizontal sprays 2 to 4 feet long in red, orange, yellow, maroon, or bicolors with large-flowered types bearing 1½- to 3-inch blossoms and leaves ½ to 1 inch wide and 2 to 3 feet long; 'Aurantiaca' has deep orange flowers; 'Venus' has peach-yellow flowers; Zones 6-9.

C. masoniorum—3-foot unbranched stems ornamented with bright clusters of orange-scarlet flowers and 18-inch deep green, lance-shaped, leaves.

C. Hybrids—'Citronella' has yellow flowers with maroon markings in center; 'Emily McKenzie' has nodding orange flowers with splashes of red in the throat; 'Lucifer' bears fiery red blossoms on 3-foot stems.

Dahlia *(DAH-lee-a)*
DAHLIA

Hardiness: Zones 9-10

Plant type: annual, tender perennial grown as an annual

Height: 1 to 20 feet

Interest: flowers

Soil: moist, well-drained, fertile

Light: full sun

◀ *Dahlia x hybrida 'Figaro'*

The diversity of flower forms and colors of these versatile plants is staggering, and more than 20,000 cultivars have been classified. Flower sizes vary from petite pompons to giant dinner plate dahlias. Plants come in all colors but blue, and bloom from summer to frost. Dwarf dahlias are used as bedding and filler plants, while the taller, more statuesque varieties are used as transition plants at the back of borders, or even as specimens. All dahlias make dramatic, long-lasting cut flowers.

Growing conditions and maintenance

Plant tubers in spring, placing taller types 3 to 4 feet apart and 6 to 8 inches deep. Cover them with only 2 to 3 inches of soil. As shoots emerge, remove all but one or two, and add several inches of soil gradually as shoots lengthen, until soil fills the hole. Plant shorter types 2 to 3 inches deep and 1 to 2 feet apart. Mulch with 2 to 3 inches of compost. Pinch tops of young plants to encourage a bushy habit. Dahlias should be lifted in fall after the first frost and stored in a cool place over winter.

Selected species and varieties

D. x hybrida—categorized by division, type, and size including anemone-, cactus-, mignon-, miniature-, peony-, orchid-, and pomponlike flowers; 'Bishop of Llandaff' is peonylike with richly petaled wine red flowers; 'Bo Bo' is a miniature with metallic bronze flowers; 'Comet' has anemone-like red flowers; 'Dahliadel Twinkle' is orchidlike with stunning white or lavender blossoms; 'Figaro' has single scarlet flowers; 'Mannequin' has soft pink, cactuslike flowers; 'Red Riding Hood' is mignonlike with bright red single blossoms; 'Willo's Violet' has purple pomponlike flowers.

★ PRO'S PICK ★

D. x hybrida 'Ted's Choice' has clear red double flowers on sturdy stems.

Dianthus (dy-AN-thus)
PINK

Hardiness: Zones 3-9

Plant type: biennial, perennial

Height: 4 to 24 inches

Interest: flowers, foliage, fragrance

Soil: moist, well-drained, slightly alkaline

Light: full sun to partial shade

◀ *Dianthus plumarius*

Pinks derive their name from the tips of their fringed petals, which appear to have been cut by pinking shears. The five-petaled, usually fragrant flowers are borne singly or in small clusters above mats of grassy, sometimes evergreen foliage. They are used as ground covers, as edging or fillers in borders or rock gardens, and as colorful cascades for walls.

Growing conditions and maintenance

Pinks grow best in areas with cool summers and moderate winters. In regions subject to hot summers they should be planted in partial shade. A light mulch of pine boughs applied after the ground has frozen reduces winter damage in northern areas. Space plants 12 to 18 inches apart and divide every 2 to 3 years to maintain vigor and maximize flower production. Propagate by seed sown in early spring, by springtime division of plants, or by transplanting self-sown seedlings. Cuttings can be made in early summer.

Selected species and varieties

D. x allwoodii (Allwood pink)—4- to 20-inch mounds of blue-gray foliage above single or double 1- to 2-inch light pink, rose, or deep red flowers from late spring through midsummer.

D. barbatus (sweet William)—1- to 2-foot short-lived perennial with scentless, 1- to 2-inch flowers in solid or multicolored patterns of red, white, pink, or lavender from late spring through summer, and bright green foliage; self-sows freely; Zones 4-9.

D. deltoides (maiden pink)—6- to 12-inch mats of grass-green leaves, and dainty, 1/2- to 3/4-inch red or pink flowers in early summer on stems 1 foot above foliage; Zones 3-7.

D. plumarius (cottage pink)—a parent of Allwood pink bearing very fragrant 1- to 2-inch single or semidouble flowers in shades of red, pink, white, or bicolors in summer atop 12- to 18-inch mats of grassy evergreen leaves.

Dicentra (dy-SEN-tra)
BLEEDING HEART

Hardiness: Zones 3-9

Plant type: perennial

Height: 4 inches to 3 feet

Interest: flowers, foliage

Soil: moist, well-drained

Light: partial to full shade

◀ *Dicentra spectabilis*

Bleeding hearts have long panicles of ornate, symmetrical flowers that dangle on arching stems above layers of soft, lacy foliage. The many Asian and North American species produce attractive flowers in spring and summer. In summer, the gray-green foliage of most species fades as the plants become dormant. *D. eximia* and *D. formosa* retain their attractive foliage until frost. Bleeding hearts make excellent additions to woodland borders and shady wildflower gardens.

Growing conditions and maintenance

Bleeding hearts thrive in the dappled shade beneath tall trees. Plant *D. spectabilis* 2 to 3 feet apart and other species 1 to 2 feet apart. They will spread slowly by small tubers, self-sowing, or offsets. Cut back old flower shoots of *D. eximia* and *D. formosa* after they flower in late spring to encourage rebloom in the fall. Propagate by division when plants are dormant.

Selected species and varieties

D. canadensis (squirrel corn)—6 to 10 inches with blue-gray leaves, 1/2-inch, heart-shaped, white flowers in late spring, and tubers that look like kernels of corn; Zones 3-7.

D. cucullaria (Dutchman's-breeches)—4 to 10 inches with 1/2-inch, yellow-tipped, double-spurred, fragrant white flowers in spring resembling pantaloons, and small pink tubers; Zones 3-7.

D. eximia (wild bleeding heart)—1/2-inch, heart-shaped, magenta to pink flowers from spring to fall on 12- to 18-inch stems above mounds of blue-green foliage; Zones 4-8.

D. formosa (western bleeding heart)—1/2-inch, heart-shaped, rose-purple to yellow flowers in early summer on 9- to 12-inch stems above mounds of bright green foliage; Zones 4-9.

D. spectabilis (bleeding heart)—1- to 1 1/2-inch pink-and-white or all-white flowers from spring to early summer on 2- to 3-foot stalks above feathery foliage; Zones 4-8.

Digitalis (di-ji-TAL-us)
FOXGLOVE

Hardiness: Zones 3-9

Plant type: biennial or perennial

Height: 2 to 5 feet

Interest: flowers, foliage

Soil: moist, well-drained, acid

Light: full sun to partial shade

◀ *Digitalis x mertonensis*

Foxgloves produce 2- to 3-inch spotted, tubular flowers that crowd along a stiff stalk from late spring to early summer. These short-lived perennials or biennials overwinter as a clump of attractive light green leaves. Evocative of English cottage gardens, foxgloves provide strong vertical accents for beds and borders. They are most effective when planted in clumps. They grow well in coastal gardens, and make excellent cut flowers if picked when partially open.

Growing conditions and maintenance

Foxgloves flower most abundantly when planted in light shade. Space established plants 12 to 18 inches apart. Propagate by seed sown ¼ inch deep in late summer, by division in the fall, or by transplanted self-sown seedlings in early spring. *D. purpurea* usually self-sows abundantly.

Selected species and varieties

D. grandiflora (yellow foxglove)—perennial with brown-spotted yellow flowers on 3-foot stalks, needing partial shade; 'Temple Bells' has large flowers.

D. x mertonensis (strawberry foxglove)—perennial with dark strawberry pink flowers neatly layered on 4-foot stems; grown as a cool-season annual In the Southeast.

D. purpurea—biennial with purple, pink, cream, or brownish red drooping flowers on 2- to 5-foot stems, preferring partial shade; 'Alba' has clear white flowers.

> ★ **PRO'S PICK** ★
>
> **D. purpurea** var. **gloxiniiflora** has 4-inch gloxinia-shaped white, rose, purple, or yellow flowers on robust 4-foot stems.
>
>

★ **Point of interest:** *Foxglove is the source of digitalis, a medication used to treat heart disease.*

Doronicum (do-RON-i-kum)
LEOPARD'S-BANE

Hardiness: Zones 4-8

Plant type: perennial

Height: 1 to 4 feet

Interest: flowers

Soil: moist

Light: full sun to partial shade

◀ *Doronicum cordatum*

Leopard's-bane bursts forth in early spring with yellow daisylike flowers on tall stems. The delicate flowers contrast well with the bold mounds of heart-shaped or rounded dark green leaves below. The flowering season is relatively long. Leopard's-bane is effective planted in beds either singly or in groups, or for naturalizing in meadows, where both its flowers and its foliage add interesting accents to grasses and other flowers.

Growing conditions and maintenance

Space leopard's-bane 1 to 2 feet apart in partial shade in hot climates or in full sun in cool regions. Its shallow roots need constant moisture, and benefit from additions of compost and mulch. The flowering season can be extended by deadheading before plants set seed. If you have planted leopard's-bane in a meadow or other location that will be mowed, delay disturbing the plants until the foliage dies back in early summer. Propagate by division in the fall every 2 to 3 years.

Selected species and varieties

D. cordatum [also listed as **D. caucasicum** or **D. orientale**] (Caucasian leopard's-bane)—2- to 3-inch flowers on 1- to 2-foot stems above clumps of 2- to 4-inch heart-shaped, toothed leaves; 'Finesse' blooms later than the species and has 3-inch flowers on 18- to 24-inch stems; 'Madame Mason' has large flowers with foliage that may remain throughout most of the summer; 'Spring Beauty' grows to 18 inches tall with very early double flowers.

D. plantagineum (plantain leopard's-bane)—3- to 4-inch bright yellow flowers on 4-foot stems, and long-stalked oval or rounded leaves.

Dyssodia *(dis-OH-dee-ah)*
DAHLBERG DAISY

Hardiness: Zones 9-10

Plant type: tender perennial grown as an annual

Height: 4 to 12 inches

Interest: flowers, foliage, fragrance

Soil: dry, well-drained

Light: full sun

◀ *Dyssodia tenuiloba*

Dahlberg daisy blooms from summer to fall with petite yellow flowers at the tips of 3-inch-long branches. The highly dissected foliage has a pleasant fragrance reminiscent of thyme. The medium-green leaves are short and finely divided into feathery segments. This native of southern Texas and Mexico is an exquisite plant for rock gardens, sunny borders, and containers, or as edging for pathways.

Growing conditions and maintenance

Sow indoors in late winter and plant in the garden after danger of frost has passed. Or sow directly in the garden after the last frost spacing plants 9 to 18 inches apart. Dahlberg daisy is heat and drought tolerant and may self-sow in dry, gravelly soil.

Selected species and varieties

D. tenuiloba [also listed as **Thymophylla tenuiloba**] (Dahlberg daisy, golden fleece)—½-inch flower heads with bright yellow centers and stubby yellow, gold, orange, or red petals with lighter-shaded tips and feathery 1-inch leaves covered with very fine hairs.

Echinacea *(ek-i-NAY-see-a)*
PURPLE CONEFLOWER

Hardiness: Zones 3-8

Plant type: perennial

Height: 1½ to 4 feet

Interest: flowers

Soil: well-drained

Light: full sun to partial shade

◀ *Echinacea purpurea*

Purple coneflowers are robust natives of the eastern United States that look equally at home in borders, massed in beds or herb gardens, or naturalized in meadows. Their daisylike flowers have softly drooping pink to purple petals surrounding spiny, conical centers that glow purple, orange, or bronze depending on how the sunlight strikes them. Plants flower from early summer to fall, and make excellent cut flowers.

Growing conditions and maintenance

Purple coneflowers grow best in full sun, but in hot climates the flower color will be more intense if the plants are grown in light shade. Propagate in spring by division, seed, or self-sown seedlings. Space plants 2 feet apart. Wear gloves if collecting the prickly seeds, and gently tap the seed heads with a hammer to extract them.

Selected species and varieties

E. angustifolia (narrow-leaved purple coneflower)—1- to 2-inch lavender to rosy pink summer flowers with slightly drooping petals and dark centers, and long, slender leaves.

E. pallida (pale coneflower)—rosy purple or white flowers up to 3½ inches wide in late summer on 3- to 4-foot stems with broad leaves; Zones 4-8.

E. purpurea (purple coneflower)—pink, purple, or white flowers 2 to 4 inches across in summer and fall on strong 2- to 4-foot stems, and broad, pointed, tooth-edged leaves; 'Magnus' has brilliant rosy pink flowers; 'Monk's Silver' produces deep purple flowers; 'The King' bears large, deep carmine blossoms; 'White Swan' has snow white flowers; Zones 5-8.

★ **Point of interest:** *Purple coneflowers have been used in herbal remedies that are said to strengthen the immune system.*

Echinops (EK-in-ops)
GLOBE THISTLE

Hardiness: Zones 3-8

Plant type: perennial

Height: 6 inches to 8 feet

Interest: flowers, foliage

Soil: moist to dry, well-drained

Light: full sun to partial shade

◀ *Echinops ritro 'Veitch's Blue'*

Globe thistles have bold, slightly wild-looking foliage that contrasts with the refined look of its ornate, spherical summer-blooming flowers, adding a unique aspect to borders. The stiff stalks are lined with thick, hairy, deeply lobed leaves bearing metallic-blue spines at their tips, and topped with soft blue to white flowers that bloom for 2 months. These plants attract butterflies and honeybees to the garden, and makes an excellent dried flower.

Growing conditions and maintenance

Globe thistles are drought and heat tolerant, although the flower color is less intense under these conditions. Space plants 18 to 24 inches apart. Propagate by division in early spring. Plants grown from seed are often inferior to their parents in form and flower color. Wear gloves when handling these plants.

Selected species and varieties

E. humilis—6 to 12 inches tall with pale green spiny-toothed leaves and round, 1½-inch steel-blue flower heads.

E. niveus—3-foot stems topped with rounded clusters of blue flowers above spiny, deeply lobed leaves with fuzzy undersides.

E. ritro (small globe thistle)— blue-violet or deep blue flowers, rarely white, in 2-inch spheres on 2- to 5-foot white, woolly stems, and 8-inch, glossy, dark green leaves with white undersides; 'Veitch's Blue' has lapis blue flowers on strong 3- to 4-foot stems.

E. sphaerocephalus (great globe thistle)—5- to 8-foot stems bearing pale blue or white 2- to 2½-inch-wide globular flower clusters, and 14-inch rough green leaves with woolly undersides.

★ **Point of interest:** *Some people develop a rash if scratched by the spines of the thistle.*

Epimedium (ep-i-MEE-dee-um)
EPIMEDIUM

Hardiness: Zones 4-8

Plant type: perennial

Height: 3 to 12 inches

Interest: flowers, foliage

Soil: well-drained, moist, fertile

Light: partial to full shade

◀ *Epimedium grandiflorum*

Epimediums have sprays of waxy bicolored flowers with downward curving spurs that appear in mid-spring before the small, heart-shaped leaves emerge. New leaves are pale green or red as they unfurl, turn medium green in summer and bronze in fall, and remain throughout the winter in warmer regions. Epimediums are popular plants for shady rock gardens. Planted in large groups, they can be used as a slowly creeping ground cover for shady areas.

Growing conditions and maintenance

Epimediums prefer moist, peaty loam, but tolerate dry shade once established. Add compost or peat moss before planting 8 to 10 inches apart. Remove dead foliage in early spring before new growth starts. Propagate by division of rhizomes in late summer.

Selected species and varieties

E. alpinum (red Alpine epimedium)—1-foot masses of reddish green leaves and slipper-shaped yellow-and-red flowers.

E. grandiflorum (longspur epimedium, bishop's hat)—1-foot tall with 1- to 2-inch red, pink, lavender, or white spurred flowers with red sepals and 2- to 3-inch leaves; 'Nanum' is 3 inches tall; 'Violaceum' has pale purple flowers; 'White Queen' has white flowers.

E. pinnatum (Persian epimedium)—9 to 12 inches tall with bright yellow flowers and red spurs from mid-spring to mid-summer; Zones 5-8.

★ PRO'S PICK ★

E. grandiflorum 'Rose Queen' has large, deep pink flowers and foliage that emerges reddish and turns dark green as it matures.

Erythronium *(er-i-THRO-nee-um)*
TROUT LILY

Hardiness: Zones 3-9

Plant type: bulb

Height: 3 to 16 inches

Interest: flowers, foliage

Soil: well-drained, moist

Light: full sun to full shade

◀ *Erythronium nudopetalum*

Trout lilies have nodding, lilylike flowers with narrow reflexed petals and prominent stamens in early spring. The lance-shaped, paired leaves are commonly mottled with brown in patterns resembling the back of trout. All trout lilies rise from small corms. *E. americanum* is above ground for only about a month in the spring before it dies back to its corm, but other trout lilies have a longer flowering period. These plants often form large, exclusive mats in moist deciduous woodlands, and make excellent plants for wildflower gardens.

Growing conditions and maintenance

Trout lilies will grow in nearly any light conditions except the deep shade of evergreens. Plant corms in summer or fall, 2 to 3 inches deep and 4 to 6 inches apart. The first year after planting the corm will send up a single leaf and no flower. In subsequent years a pair of leaves will arise accompanied by one or two flower stems. Propagate by separating the small cormels that develop at the base of mature corms in fall.

Selected species and varieties

E. albidum (white dog-tooth violet)—nodding, 1½-inch white to light pink flowers above a pair of deep green, wavy-edged leaves mottled with brown; Zones 4-9.

E. americanum (eastern trout lily)—native to deciduous forests of the eastern United States, 3- to 8-inch stems bearing one or two 1- to 1½-inch chrome yellow flowers with either yellow or brown stamens, and a pair of fleshy, mottled, 3- to 6-inch leaves.

E. nudopetalum—plain green leaves beneath 1-inch yellow flowers with reflexed petals and white anthers; Zones 5-8.

E. revolutum (mahogany fawn lily, coast fawn lily)—Pacific Coast native with 1½-inch white, pink, or pale lavender flowers aging to purple, and 12- to 16-inch stems; Zones 5-8.

★ **Point of interest:** *There is evidence that placing a large, flat rock 3 inches below newly planted corms of E. americanum will hasten flowering.*

Eupatorium *(yew-pa-TOR-ee-um)*
JOE-PYE WEED

Hardiness: Zones 3-9

Plant type: perennial

Height: 2 to 6 feet

Interest: flowers, foliage

Soil: moist, well-drained

Light: full sun to partial shade

◀ *Eupatoruim maculatum 'Atropurpureum'*

These stately, robust natives of eastern North American wetlands display rounded clusters of small, misty, purplish pink or white flowers that attract honeybees, butterflies, and hummingbirds in late summer. Joe-Pye weed is ideal for planting near water elements or in bog gardens, or for naturalizing in wet meadows.

Growing conditions and maintenance

Plant Joe-Pye weed in spring or fall, spacing plants 2 to 3 feet apart. Divide clumps every 3 years in spring. Joe-Pye weed does not need mulching or fertilizing and is virtually pest free.

Selected species and varieties

E. maculatum (spotted Joe-Pye weed)—flat-topped clusters of pink or purple late summer flowers on 4- to 6-foot stems spotted with purple, and 10-inch, coarsely toothed leaves; 'Atropurpureum' has wine-red flowers; Zones 3-6.

E. perfoliatum (boneset)—loose clusters of antique white flowers from late summer to fall on 2- to 5-foot hairy stems piercing the base of the paired, stemless, bright green leaves.

E. purpureum (Joe-Pye weed)—dome-topped clusters of pale pink to green-yellow or rose-purple flowers from late summer to fall on 3- to 6-foot green and purple stems above whorls of vanilla-scented leaves; Zones 4-9.

E. rugosum (white snakeroot)—hairy, to 5 feet with 7-inch, toothed, heart-shaped leaves and drooping terminal clusters of tiny white flowers from mid-summer to early fall.

Filipendula   *(fil-i-PEN-dew-la)*
MEADOWSWEET

◀ *Filipendula rubra 'Venusta'*

Hardiness: Zones 3-8

Plant type: perennial

Height: 1 to 8 feet

Interest: flowers, foliage

Soil: moist, well-drained

Light: full sun to partial shade

Meadowsweets have long-lasting feathery plumes of mid-summer flowers that rise above thick clumps of reddish green compound leaves. These tall, stately plants are especially striking when massed at the back of borders, or naturalized in meadows or fields.

Growing conditions and maintenance

Meadowsweets benefit from additions of compost and organic mulch in spring. Plant in spring or fall, spacing plants 1 to 2 feet apart. Add a thin layer of mulch again in fall. Divide clumps every 3 to 4 years in the spring by cutting the rhizome that connects the main clump to the new shoots. Plant the divisions about 2 inches deep. Cut foliage to the ground in late summer or early fall when the leaves begin to turn brown.

Selected species and varieties

F. palmata (meadowsweet)—large clusters of small pink flowers fading to snowy white on 2- to 3-foot stems with seven to nine lobed, dark green leaves with pale undersides; 'Rubra' has dark red flowers.

F. rubra (queen-of-the-prairie)—very ornamental pink flowers in 4- to 8-inch clusters on sturdy 4- to 8-foot stems bearing 6- to 10-inch deeply lobed leaves; 'Venusta' has plumes of rosy pink flowers on 6-foot stems.

F. ulmaria (queen-of-the-meadow)—creamy white flower clusters in summer on 3- to 6-foot stems bearing large compound leaves that are green above and white below; 'Variegata' has leaves marked with a prominent yellow stripe.

F. vulgaris (dropwort)—finely cut, fernlike, dark green leaves, and 2- to 3-foot arching stems topped with loose panicles of vanilla-colored flowers.

★ **Point of interest:** *An oil with an aroma similar to wintergreen can be produced from the flowers of meadowsweet.*

Galanthus   *(ga-LAN-thus)*
SNOWDROP

◀ *Galanthus nivalis*

Hardiness: Zones 3-8

Plant type: bulb

Height: 4 to 12 inches

Interest: flowers

Soil: moist, well-drained, fertile

Light: full sun to partial shade

Among the earliest of spring-flowering bulbs, snowdrops often bloom while their leaves and flowers are still dusted with late winter snow. The solitary, pendant flowers have three outer petal-like segments that hang over a shorter, green-tipped tube. The leaves are glossy green and straplike. Plant snowdrops in rock gardens, along pathways or at foundations, or naturalize in lawns or under deciduous trees and shrubs.

Growing conditions and maintenance

In late summer or fall, work peat moss or compost into the soil and plant bulbs 3 inches deep and 3 inches apart and mark their locations. Snowdrop bulbs multiply quickly and can be divided every 3 to 4 years. Divide clumps of bulbs in late spring after the leaves have yellowed. To force snowdrops, plant four to six bulbs 1 inch deep in a 4-inch pot in late fall. In cold regions leave the pot outdoors under a mound of dry mulch, or chill in the refrigerator for 6 to 8 weeks. Once returned to a warm spot, the bulbs will bloom in a few weeks.

Selected species and varieties

G. x grandiflorus—10-inch flat, glossy green leaves beneath nodding white flowers tipped with green in late winter.

G. ikariae—1¾-inch white late-winter flowers tinged with green, and deep green 5½-inch long, narrow leaves.

G. nivalis—single, nodding, 1-inch early spring white flowers on 4- to 6-inch stems with 9-inch narrow leaves.

> ★ **PRO'S PICK** ★
>
> **G. elwesii** (giant snowdrop) has 1½-inch flowers with pairs of narrow, blue-green leaves and 9- to 12-inch stems, making it the tallest of the spreading species.
>
>

Galega (gal-EE-ga)
GOAT'S RUE

Hardiness: Zones 4-10

Plant type: perennial

Height: 1½ to 5 feet

Interest: flowers, foliage

Soil: well-drained

Light: full sun to partial shade

◀ *Galega officinalis*

Goat's rues are rambling members of the bean family with upright clusters of white, lavender, or violet-blue pealike flowers in summer on erect stems. Their bold, featherlike compound leaves have oval leaflets and form dense mounds that completely cover the ground. A robust growth habit makes them useful at the back of borders or naturalized in wild gardens. Goat's rues make good cut flowers.

Growing conditions and maintenance

Goat's rues should have afternoon shade in regions with hot summers. Plant in spring or fall 2 inches deep and 1 to 2 feet apart, and mulch lightly. Propagate in early spring from seed sown where plants are desired, or by dividing root crowns.

Selected species and varieties

G. officinalis—sprays of white, lilac, pink, or lavender flowers on 2- to-5-foot stems from summer to early fall, and five to eight narrow, blue-green leaflets with pointed tips; 'Lady Wilson' has fine, slender spikes of lilac-blue flowers.

G. orientalis—a more compact species with 1½-foot stems spreading to 2 feet, and violet flowers tinged with blue in early summer; Zones 6-10.

★ **PRO'S PICK** ★

G. officinalis 'Carnea' has rosy pink flowers that contrast beautifully with its blue-green leaves.

Gaura (GAW-ra)
GAURA

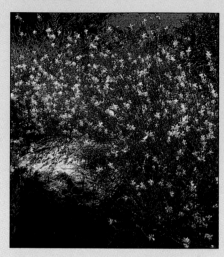

Hardiness: Zones 5-9

Plant type: perennial, biennial

Height: 2½ to 3 feet

Interest: flowers

Soil: well-drained, sandy

Light: full sun

◀ *Gaura lindheimeri*

Gauras have airy mounds of lance-shaped leaves and pale pink tubular flowers from summer to fall. The unique blossoms have four spatula-shaped white petals that contrast with the long red stamens. Gauras are members of the evening primrose family, and are useful for coastal gardens, naturalizing, or informal borders.

Growing conditions and maintenance

Space plants 2 to 4 feet apart. Water during hot, dry periods or plants will go dormant before flowering. Propagate by seed indoors in late winter or sow in mid-spring. Seedlings will grow to flowering-sized plants the first season. Gaura also can be propagated from softwood cuttings in summer.

Selected species and varieties

G. biennis—airy clusters of white tubular flowers opening at dusk and fading to red in summer to early fall, on 3- to 5-foot branched stems with narrow, elliptical leaves.

G. lindheimeri—loose panicles of white tubular flowers that open at dawn, touched with pale pink and fading to coral, in late summer to fall, on lanky, 2- to 5-foot stems with alternate, lance-shaped 3½-inch leaves and spreading clumps of carrotlike taproots; 'Corre's Gold' has white flowers on 2-foot stems, and green leaves edged with gold; 'Siskiyou Pink' has maroon buds and pink blossoms.

★ **Point of interest:** *Gather the ribbed, nutlike fruits of gaura in fall, place on a large sheet of paper, and gently tap with a wooden mallet to dislodge the seeds.*

Gentiana   *(jen-she-AY-na)*
GENTIAN

Hardiness: Zones 3-8

Plant type: perennial

Height: 2 inches to 3 feet

Interest: flowers

Soil: moist, well-drained

Light: full sun to partial shade

◀ *Gentiana septemfida var. lagodechiana*

Gentians are noted for their unique blossoms, which range from flaring, bell-shaped forms of brilliant sapphire blue to modest white flowers that resemble unopened buds. The variability of this genus provides the gardener with plants that thrive in rock gardens, borders, or slightly alkaline fields.

Growing conditions and maintenance

Plant larger species 1 to 1½ feet apart and smaller ones 4 to 12 inches apart. Propagate plants by mixing the fresh seed with dry, fine sand and spreading the mixture on the surface of the garden in spring. The seeds need light to germinate, so do not cover with soil. Divide clumps in early spring.

Selected species and varieties

G. acaulis (stemless gentian)— 2-inch bell-shaped, sky-blue flowers spotted with yellow in spring above thick rosettes of 2-inch leaves and 4-inch stems; 'Trotter's Variety' flowers in spring and fall; Zones 4-8.

G. andrewsii (closed gentian, bottle gentian)—clusters of closed blue flowers in late summer and fall that become purplish with age, and 1- to 2-foot stems with whorls of 3- to 4-inch lance-shaped leaves; var. **albiflora** has white flowers; Zones 5-8.

G. asclepiadea (willow gentian)—1½-inch bell-shaped, single, azure blue flowers with white throat stripes from mid-summer to early fall on 1- to 3-foot stems, and pairs of 3-inch leaves; Zones 5-8.

G. septemfida (crested gentian)—small, terminal clusters of 2-inch bell-shaped, pleated blue flowers from mid- to late summer on 8- to 12-inch stems with erect or arching clumps; var. **lagodechiana** has deep blue flowers on 6- to 8-inch stems.

Geranium   *(jer-AY-nee-um)*
CRANESBILL

Hardiness: Zones 3-10

Plant type: perennial

Height: 9 inches to 2 feet

Interest: flowers, foliage, fragrance

Soil: dry to moist, well-drained

Light: full sun to partial shade

◀ *Geranium sanguineum*

Cranesbills have long been garden favorites for their bright, five-petaled flowers in spring and summer and their spreading mounds of foliage. All have palmately lobed leaves, and some, such as *G. macrorrhizum*, which is the source of geranium oil, have strongly aromatic foliage. Cranesbills are a versatile group of plants used in rock gardens and borders, as ground covers, or naturalized in meadows or woodland gardens. They sometimes are called hardy geraniums to distinguish them from the genus *Pelargonium*, also known as zonal geraniums.

Growing conditions and maintenance

Plant cranesbills in spring or fall, spacing them 1½ to 2 feet apart. Mulch after planting and fertilize lightly in spring. In regions with hot summers they benefit from afternoon shade and supplemental water. Propagate cranesbills by dividing clumps in spring every 3 to 4 years.

Selected species and varieties

G. x cantabrigiense 'Biokovo'— 1-inch white spring flowers tinged in the center with bright green 1- to 3-inch lobed, bright green leaves that release a pleasing fragrance when rubbed.

G. endressii 'Wargrave Pink'— 1- to 1½-inch bluish pink flowers with ragged 2- to 4-inch leaves divided into five segments and blossoming from spring to fall where summers are hot; Zones 4-8.

G. ibericum (Iberian cranesbill)—1- to 2-inch purple flowers from spring through summer on 1- to 1½-foot hairy stems clad with deeply lobed leaves; 'Album' has white flowers; Zones 5-8.

G. x 'Johnson's Blue'—15- to 18-inch leafy mounds decorated with 1½- to 2-inch lavender-blue flowers traced with darker blue veins from spring to summer; Zones 5-8.

G. macrorrhizum (bigroot geranium)—10- to 12-inch creeping stems bearing magenta flowers from late spring to early summer with very aromatic maple-shaped leaves turning bright red in fall; 'Album' has white flowers; 'Bevan's Variety', deep magenta flowers; Zones 3-8.   *Continued* ▶

G. maculatum (wild geranium, wild cranesbill, spotted cranesbill)—grayish, maplelike leaves on 1- to 2-foot openly branched stems with 1-inch rose-purple to pale lilac flowers in late spring or early summer; Zones 3-7.

G. x oxonianum—2 to 3 feet tall with slightly wrinkled toothed leaves and pink summer flowers accented with darker colored veins; 'A.T. Johnson' has pink flowers with a light silver cast; 'Rose Clair' has porcelain pink flowers in July on 1- to 2-foot stems; Zones 5-7.

G. psilostemon (Armenian cranesbill)—2 to 4 feet tall and 3 to 4 feet wide with mounds of deeply toothed green leaves peppered in summer with bold magenta flowers marked with a prominent black eye; 'Bressingham Flair' has pink flowers on 1- to 3-foot stems; Zones 5-7.

G. sanguineum (bloody cranesbill, blood-red cranesbill)—solitary, 1- to 1½-inch crimson flowers in spring and summer on 24-inch-wide mounds of gray-green leaves that turn red in fall; 'Album' has pure white flowers on 8- to 10-inch stems; 'Alpenglow' has dark green leaves and bright rose-red flowers; 'Glenluce' bears clear pink blossoms on dense mounds of medium green leaves; 'Minitum' is low growing with tiny leaves and pink flowers; var. **striatum** is a dwarf with soft pink flowers and purple veins; 'Splendens' is a vigorous grower with pearl-pink flowers accented with purple-red veins; Zones 4-9.

Geranium sanguineum 'Album'

G. sylvaticum (wood cranesbill)—crowded clusters of 1- to 1½-inch pinkish purple, violet-blue, or white flowers atop 1½- to 2-foot stems in late spring and summer; 'Mayflower' has rich violet-blue flowers with white zones in the center; 'Nanum' has a low-growing, compact habit and rosy red flowers; 'Silva' has dark green leaves and pale blue flowers; Zones 5-9.

G. traversii var. **elegans**—1- to 1½-feet tall with silver-green leaves and small 1-inch wide white or muted pink flowers in summer; Zones 8-10.

G. wallichianum—prostrate stems to 2 feet long with rose-purple flowers from summer through early fall; 'Buxton's Variety' has small leaves marbled with white and stunning china blue flowers marked with a discrete white center; Zones 7-9.

Helenium (he-LEE-nee-um)
SNEEZEWEED

Hardiness: Zones 3-10

Plant type: perennial

Height: 2½ to 6 feet

Interest: flowers, foliage

Soil: moist, well-drained

Light: full sun

◄ *Helenium autumnale 'Brilliant'*

Sneezeweeds provide masses of vividly colored daisylike flowers from late spring through early fall, when most perennials have long since stopped flowering. The yellow, orange, or red fan-shaped petals surround a prominent, burnt red center, and willowy green leaves cling to 2- to 6-foot stems. Sneezeweeds are native to streamsides and wet meadows in much of the United States, and are stunning when naturalized or planted in borders.

Growing conditions and maintenance

Sneezeweeds are bothered by few garden pests and are heat and drought tolerant. Space plants 18 to 24 inches apart in spring or fall. Pinch stems in spring to promote bushy growth and more flowers, and fertilize lightly. Propagate by division of clumps every 3 to 4 years.

Selected species and varieties

H. autumnale (yellow star)—2-inch flaring, slightly reflexed yellow petals surrounding a raised yellow disk on branched stems up to 6 feet; 'Brilliant' has bright red-orange flowers that fade to lighter watercolor shades on 3-foot stems; 'Bruno' has 4-foot stems with mahogany flowers 'Butterpat' produces light yellow petals surrounding a bronze disk; 'Wyndley' has red-orange blossoms.

H. bigelovii (Bigelow sneezeweed)—2- to 3-inch yellow flowers with yellowish brown centers on 3- to 4-foot stems with lance-shaped leaves; Zones 8-10.

H. hoopesii (orange sneezeweed)—2-inch, slightly reflexed orange-yellow petals surrounding a raised yellow disk from spring to fall on strong 3-foot stems with 10-inch, narrow leaves.

Helleborus (hell-e-BOR-us)
HELLEBORE

Hardiness: Zones 4-9

Plant type: perennial

Height: 2 to 18 inches

Interest: flowers, foliage

Soil: moist, well-drained, slightly alkaline

Light: partial to full shade

◀ *Helleborus orientalis*

Hellebores are members of the buttercup family with 2- to 3-inch cup-shaped flowers in subtle hues of creamy white, pink, and deep maroon nestled around attractive, deeply lobed evergreen leaves. They are valued for late winter or early spring flowering, when little else is in bloom. Hellebores are excellent for borders and paths, and can be massed as a ground cover. The solitary blossoms make long-lasting cut flowers.

Growing conditions and maintenance

Plant hellebores in spring in the North and in fall in the South, spacing them 1 to 2 feet apart. Mulch lightly in spring and again in fall. Give extra water during hot, dry periods. Propagate by seed or division in early summer, being careful not to damage the fragile roots. Plants also self-sow. It usually takes several years for plants from seed or division to reach flowering size.

Selected species and varieties

H. niger (Christmas rose)—12 to 15 inches tall with nodding, creamy white flowers tinged with pink around prominent yellow stamens in late fall in the South and early spring in the North; 'Louis Cobbett' has white flowers stained with pink; Zones 5-8.

H. orientalis (Lenten rose)—15 to 18 inches tall with nodding clusters of two to six 2-inch cream, pink, maroon, or plum flowers from early to mid-spring; 'Atrorubens' bears blood red flowers; 'Zodiac' has pink flowers densely speckled with red.

★ PRO'S PICK ★

H. orientalis 'Queen of the Night' has clusters of spectacular blossoms with velvety, deep red petals and a shower of bright yellow stamens surrounded by black nectaries at the center of the flowers.

Hemerocallis (hem-er-o-KAL-lis)
DAYLILY

Hardiness: Zones 3-10

Plant type: perennial

Height: 1 to 6 feet

Interest: flowers, foliage, fragrance

Soil: moist, well-drained

Light: full sun to partial shade

◀ *Hemorocallis 'Stella d'Oro'*

Daylilies are old-fashioned, easy-to-care-for favorites. The original 15 species have yielded more than 26,000 varieties with flowers in every color except blue. So many cultivars and hybrids allow one to create beds and borders graced with daylily flowers from late spring to fall. In northern regions the long, grasslike leaves die back to the ground in fall, while in the South some varieties are evergreen. The flowers are borne on stems that often are twice as tall as the mounds of foliage. Each flower lasts from 1 to 2 days, but the numerous buds keep daylilies blooming for many weeks.

Growing conditions and maintenance

Plant daylily crowns 1 inch below the soil surface, 18 to 24 inches apart for smaller types and 2 to 3 feet apart for taller ones in spring, summer, or fall. Provide organic mulch to conserve water and prevent frost heaving where winters are cold, and afternoon shade where summers are hot and dry. A light application of fertilizer in spring is helpful. Rejuvenate established plants by dividing clumps every 3 to 6 years in early spring, or after flowering in late summer or fall.

Selected species and varieties

H. altissima—very strong 5- to 6-foot stems holding fragrant, pale yellow flowers in mid-summer; Zones 6-9.

H. citrina (citron daylily)—2 to 3 feet tall with fragrant, light yellow, 5- to 6-inch blossoms opening on mid-summer evenings.

H. fulva (orange daylily, tawny daylily)—vigorous, 4 feet tall with clusters of six to 12 tawny orange 4- to 5-inch flowers in mid-summer; 'Europa' has naturalized in many areas of the country, forming dense ground covers.

H. lilioasphodelus [also listed as *H. flava*] (lemon daylily)—3- to 4-inch deliciously fragrant lemon yellow flowers on delicate, arching, 2-foot scapes in late spring or early summer.

H. 'Stella d'Oro'—nearly ever-blooming miniature hybrid with 2½-inch, slightly ruffled, orange-throated canary yellow flowers on 12- to 18-inch scapes from late spring to late summer.

Hydrangea (hy-DRANE-jee-a)
HYDRANGEA

Hardiness: Zones 3-9

Plant type: shrub, small tree

Height: 3 to 20 feet

Interest: flowers, foliage, bark

Soil: moist, well-drained, fertile

Light: full sun to shade

◀ *Hydrangea macrophylla*

Hydrangea's large, showy flower clusters, bold foliage, and interesting reddish brown bark give these shrubs year-round garden interest. There are sterile and fertile flowers in each cluster. The sterile blossoms are 1 to 1½ inches wide with four to six petals surrounding smaller, fertile blossoms. The leaves are usually rounded, and turn attractive shades of yellow, red, or lavender in the fall.

Growing conditions and maintenance

These drought-intolerant shrubs need even moisture, and thrive on additional compost. Flower color of *H. macrophylla* is pH related. To produce blue blossoms, add sulfur to make the soil more acid. Ground limestone will make it more alkaline and produce pink flowers. Plant hydrangeas in spring or fall in full sun in northern areas, and in light shade in southern areas. Mulch with bark chips. Prune *H. quercifolia* and *H. macrophylla* after flowering, and other species in late winter. Propagate by softwood cuttings in late spring.

Selected species and varieties

H. anomala ssp. *petiolaris* (climbing hydrangea)—climbing without support to 60 feet or more with fragrant, white, early summer flowers 6 to 12 inches wide, and attractive exfoliating bark; Zones 4-7.

H. macrophylla (bigleaf hydrangea, hortensis hydrangea)—3 to 6 feet tall with equal or greater spread, 8-inch leaves, and globular, 5-inch flower heads in summer; Zones 6-9.

H. paniculata 'Grandiflora' (peegee hydrangea)—large shrub or small tree 10 to 25 feet tall and 10 to 20 feet wide with 12- to 18-inch white to russet flower clusters in summer above dark green 3- to 6-inch leaves; Zones 3-8.

H. quercifolia (oakleaf hydrangea)—4 to 6 feet tall and wide with 12- to 15-inch conical flower clusters changing from white to tan or pink in late summer, and 3- to 8-inch deep green oak-lobed leaves turning reddish purple in fall; Zones 5-9.

Hypericum (hy-PER-i-kum)
ST.-JOHN'S-WORT

Hardiness: Zones 3-8

Plant type: perennial, shrub

Height: 1 to 4 feet

Interest: flowers, foliage, fruit

Soil: well-drained, dry, slightly alkaline

Light: full sun to partial shade

◀ *Hypericum calycinum*

St.-John's-worts have long-lasting sunny yellow flowers accented by a pincushion clump of central stamens. In fall the old flower stems hold interesting winged fruit capsules that persist into winter. *H. calycinum* is an excellent long-flowering ground cover, and *H. prolificum* is a vigorous addition to shrub borders.

Growing conditions and maintenance

Plant St.-John's-worts in gravelly, limestone-rich soil, or amend slightly acid soil with a dusting of ground limestone a few weeks before planting in spring. Space *H. prolificum* 2 to 3 feet apart and *H. calycinum* 1 to 1½ feet apart. Propagate by division in spring or by softwood cuttings in early summer.

Selected species and varieties

H. androsaemum (Tutsan)—¾-inch yellow summer flowers in clusters of three to nine with large, 3½- to 4-inch leaves and fruit that ripens to bright red.

H. calycinum (creeping St.-John's-wort, Aaron's beard)—2- to 3-inch vivid yellow flowers with bright red anthers from summer to early fall, and creeping stems with dark green semi-evergreen leaves that turn purplish in fall; Zones 6-8.

H. prolificum (shrubby St.-John's-wort, broombrush)—1 to 4 feet tall with bright yellow ¾- to 1-inch flowers in summer, light brown exfoliating bark, and 2- to 3-inch blue-green leaves, and three-valved capsules that persist in winter.

Iris *(EYE-ris)*

IRIS

Hardiness: Zones 3-10

Plant type: bulb, perennial

Height: 4 inches to 5 feet

Interest: flowers, foliage

Soil: moist to wet, well-drained

Light: full sun to partial shade

◀ *Iris ensata*

Irises blossom in spring and summer. The flowers are held above clumps of flat, sword-shaped foliage on strong stems. Some spread from rhizomes, while others grow from bulbs. Irises can be used in borders or rock gardens, or naturalized in woodland settings. Many irises are quite fragrant, and those with long stalks make good cut flowers.

Growing conditions and maintenance

Plant irises in summer in the North and in fall in the South, spacing smaller types 1 foot apart and taller varieties 1½ feet apart. Dig a hole and refill until the top of the mound of soil is at ground level. Place rhizomes on mounds and spread roots. Finish filling the hole and gently tamp the soil. Bearded iris should have the top half of the rhizomes above soil level. *I. pseudacorus* prefers wet meadows or the shallow edges of ponds.

How to: Propagate rhizomatous irises after flowering by first trimming foliage to a 6-inch fan of leaves. Divide rhizomes by cutting them with a sharp, clean knife, being sure each rhizome piece has several buds and healthy roots.

Selected species and varieties

I. bearded Hybrids—3- to 5-inch white to purple flowers with yellow beards on 2- to 3-foot stems, and clumps of light green leaves in summer; 'Austrian Sky' has sky blue flowers with navy blue falls; 'Broadway' has golden standards and white falls; 'Marmalade Skies' is apricot-orange; 'Silent Strings' has clear blue blossoms; 'Smarty Pants', yellow flowers with red stripes on falls; 'Vanity' has light pink flowers splashed with white.

Iris bearded hybrid

I. cristata (crested iris, dwarf crested iris)—small, spreading rhizomes producing grassy, 6-inch leaves and 2-inch white or blue-violet flowers crested in yellow or white in mid-spring on 4-inch stems; 'Shenandoah Sky' has pale blue flowers; 'Summer Storm', dark blue blossoms.

I. ensata [also listed as ***I. kaempferi***] (Japanese iris)—graceful, stiff, 2-foot leaves with beardless 3- to 6-inch flowers in many different colors on 4-foot stalks in summer; 'August Emperor' has giant, deep red flowers in late summer; 'Pink Triumph', 8-inch deep pink, double-petaled flowers; 'Royal Crown', red-and-white flowers.

I. pallida 'Variegata'—3 feet tall with fragrant lavender-blue flowers in early spring and lovely foliage all summer.

I. pseudacorus (yellow flag, yellow iris)—2-inch bright yellow beardless flowers from late spring to early summer on 4- to 5-foot stems, spreading vigorously from rhizomes.

I. reticulata (reticulated iris)—8- to 10-inch tall stems rising from bulbs in late winter bearing blue to red-purple flowers in early spring; 'Harmony' has 6-inch brilliant blue flowers.

I. sibirica (Siberian iris)—2- to 4-foot clumps of leaves with beardless, 3- to 5-inch late spring flowers in many colors including violet, blue, white, and red, on 3-foot stems, growing from rhizomes; 'Blue Bridge' has flowers of pale lilac stained with pastel purple; 'Eric the Red' has dark red flowers; 'Periwinkle' has powder-blue flowers; 'Super Ego' has robust 3-foot stems and striking 5-inch pale blue petals boldly etched with navy blue;

Iris sibirica

'White Dove' is tall with pure white flowers.

I. versicolor (blue flag)—2- to 3-foot tall clumps of graceful lance-shaped leaves and strong stalks bearing several showy violet-blue flowers in summer; 'Rosea' has pink flowers; Zones 3-6.

Knautia (NAW-tee-a)
KNAUTIA

Hardiness: Zones 6-10

Plant type: annual, biennial, or perennial

Height: 2 to 4 feet

Interest: flowers

Soil: well-drained

Light: full sun

◄ *Knautia macedonica*

These relatives of teasels and pincushion flowers have lilac or deep-red domed blossoms accented with white pinlike stamens from late spring to fall. The informal flowers gently sway on the long, wiry stems held high above the deeply lobed foliage. Knautias are good as fillers at the backs of borders, or for interplanting with ornamental grasses in naturalized gardens.

Growing conditions and maintenance

K. arvensis performs best in slightly alkaline, gravelly soil, while *K. macedonica* prefers sandy loams. Mulch plants in Zones 6 and 7 in fall. Propagate knautias by seed in spring, or by division or transplanting of self-sown seedlings in fall.

Selected species and varieties

K. arvensis (blue-buttons, field scabious)—2- to 4-foot stems with pairs of narrowly oval, highly dissected leaves and nearly globular 1-inch lilac or white flowers with pink anthers from mid-summer to frost.

K. macedonica [also listed as *Scabiosa macedonica* or *Scabiosa rumelica*]—1½ to 2½ feet tall with slender, curved stems, lyre-shaped pale green leaves, and 1¼-inch rounded, dark purple, red, or maroon summer flowers.

K. orientalis—annual, slender, somewhat sticky 2-foot stems with purple flowers in summer and oblong to elliptical leaves.

K. tatarica—biennial, to 6 feet tall with 10-inch toothed, oblong-elliptic leaves and 1½-inch bright yellow flowers.

★ **Point of interest:** *Knautias attract butterflies and hummingbirds to the garden throughout the summer.*

Kniphofia (ny-FO-fee-a)
RED-HOT POKER

Hardiness: Zones 5-9

Plant type: perennial

Height: 2 to 4 feet

Interest: flowers, foliage

Soil: moist, well-drained

Light: full sun

◄ *Kniphofia uvaria*

Red-hot pokers have cylindrical clusters of boldly colored orange or yellow tubular blossoms on thick stems that arc over clumps of narrow, lance-shaped leaves. They produce a succession of flower spikes from summer to early fall. Spectacular as specimens, they add a unique accent to beds and borders.

Growing conditions and maintenance

Plant red-hot pokers 1½ to 2 feet apart in sunny locations sheltered from the wind. Remove flower stalks after blossoms have faded. In late fall cut back foliage and cover with salt hay or other light mulch. Propagate by seed or division in early spring. Seedlings and offsets may require several years to reach flowering size.

Selected species and varieties

K. uvaria—many 1- to 2-inch individual blossoms forming a 6- to 10-inch bottlebrush-shaped flower cluster atop 2- to 4-foot stems and narrow, rough-textured leaves.

K. Hybrids—Little Maid' has pastel yellow flowers that fade to antique white; 'Primrose Beauty' produces light yellow flowers; 'White Fairy' is a dwarf with creamy white flowers in mid-summer.

★ **PRO'S PICK** ★

K. uvaria 'Coral Sea' is robust, with wine-colored flowers in late spring and early summer that fade to coral.

Lavandula (lav-AN-dew-la)
LAVENDER

Hardiness: Zones 5-10

Plant type: perennial

Height: 1 to 3 feet

Interest: flowers, foliage, fragrance

Soil: well-drained

Light: full sun

◄ *Lavandula dentata*

Lavender's fragrant purple flowers blossom in late spring above paired gray-green leaves that line erect, square stems. Plants form shrubby cushions of soft foliage that can be clipped into a low hedge. They also can add an informal accent to edges, borders, and rock or herb gardens.

Growing conditions and maintenance

Plant lavenders in spring, spacing them 12 to 18 inches apart in well-worked soil. Cut back to 8 inches to encourage a bushy form. Lavenders can be propagated from cuttings made in late spring or early fall, or by divisions made in early spring.

Selected species and varieties

L. angustifolia ssp. **angustifolia** [also listed as **L. officinalis**] (English lavender, true lavender)—3- to 4-inch whorls of ¼-inch flowers atop 2- to 3-foot stems with 1- to 2-inch aromatic leaves; 'Fragrance' has particularly pungent flowers; 'Munstead Dwarf' is more spreading and only 1 foot tall; 'Twickel Purple' has fan-shaped clusters of violet flower spikes.

L. dentata (French lavender)—dense, woolly gray foliage at the base of 1- to 3-foot shrubby stems, topped by 1½-inch clusters of slightly fragrant lavender-blue flowers; Zones 8-9.

L. stoechas (Spanish lavender)—spikes of rose-purple flowers atop arching 2- to 3- foot stems with narrow, aromatic gray-green leaves; Zones 8-10.

★ PRO'S PICK ★

L. angustifolia 'Hidcote' is a tightly compact dwarf with deep purple flowers and silvery foliage on 20-inch stems.

Liatris (ly-AY-tris)
GAY-FEATHER

Hardiness: Zones 3-10

Plant type: perennial

Height: 18 inches to 5 feet

Interest: flowers

Soil: well-drained

Light: full sun to light shade

◄ *Liatris spicata*

Gay-feathers have slender stalks topped with soft spikes of feathery flowers over clumps of grassy leaves. The 6- to 15-inch flower clusters open from top to bottom. They give a strong vertical accent to borders. Gay-feathers are superb for naturalizing in meadow gardens.

Growing conditions and maintenance

Plant corms 3 to 4 inches deep in spring or fall, spacing them 1 to 2 feet apart. Propagate by separating and planting the tiny cormels that develop around mature corms.

Selected species and varieties

L. ligulistylis—tufts of 3- to 5-foot stems with 1½-inch clusters of rosy purple flowers from summer to fall and deep green, narrow leaves.

L. spicata (spike gay-feather, button snakewort)—clumps 2 to 5 feet tall and 2 feet wide with very narrow, tapering, 3- to 5-inch leaves on erect, stout stems, and purple or rose flowers from mid- to late summer; 'Alba' is pure white.

★ PRO'S PICK ★

L. spicata 'Kobold' is an 18- to 24-inch dwarf with dense heads of purple flowers tinged with burgundy.

Lilium   *(LIL-ee-um)*
LILY

Hardiness: Zones 3-9

Plant type: bulb

Height: 2 to 8 feet

Interest: flowers

Soil: moist, well-drained, fertile

Light: full sun to partial shade

◀ *Lilium auratum 'Malta'*

The eye-catching flowers of lilies range from modest single blossoms to showy clusters of up to 50. Each flower has six overlapping petals called tepals that can be either wavy or smooth, some with solid colors, others flecked with spots. The shapes range from flat or bowl-shaped to trumpets and turbans. There are many choices for size and season of bloom, making lilies versatile as specimens, as spreading clumps in borders, as naturalizing plants, or as transitional plants in front of shrubs.

Growing conditions and maintenance

Plant bulbs in spring or fall, spacing them 6 inches to 1 foot apart and 4 to 6 inches deep, according to bulb size. Mulch in spring and fall. Propagate from bulblets that form at the base of mature bulbs, or from the pea-sized black bulbils that form in the leaf joints of some species.

Selected species and varieties

L. Asiatic Hybrids—4- to 6-inch single or clustered flowers in any color but blue facing outward or upward from the tops of compact 2- to 4-foot stems from late spring to early summer.

L. auratum (gold-banded lily)—8 feet tall with purple-green, lance-shaped, 9-inch leaves and slightly pendulous, fragrant, white mid- to late-summer flowers with yellow or crimson streaks; 'Malta' has deep pink flowers.

L. martagon (Martagon lily, Turk's-cap lily)—4 to 6 feet tall bearing tiered clusters of up to 50 nodding, dull pink, 1½-inch fragrant flowers spotted with purple in mid-summer.

L. superbum (American Turk's-cap lily)—5 to 8 feet with clusters of 3-inch nodding, deep yellow-orange flowers with maroon spots in mid-summer.

L. Trumpet Hybrids [also known as Aurelian Hybrids]—4 to 5 feet tall with 6- to 10-inch somewhat fragrant white, gold, or pink flowers in trumpet, starburst, or bowl shapes, pointing outward or nodding, from mid- to late summer.

Lobelia   *(lo-BEE-lee-a)*
LOBELIA

Hardiness: Zones 3-10

Plant type: perennial, tender perennial grown as an annual

Height: 4 inches to 3 feet

Interest: flowers

Soil: moist, well-drained, fertile

Light: full sun to partial shade

◀ *Lobelia erinus*

Lobelias are free-flowering plants ranging from mounding, compact annuals to erect perennials with 3-foot stems and showy spires of five-lobed, two-lipped blossoms from summer through fall. *L. erinus* is popular for edging, walls, planters, and rock gardens. *L. cardinalis* and *L. siphilitica* are used as bedding and border plants, or in wet meadows or near water.

Growing conditions and maintenance

Plant lobelias in spring, spacing smaller species 4 inches apart and larger types 1 foot apart. Lobelias respond well to periodic additions of organic mulch and compost. The best flower colors result when they are grown in partial shade. Cut back *L. erinus* after its first flowering to encourage reblooming. All species can be propagated by seed, and perennial types also can be propagated by layering or division in early spring.

Selected species and varieties

L. cardinalis (cardinal flower)—2- to 3-foot unbranched stalks of brilliant red flowers above dark green leaves from late spring through fall.

L. erinus (edging lobelia, trailing lobelia)—tender perennial producing mounds of 4- to 8-inch stems with blue or white ½-inch flowers from summer to frost and thin, ½-inch leaves; 'Cambridge Blue' has light green foliage and light blue flowers; 'Crystal Palace' has dark blue flowers.

L. siphilitica (great blue lobelia, blue cardinal flower)—1-inch lavender to blue flowers on stiff, 2- to 3-foot stems from summer to fall; Zones 4-7.

L. spicata (pale-spike lobelia)—18- to 24-inch slender stems lightly ornamented with oblong leaves and topped with tightly clustered spikes of tiny blue flowers in summer; Zones 4-8.

★ **Point of interest:** *Cardinal flower's crimson blossoms are irresistible to hummingbirds.*

Lobularia (lob-yew-LAIR-ee-a)
SWEET ALYSSUM

Hardiness: Zones 9-10

Plant type: tender perennial grown as an annual

Height: 3 to 6 inches

Interest: flowers

Soil: well-drained

Light: full sun to partial shade

◀ *Lobularia maritima*

Sweet alyssum produces robust mounds of narrow, lance-shaped, gray-green leaves that are usually hidden beneath masses of petite, fragrant four-petaled flowers from spring to frost. Long a favorite for beds, borders, rock gardens, and containers and as a cover for the withering foliage of spring bulbs, it is usually grown as an annual except in warmer climates.

Growing conditions and maintenance

Propagate from seed sown indoors 6 to 8 weeks before the last frost, or outdoors after danger of frost has passed. Thin seedlings to 6 inches apart. Young plants will spread quickly and flower rapidly if kept moist and cool. Periodic shearing of old blossoms during summer will stimulate further flowering. In warm climates they will self-sow.

Selected species and varieties

L. maritima [also listed as *Alyssum maritimum*]—3 to 6 inches tall with white, pink, or violet flowers; 'Pastel Carpet' has flowers with a variety of pastel shades and white centers; 'Royal Carpet' has violet-purple flowers; 'Tiny Tim' is 3 inches tall with white flowers.

★ **PRO'S PICK** ★

L. maritima 'Little Dorrit' has a greater abundance of more densely packed clusters of flowers and a more compact form than many other sweet alyssums.

Magnolia (mag-NO-lee-a)
MAGNOLIA

Hardiness: Zones 4-9

Plant type: shrub, tree

Height: 20 to 80 feet

Interest: flowers, foliage, fragrance, fruit

Soil: moist, well-drained, acid

Light: full sun to partial shade

◀ *Magnolia liliiflora*

Magnolias are renowned for their masses of showy, often fragrant flowers. In spring or summer they produce broad, cup- or star-shaped pure white to deep purple blooms that often ripen into ornamental, conelike fruit with red seeds. Magnolias are either evergreen or deciduous, and make excellent specimen plants.

Growing conditions and maintenance

Plant in spring or fall in soil amended with peat moss or compost. Fertilize in spring and mulch around the base of the trunk. Many species are susceptible to leaf spot, which defaces the leaves in late summer but does not damage the health of the plants. Water during hot, dry periods. Propagate by collecting fresh seed in fall and chilling for 4 months. Sow in spring.

Selected species and varieties

M. grandiflora (southern magnolia)—60- to 80-foot low-branching, pyramidal evergreen tree with shiny, leathery, 5- to 8-inch leaves, fragrant 8- to 12-inch cream-colored flowers in spring, and fruit pods with scarlet seeds in fall; Zones 7-9.

M. liliiflora (lily magnolia)—15-foot deciduous tree with medium green 6-inch elliptical leaves and narrow-petaled, lilylike, fragrant reddish purple spring flowers.

M. x soulangiana (saucer magnolia)—30-foot deciduous tree with 6-inch dark green, oval leaves, and large, cup-shaped flowers in spring.

M. stellata (star magnolia)—deciduous shrub or tree to 20 feet tall with fragrant 4-inch white late spring flowers tinged with pink; Zones 5-9.

M. virginiana (sweet bay)—deciduous shrub or tree to 20 feet tall in the North, but growing as a pyramidal deciduous or evergreen tree to 60 feet in the South, with lemon-scented, waxy, 3-inch white flowers from spring through summer; Zones 5-9.

Malus *(MAY-lus)*
CRAB APPLE

◀ *Malus floribunda*

Hardiness: Zones 2-8

Plant type: shrub, tree

Height: 6 to 50 feet

Interest: flowers, foliage, fragrance, form

Soil: moist, well-drained, acid

Light: full sun

Crab apples are popular ornamental shrubs and trees that bear clusters of white to red spring blossoms before leaves appear. Small green, yellow, or red applelike fruit is produced in summer and often persist into fall. Crab apples are excellent specimen trees and make good additions to shrub borders.

Growing conditions and maintenance

Prune crab apples each year immediately after flowering to maintain shape, and remove suckers. Feed in spring with a balanced fertilizer, and mulch with compost.

Selected species and varieties

M. baccata (Siberian crab apple)—very hardy 30- to 50-foot tree with pure white, deliciously scented flowers and reddish yellow fruit; var. **gracilis** has graceful, slightly pendant branches ornamented in spring with 1½-inch fragrant white flowers and in fall with reddish orange fruit.

M. coronaria (American crab apple)—20- to 30-foot tree with wide-spreading branches bearing pink buds opening to white flowers in late spring, and 1- to 1½-inch yellowish green, very sour fruit; 'Charlottae' has pale pink double flowers and attractive fall foliage.

M. floribunda (Japanese flowering crab apple)—rounded, 15- to 25-foot tree with pink to red buds opening to white or pink fragrant flowers, followed by red or yellow fruit; Zones 5-8.

M. sargentii (Sargent crab apple)—spreading, densely branched, 6 to 8 feet tall with clusters of red buds opening to ½-inch to 1-inch highly fragrant white flowers, and bright red ¼-inch fruit.

Mertensia *(mer-TEN-see-a)*
BLUEBELLS

◀ *Mertensia virginica*

Hardiness: Zones 3-8

Plant type: perennial

Height: 1 to 3 feet

Interest: flowers, foliage

Soil: moist to wet, well-drained, fertile

Light: full sun to shade

These North American natives have long been grown in gardens for their springtime displays of pale blue trumpet-shaped flowers. Their leaves emerge in spring with a distinctive purplish sheen, and mature to pale blue-green. The flower shoots bear nodding clusters of pink buds that open to powder blue and fade to lilac. Bluebells enter dormancy shortly after flowering, and should be planted with companions such as ferns to fill in the vacant spaces. These plants are effective grown in large clumps in borders and rock gardens, or naturalized in woodland and streamside settings.

Growing conditions and maintenance

Propagate by sowing fresh seed in early summer, or by dividing the root mass immediately after flowers fade and leaves turn yellow. It may be difficult to locate the dormant roots, so mark their locations to avoid damaging them later. Replant divisions, spacing them 18 inches apart and setting the root crowns at the soil surface.

Selected species and varieties

M. ciliata (mountain bluebells, Rocky Mountain bluebells)—clumping, 1 to 3 feet high with 2- to 6-inch smooth, succulent leaves and slightly fragrant ¾-inch flowers in late spring and summer; foliage persists longer than that of **M. virginica**.

M. virginica (Virginia bluebells, Virginia cowslip)—18- to 24-inch shoots bearing 2- to 5-inch thick, elliptical leaves and clusters of 1-inch flowers in mid-spring, and receding into its roots by early summer; 'Alba' has white flowers.

★ **Point of interest:** *Bluebells frequently are visited by bumblebees, and provide nectar for hummingbirds in the spring.*

Monarda (mo-NAR-da)
BEE BALM

Hardiness: Zones 4-9

Plant type: perennial

Height: 3 feet

Interest: flowers, foliage, fragrance

Soil: moist, well-drained

Light: full sun to partial shade

◀ *Monarda didyma 'Cambridge Scarlet'*

Bee balms have clusters of purple, lilac, red, pink, or white tubular, two-lipped flowers arranged in moplike tufts at the tops of tall, leafy stems. Their lance-shaped leaves are aromatic when crushed, and are used to make refreshing teas. Bee balms are members of the mint family, and are excellent for planting in beds and borders or naturalizing in woodland plantings.

Growing conditions and maintenance

Plant in spring or fall. Space plants 1½ to 2 feet apart. Prune withering flower heads to prolong the flowering season. Propagate by seed or division every few years in early spring, or from cuttings made in early summer. Bee balms are prone to mildew, so plant them where they will get good air circulation. Water during hot, dry periods.

Selected species and varieties

M. didyma (bee balm, Oswego tea)—1- to 2-inch scarlet flowers in rounded, 2- to 3-inch-wide clusters from late spring to late summer on 3- to 4-foot stems; 'Cambridge Scarlet' is wine red; 'Croftway Pink', rosy pink; 'Granite Pink' is a dwarf with pink flowers; 'Mahogany' has dark red flowers; 'Marshall's Delight' is mildew resistant and bears large pink flowers over a longer season; 'Salmonea' has salmon-pink flowers; 'Snow Queen' has icy white blossoms.

M. fistulosa (wild bergamot)— 2- to 4-inch pomponlike clusters of lilac to pink flowers from mid- to late summer on 2- to 4-foot stems and slightly fuzzier leaves with a sweeter fragrance; forma *albescens* has white flowers.

M. punctata (spotted bee balm, horsemint)—2- to 3-foot stems bearing whorls of ¾-inch-long yellow blossoms with purple spots in late summer.

★ **Point of interest:** *Bee balm is attractive to bees, butterflies, and hummingbirds.*

Narcissus (nar-SIS-us)
DAFFODIL

Hardiness: Zones 3-10

Plant type: bulb

Height: 8 to 16 inches

Interest: flowers, fragrance

Soil: well-drained

Light: full sun to partial shade

◀ *Narcissus jonquilla*

The bright, perky flowers of these heralds of the new growing season make them favorites for massing in beds, borders, or naturalized in lawns. The 1- to 4-inch flowers, which emerge in late winter through early spring, face out, arch up, or nod downward, and consist of an outer ring of six pointed or rounded petals, and a raised center or corona that may be a small cup or a long trumpet. Narcissus petals and coronas may be ruffled, fringed, or flared, and come in colors ranging from traditional yellow to orange or white. Some species have sweetly fragrant flowers. They are excellent as cut flowers and for forcing.

Growing conditions and maintenance

The tops of daffodils die back to the bulbs in late spring. Allow foliage to turn completely yellow, which can take 6 weeks, before removing it. Plant in fall, a few weeks before soil freezes, setting bulbs one and a half to three times the width of the bulb, and spacing them 1 to 3 inches apart. Propagate by replanting bulblets from the bases of mature bulbs. They take several years to reach blooming size. Divide bulbs if they become overcrowded and flowering decreases.

Selected species and varieties

N. jonquilla (jonquil)—2-inch very fragrant golden yellow flowers with flat coronas in clusters on 12-inch stems; Zones 5-9

N. poeticus (pheasant's-eye)— very fragrant 1½- to 3-inch mid-spring blossoms with back-swept white petals, and flat, disk-shaped, yellow coronas rimmed with red on 8- to 16-inch stems.

N. pseudonarcissus—2- to 3-inch deep yellow blossoms with ruffled and flared trumpets on 10-inch stems in spring.

★ **PRO'S PICK** ★

N. poeticus 'Actea' thrives in the wet soils of meadows and other poorly drained areas where other Narcissus would not survive.

Nepeta (NEP-e-ta)
CATMINT

Hardiness: Zones 3-9

Plant type: perennial

Height: 12 inches to 3 feet

Interest: flowers, foliage, fragrance

Soil: well-drained

Light: full sun

◀ *Nepeta x faassenii*

Catmints have fragrant, soft, dusty green, heart-shaped leaves and square stems topped by spikes of tiny white or blue flowers. Catmints flower nearly all summer. They are excellent as ground covers, in rock or herb gardens, or as edging.

Growing conditions and maintenance

Plant catmints in spring, spacing them 1 to 1½ feet apart. Shear plants after flowering to encourage rebloom. To propagate, take softwood cuttings in summer from nonflowering shoots and stick directly in moist sand away from direct sunlight.

Selected species and varieties

N. cataria (catnip)—spreading, 24-inch clumps of pliant stems covered with gray-green leaves and topped with narrow spikes of white and violet flowers; 'Citriodora' has tart, lemon-scented leaves.

N. x faassenii (blue catmint)—18- to 24-inch mounds of 1-inch silvery gray leaves, and ½-inch lavender-blue sterile flowers from spring to summer; 'Dropmore' has upright stems with lavender flowers; 'Porzellan' has narrow, gray-green leaves and Wedgwood blue flowers; 'Snowflake' is a dwarf with pewter green leaves and pure white flowers; 'Superba' has spreading branches covered with gray-green leaves and abundant dark blue flowers; Zones 4-9.

N. mussinii (Persian catmint)—1 foot tall, sprawling, gray-green foliage with ¼-inch-long lavender flowers in summer; 'Blue Wonder' has deep blue flowers on 12-inch stems.

★ PRO'S PICK ★

N. x faassenii 'Six Hills Giant' is robust, very hardy, and grows to 3 feet tall with large sprays of deep blue flowers.

Nicotiana (ni-ko-she-AN-a)
FLOWERING TOBACCO

Hardiness: Zones 7-10

Plant type: annual, tender perennial grown as an annual

Height: 1 to 6 feet

Interest: flowers, foliage, fragrance

Soil: moist, well-drained

Light: full sun to partial shade

◀ *Nicotiana alata*

The blossoms of many flowering tobaccos species open in late afternoon and fill the evening with a heavy, sweet perfume. Erect stems arise from coarse clumps of large, sticky leaves and are topped by loose clusters of long, tubular flowers that are pollinated by honeybees, hummingbirds, and nocturnal moths. Flowering tobacco makes an excellent border filler or specimen for the back of beds.

Growing conditions and maintenance

Propagate flowering tobaccos by seed, sowing seeds indoors 6 to 8 weeks before the last frost. Seeds need light to germinate, so sprinkle them on top of the soil, moisten, and cover the container with plastic wrap. Space transplants 1 foot apart. Remove dead flowers before they set seed to encourage further blooming.

Selected species and varieties

N. alata (jasmine tobacco, flowering tobacco)—1- to 4-foot clumps bearing 2- to 4-inch flowers from spring to fall above 4- to 10-inch leaves; 'Daylight Sensation' has flowers in shades of lilac, white, purple, and rose that open at dawn; 'Fragrant Cloud' has heavily scented snow-white blossoms that open in the evening; 'Lime Green' has bright yellow-green flowers from summer to fall on 18-inch stems; 'Nikki' series produces bushy, 18- to 24-inch plants with flowers in a range of colors that includes shades of pink, red, white, and yellow.

N. langsdorffii—3- to 5-foot annual with nodding, 2-inch, bell-shaped, yellow-green flowers and turquoise anthers in summer; Zones 9-10.

N. sylvestris (woodland tobacco)—3- to 6-foot annual with 1-foot leaves and drooping, 3- to 4-inch fragrant white summer flowers tinged with pink or purple; 'Only the Lonely' has 4- to 5-foot stalks, each bearing up to 30 tubular flowers; Zones 8-10.

★ **Point of interest:** *N. sylvestris is a pungent night-bloomer that also opens on cloudy days.*

Paeonia (pee-O-nee-a)
PEONY

Hardiness: Zones 3-8

Plant type: perennial, shrub

Height: 1½ to 5 feet

Interest: flowers, foliage, fragrance

Soil: moist, well-drained, fertile

Light: full sun to partial shade

◀ *Paeonia suffruticosa*

The showy blossoms of peonies grace the garden in spring and early summer. The flowers, borne at the tips of branches, have either single petals and clusters of golden stamens, or double petals that fill the entire flower with soft colors. *P. lactiflora* is herbaceous, with broad, deeply lobed leaves that remain attractive into fall, while *P. suffruticosa* is a small, woody shrub. Peonies are long-lived perennials that are excellent for borders or as specimens and make long-lasting cut flowers.

Growing conditions and maintenance

Plant container-grown peonies in spring in soil amended with compost. Provide extra water in hot, dry periods. Peonies prefer to remain undisturbed, but can be propagated by dividing tuberous roots in fall, setting pieces with three to five eyes 1 to 2 inches deep and 4 feet apart.

Selected species and varieties

P. lactiflora (Chinese peony)— 3 to 6 inches wide double or single white, pink, or red blossoms from late spring to early summer on 1½- to 3-foot stems; 'Auguste Dessert' has salmon rose flowers edged in silver; 'Calypso', faded pink flowers with yellow stamens; 'Carnival', pale rose blossoms edged in pink; 'Hidcote Purple' has dark purple flowers; 'Poetic' has deep crimson flowers; 'Sarah Bernhardt' is apple blossom pink.

P. suffruticosa (tree peony)— 6- to 10-inch-wide mid-spring flowers from white to pink to deep red and yellow with crinkled, satiny petals often bearing a red blotch at their bases, and 4- to 5-foot woody stems.

★ PRO'S PICK ★

P. lactiflora 'Bowl of Beauty' is a single peony with 9-inch flowers made up of several rows of pink petals surrounding frothy, creamy white petal-like filaments. The sturdy 2½-foot stems hold the dark green foliage long after flowers fade.

Perovskia (per-OV-skee-a)
RUSSIAN SAGE

Hardiness: Zones 5-8

Plant type: perennial

Height: 2 to 3 feet

Interest: flowers, foliage, fragrance

Soil: well-drained

Light: full sun

◀ *Perovskia atriplicifolia*

Russian sage is a low, shrubby perennial bearing long clusters of small, soft, somewhat hairy blue-violet flowers from late summer to early fall. It forms somewhat woody clumps with fine-textured, aromatic, gray-green foliage. The leaves have a sagelike fragrance when bruised. Russian sage is most effective when massed in mixed borders with ornamental grasses.

Growing conditions and maintenance

Plant Russian sages 2 to 3 feet apart and lightly fertilize in spring. To promote bushy form, cut woody stems back in spring before new growth begins. Propagate by seed.

Selected species and varieties

P. atriplicifolia (Russian sage, azure sage)—tiny, lavender-blue, two-lipped summer to fall flowers on 12-inch spikes, and 1½-inch downy, toothed, finely divided gray leaves on woody stems; 'Blue Mist' has pale blue flowers in summer; 'Filagran' has fine-textured foliage and blue flowers from summer to fall; 'Longin' has erect 3-foot stems and blue flowers.

P. scrophulariifolia—24- to 36-inch stems with oval leaves and sprays of light blue flowers from late spring to early summer.

★ PRO'S PICK ★

P. atriplicifolia 'Blue Spire' is more hardy than the species with deeply cleft leaves and abundant 12- to 14-inch clusters of lavender-blue flowers.

Petunia   (pe-TOO-nya)
PETUNIA

Hardiness: half-hardy

Plant type: annual

Height: 6 inches to 2 feet

Interest: flowers

Soil: well-drained

Light: full sun

◀ *Petunia x hybrida*

Petunias, among the most popular of annuals, are renowned for producing a profusion of trumpet-shaped blooms in a wide variety of colors from summer to frost. The trailing or upright stems are slender, with small, pointed leaves covered with soft, sticky hairs. Dwarf varieties grow 6 to 12 inches tall, while bedding varieties can attain heights of 2 feet. Hybrid grandiflora varieties produce single ruffled or fringed flowers 4 to 6 inches across. Hybrid multiflora varieties produce smaller flowers, but in greater abundance. Petunias are effective as bedding plants, as borders, cascading over walls and banks, or as container plants.

Growing conditions and maintenance

Start petunias indoors from seed 10 to 12 weeks before the last frost. Pinch some of the shoots of young plants to encourage a bushy form. Remove withered flowers before they set seed to encourage further flowering.

Selected species and varieties

P. x hybrida—white, yellow, pink, red, purple, blue-purple, or lavender flowers with ruffled, fringed, or deeply veined petals; 'Blue Danube', a double grandiflora with fringed blue petals; 'Flaming Velvet', a very deep red bedding petunia; 'Purple Wave' has a compact habit and violet-purple flowers; 'Satin Series' is a multiflora with solid colors.

★ PRO'S PICK ★

Petunia 'Star Series' (hybrid grandiflora) is bushy, 6 to 12 inches tall, with large, flaring, single flowers and petals that are various pure colors striped with white.

Phlox   (flox)
PHLOX

Hardiness: Zones 3-9

Plant type: half-hardy annual, perennial

Height: 6 inches to 4 feet

Interest: flowers, foliage, fragrance

Soil: dry to moist, well-drained

Light: full sun to shade

◀ *Phlox drummondii* 'Dwarf Beauty'

The many species of phlox can provide bright color in the garden from spring through frost. All species have similar clusters of trumpet-shaped, five-petaled flowers with flaring faces and often with a dark eye. Their sizes and flowering seasons, however, range from *P. stolonifera*, which forms 8-inch-tall mats of soft evergreen foliage and flowers in spring, to the upright, 3-foot clumps of *P. paniculata,* which flowers from late summer to fall and has deciduous leaves. The taller types are effective fillers for massing in beds and borders, while the mat-forming species are used in rock gardens and walls, and as ground covers. *P. drummondii* has compact cultivars that are excellent for container plants.

Growing conditions and maintenance

Phlox species have different cultural requirements. *P. drummondii* grows best in well-drained, sandy soil in sunny locations. *P. divaricata* needs shady, moist conditions, while *P. maculata* and *P. paniculata* need full sun with ample moisture and *P. stolonifera* grows well in sun or shade. Perennial varieties benefit from annual additions of compost. Space lower forms 12 to 18 inches apart and taller ones 2 feet apart. Propagate perennials by division in early spring before growth starts. *P. drummondii* must be propagated by seed started indoors 6 weeks before the last frost in cold climates, and sown directly outdoors in regions with warm winters. Phlox needs good air circulation to prevent mildew. Remove withered flowers to prolong blooming season. *Continued* ▶

Selected species and varieties

P. carolina (thick-leaf phlox)—
24- to 36-inch sturdy stems
draped with dark green, lance-
shaped leaves and dense clusters
of pink or purple flowers from
spring to early summer; 'Gloriosa'
has salmon-pink flowers; 'Miss
Lingard' has pure white flowers
on 36-inch stems; Zones 3-8.

P. divaricata (wild blue phlox,
woodland phlox)—12- to 15-inch
spring-blooming perennial with
semievergreen oval leaves and
scapes topped with loose clusters of fragrant blue, purple, or
white flowers with darker eyes
and notched petals; ssp.
laphamii has rich blue-violet
flowers; Zones 4-9.

P. drummondii (annual phlox,
Drummond's phlox)—6- to
20-inch annual bearing 1-inch
pink, red, lavender, purple, or
white flowers from late spring
through summer; 'Beauty Series'
has a dwarf habit with pink,
white, red, lilac, and purple
flowers; 'Petticoat' has mixed-
color flowers; 'Twinkle Series'
has fringed petals.

P. maculata (wild sweet
William, spotted phlox)—2- to
4-foot perennial, often with
purple-spotted stems and elegant
cylindrical flower clusters in
shades of pink to white from
midsummer through early fall;
'Alpha' has bright pink flowers.

★ PRO'S PICK ★

P. paniculata 'Bright Eyes'
produces dense clusters of pale
pink flowers with deep crimson throats. Flowers contrast
beautifully with the dark green
foliage borne on 3-foot stems.

P. paniculata (summer phlox)—
2- to 4-foot clump-forming
perennial bearing pyramidal, 4- to
8-inch clusters of fragrant, 1-inch
white, lavender, pink, purple, red,
salmon, or bicolored flowers in
late summer and fall; 'David' has
a long season of bright white
flowers; 'Eva Cullum' has long-
blooming flowers of faded pink
accented by a deep red eye;
'Franz Schubert' has lavender-
pink flowers with a deep pink,
star-shaped eye; 'Starfire' has
bright scarlet flowers; Zones 3-8.

P. stolonifera (creeping
phlox)—5- to 10-inch creeping
perennial with evergreen leaves
forming mats of blue, pink, or
white flowers in spring; 'Blue
Ridge' bears lavender-blue flowers; 'Bruce's White' has white
flowers; Zones 3-8.

P. subulata (moss pink)—4- to
6-inch creeping ground cover
with abundant white or pink
flowers in early spring; 'Brilliant'
has bright pink flowers.

Phygelius (fye-JEEL-ee-us)
CAPE FUCHSIA

◀ *Phygelius aequalis*
'Yellow Trumpet'

Hardiness: Zones
7-10

Plant type: perennial,
shrub

Height: 2 to 6 feet

Interest: flowers

Soil: well-drained

Light: full sun to
light shade

Cape fuchsias have dramatic clusters of dangling, colorful, five-
lobed tubular flowers and pairs of dark green, triangular to
lance-shaped leaves that are most dense toward the base of the
stems. These woody-based perennials will grow as small shrubs
where winters are mild, but are killed back in colder regions to
resprout in spring. They also can be used as houseplants, since
they do not grow as large indoors as in gardens. Cape fuchsias
attract sunbirds in their native South Africa, and hummingbirds
in North America.

Growing conditions and maintenance

The long flower clusters of cape fuchsias need to be sheltered
from the wind. In Zones 7 to 8 the entire plant should be protected from cold winter winds as well. They benefit from additional water and fertilizer. Prune old stems and winter-damaged
shoots in very early spring. Propagate by seed or softwood cuttings made in late autumn or spring.

Selected species and varieties

P. aequalis—3 to 4 feet tall
with dense, cylindrical clusters
of 2-inch brown, red, or dusky
pink late summer flowers;
'Yellow Trumpet' has a dense,
bushy habit and creamy yellow
flowers; Zones 8-10.

P. capensis—2- to 3-foot sprawling, four-angled or narrowly
winged stems with
1½-foot pyramidal clusters of
1½-inch yellow-throated red,
orange, or yellow flowers on the
top half of the branches from
mid-summer to fall, and spreading

by underground stolons; 'Coccineus' has bright orange flowers
accented with sunset red.

P. x rectus—3 to 4 feet tall with
pendulous clusters of light red
summer to fall flowers and lance-
shaped, slightly toothed leaves;
'Devil's Tears' has deep red
flowers with a yellow throat;
'Moonraker' flowers are pale
yellow; 'Pink Elf' is a dwarf with
crimson lobes and pink flowers;
Zones 8-10.

Physostegia (fy-so-STEE-gee-a)
OBEDIENT PLANT

Hardiness: Zones 4-10

Plant type: perennial

Height: 18 inches to 4 feet

Interest: flowers, foliage

Soil: dry to moist, well-drained

Light: full sun to partial shade

◀ *Physostegia virginiana 'Vivid'*

The wandlike stems of obedient plants, topped with conical spikes of delicate pink, lavender, or white flowers, grow in spreading clumps. The flower spikes have four vertical rows of tubular flowers that look like miniature snapdragons. Pairs of smooth, dark green, sharp-toothed leaves clasp the four-sided stems. *Physostegia* is called obedient plant because its flowers stay put when moved laterally, rather than springing back to their original positions. Obedient plants make excellent cut flowers, and are used as a filler in beds and borders or for naturalizing in meadows. They are native to prairies and fields in eastern North America, where they attract bees and hummingbirds.

Growing conditions and maintenance

Obedient plants tolerate most growing conditions but can be invasive when grown in sunny, moist borders because of their vigorously spreading stolons. Space plants 1½ to 2 feet apart. Propagate by seed or division in early spring or late fall.

Selected species and varieties

P. digitalis—3 to 4 feet with spikes of pale lavender to off-white flowers spotted with purple in midsummer; Zones 8-10.

P. virginiana (obedience, false dragonhead)—2 to 4 feet with dense clusters of 8- to 12-inch, two-lipped white, deep pink, or lavender-pink summer flowers and dark green, wavy-edged narrowly lance-shaped leaves; 'Bouquet Rose' has light pink flowers; 'Summer Spire', deep pink flowers; 'Variegata', dark green leaves edged in creamy white beneath light pink flowers.

★ PRO'S PICK ★

P. virginiana 'Summer Snow' has pure white flowers in long spires on 1½- to 2½-foot stems in June and July.

Platycodon (plat-i-KO-don)
BALLOON FLOWER

Hardiness: Zones 4-9

Plant type: perennial

Height: 1 to 3 feet

Interest: flowers

Soil: well-drained, acid

Light: full sun to partial shade

◀ *Platycodon grandiflorus*

Balloon flowers have inflated buds that form cup-shaped, 2- to 3-inch-wide blossoms with pointed, translucent petals. Flowers are usually blue, but cultivars with white or pink blossoms also are available. The branched shoots appear in late spring and quickly grow to 2 or 3 feet. The 3-inch oval, toothed leaves grow in erect clumps. Taller varieties may need staking. Balloon flowers are excellent for massing and borders, while dwarf cultivars can be used in rock gardens. Taller varieties make good cut flowers.

Growing conditions and maintenance

While balloon flowers grow well in full sun, the pink varieties have best color in shade. These slow-growers do not need much attention or division. Propagate by seed or division in early spring or late autumn. Since shoots are late to emerge in spring, mark the locations of plants during the summer so plants are not damaged when soil is cultivated the following spring. Space plants 18 inches apart. It usually takes 2 years for seedlings to reach flowering size.

Selected species and varieties

P. grandiflorus (balloon flower, Japanese bellflower)—deep blue flowers on slender, 2- to 3-foot stems above neat clumps of blue-green leaves from mid- to late summer; 'Album' has white flowers; 'Shell Pink' and 'Mother-of-Pearl' have pale pink flowers; 'Sentimental Blue' has bright blue flowers on 15-inch stems; 'Apoyama' grows 6 inches in a container and 1 foot in the garden; 'Komachi' has flowers that retain their balloon shape, never fully opening.

★ PRO'S PICK ★

P. grandiflorus var. *mariessii* is a dwarf with 1- to 1½-foot stems that do not require staking. It is a superb addition to a rock garden.

Pulmonaria (pul-mo-NAY-ree-a)
LUNGWORT, PULMONARIA

Hardiness: Zones 3-8

Plant type: perennial

Height: 6 to 18 inches

Interest: flowers, foliage

Soil: moist, well-drained

Light: partial to full shade

◀ *Pulmonaria saccharata* 'Dora Bieleveld'

While grown primarily for their clumps of broadly oval, hairy leaves mottled with silvery white spots, lungworts also bear clusters of blue or white trumpet-shaped flowers that nod from the tops of arching stems in the spring. Lungworts are effective as coarse, slowly spreading ground covers. Their foliage emerges in early spring and remains green until fall. They also can be used as accents in shady borders and beds.

Growing conditions and maintenance

Lungwort foliage looks raggedy and bleached if grown in full sun. Plants benefit from periodic additions of compost and supplemental water during dry spells. Space plants 1 to 1½ feet apart. Cut flowering stems back as blossoms fade to promote vigorous growth. Propagate by seed or division in fall.

Selected species and varieties

P. angustifolia—lance-shaped green leaves beneath sapphire blue flowers; 'Azurea' has pinkish blue buds that open to flowers of bright blue; 'Johnson's Blue' is a dwarf with sky blue flowers.

P. saccharata (Bethlehem sage)—pink flowers opening to blue or white on 6- to 18-inch stems above mottled green and white leaves; 'Dora Bieleveld' has rosy pink flowers; 'Sissinghurst White' has early-flowering white blossoms and well-spotted leaves; 'Highdown' has leaves tinged with silver and deep lapis blue flowers; 'Leopard' produces pale pink flowers and green leaves spotted with white.

> ★ PRO'S PICK ★
>
> **P. saccharata** 'Mrs. Moon' has robust, 12-inch silvery gray leaves, and produces abundant 2- to 4-inch-long clusters of bright blue flowers.

Rudbeckia (rood-BEK-ee-a)
CONEFLOWER

Hardiness: tender or Zones 4-9

Plant type: annual, biennial, or perennial

Height: 10 inches to 7 feet

Interest: flowers, foliage

Soil: well-drained

Light: full sun to partial shade

◀ *Rudbeckia hirta* 'Goldilocks'

Coneflowers are prolific bloomers from early summer to frost. These natives of North American grasslands and meadows have daisylike flower heads with intense yellow rays that contrast with their centers. The central disk is dark brown in *R. fulgida* and *R. hirta* but bright green in *R. nitida*. All have large, hairy leaves and stiff stems. They can be used in sunny borders, combined with ornamental grasses, or naturalized in meadows.

Growing conditions and maintenance

Coneflowers produce fewer flowers in shady locations. Space plants 1½ to 2 feet apart. *R. hirta* grows as an annual, biennial, or short-lived perennial, and should be propagated by seed. Its flowering season can be prolonged by sowing seed at biweekly intervals. Other species of coneflowers can be propagated by seed or division in early spring.

Selected species and varieties

R. fulgida (orange coneflower, black-eyed Susan)—1- to 3-foot perennial with 3- to 5-inch yellow-orange flowers and dark, domed centers from early summer through fall.

R. hirta (black-eyed Susan)— 1- to 3-foot annual, biennial or short-lived perennial with 2-inch petals surrounding conical centers in late summer; 'Gloriosa Daisy' is yellow with a mahogany center; 'Goldilocks' has brilliant yellow double flowers.

R. nitida (green coneflower)— 2- to 7-foot perennial with 3- to 4-inch flowers and drooping yellow rays from mid- to late summer; Zones 6-9.

> ★ PRO'S PICK ★
>
> **R. fulgida** 'Goldsturm' has a compact, 2-foot form, and resists powdery mildew better than other selections. It is also hardy and pest free.

Salvia   (SAL-vee-a)
SAGE

Hardiness: tender or Zones 4-10

Plant type: annual or tender perennial grown as an annual

Height: 1 to 5 feet

Interest: flowers, foliage, fragrance

Soil: well-drained

Light: full sun to partial shade

◀ *Salvia leucantha*

Sages have spikes or whorls of hooded, two-lipped flowers at the tips of their branched stems, and pairs of aromatic leaves that clasp or are attached by petioles to their square stems. *S. coccinea* and *S. officinalis* are ideally suited for massing in borders, while the larger shrubby species, such as *S. greggii*, *S. guaranitica*, and *S. leucantha*, are well suited to shrub borders and filling large spaces in gardens south of Zone 7. Sages include *S. officinalis*, used in cooking; *S. leucantha*, a native of the chaparral hillsides of the Pacific Coast; and *S. coccinea*, a native of the southeastern United States along the Gulf of Mexico.

Growing conditions and maintenance

Sages tolerate drought well; they grow poorly in sites that are wet in winter. Space smaller varieties 18 inches apart, larger ones 2 to 3 feet apart. Deadheading stimulates rebloom. Prune old stems in fall or early winter. Provide tender perennials with mulch over winter in regions colder than Zone 8. Propagate *S. splendens* by seed and perennial species by division in spring or fall, or by softwood cuttings in summer. *S. coccinea* self-sows in warm regions, but should be started indoors 6 to 8 weeks before the last frost elsewhere. *S. officinalis*, *S. guaranitica*, and *S. greggii* can be grown as annuals in northern regions and as perennial shrubs in warm climates.

Selected species and varieties

S. coccinea—(Texas sage, scarlet sage)—tender perennial grown as an annual with heart-shaped leaves on 1- to 2-foot branching stems, and ¾-inch to 1-inch-long, usually deep scarlet flowers in summer with small lower lips; 'Bicolor' has a white upper lip and a carmine red lower lip; 'Lady in Red' has slender clusters of bright red flowers.

S. greggii (autumn sage)—2- to 4-foot shrubby perennial with 1-inch elongated, leathery leaves, and 1-inch red, purple-red, pink, or coral flowers in small clusters in late spring and early summer; Zones 7-10.

S. guaranitica—3- to 5-foot shrubby perennial with whorls of deep blue 2-inch flowers on fuzzy, arching spikes from summer to fall, and 5-inch dark green leaves; Zones 7-10.

S. leucantha (Mexican bush sage, white sage)—3- to 4-foot very drought-resistant shrubby perennial with white woolly leaves and long, open clusters of pink flowers; excellent for xeriscaping; Zones 7-10.

S. officinalis—1½- to 2½-foot mounding perennial with whorls of tiny white, blue, or purple flowers in short spikes in summer above hairy, aromatic gray-green leaves; 'Purpurascens' has purple-tinged leaves; 'Tricolor' has leaf veins that turn from cream to pink and red as multicolored foliage ages.

S. splendens (scarlet sage)—3- to 8-foot shrubby tender perennial grown as an annual with 3-inch tapered dark green leaves and spikes of 1½-inch bright red flowers on upright stems from summer to frost; 'Atropurpurea' bears dark violet flowers; 'Bicolor' has red-and-white flowers; 'St. John's Fire' has vivid red blossoms.

S. x superba [also listed as *S. nemorosa*] (violet sage)—1½- to 3-foot perennial with dense whorls of violet to dark blue-violet flowers above narrow leaves from late spring to early summer; Zones 5-8.

★ PRO'S PICK ★

S. x sylvestris 'Mainacht', sometimes called 'May Night', is 3 feet tall and compact, with 18-inch spikes of dark blue-violet flowers from spring to late summer.

★ **Point of interest:** *The brilliant red flowers of S. coccinea attract both hummingbirds and butterflies.*

Sanguisorba *(sang-wi-SOR-ba)*
BURNET

Hardiness: Zones 3-8

Plant type: perennial

Height: 2½ to 6 feet

Interest: flowers, foliage

Soil: moist, well-drained

Light: full sun to partial shade

◄ *Sanguisorba canadensis*

Burnets have spikes of white flowers resembling a bottlebrush on wandlike stems. The buds at the base of the flower spike open first, forming a wave of white moving upward from summer to mid-fall. The tall stems rise above the very attractive toothed, compound leaves. Native to low meadows and bogs in eastern North America, burnets are an excellent choice for perennial beds, natural gardens, and waterside plantings. They form spreading clumps over time.

Growing conditions and maintenance

Burnets adapt to most conditions as long as the soil does not dry out completely. Taller varieties may need staking, so avoid adding extra fertilizer, or plants may become even lankier than under ordinary conditions. Space plants 1½ to 2 feet apart. Propagate by division in early spring, or by seed sown in damp soil in fall or spring.

Selected species and varieties

S. canadensis (Canadian burnet, American burnet)—3 to 6 feet tall, spreading to 1 to 2 feet wide with upright, leafy-stemmed clumps, and 6- to 8-inch-long, flower spikes in summer made up of individual flowers having a four-lobed, petal-like calyx and long white stamens but no petals, and attractive compound leaves with seven to 15 oblong leaflets having sharply toothed edges.

S. minor [also listed as **Poterium sanguisorba**] (salad burnet)—2 to 3 feet tall with alternate, sharply spicy leaves, and greenish white flowers in early summer; Zones 5-8.

S. officinalis (great burnet)—3-foot stems with alternate, deep green, glossy leaves, and bottlebrush spikes of deep purple-black flowers from summer to fall.

★ **Point of interest:** *The tender young leaves of salad burnet have a clean, sharp, cucumber-like flavor that make a delicious spread when mixed with soft cheese.*

Satureja *(sat-yew-REE-jia)*
SAVORY

Hardiness: Zones 4-10

Plant type: annual or perennial

Height: 2 inches to 1½ feet

Interest: flowers, foliage, fragrance

Soil: dry, well-drained

Light: full sun

◄ *Satureja montana*

While most familiar in the herb garden, savories have distinctive gray-green foliage and masses of delicate, subtle-hued flowers that make them deserving of use in rock gardens and borders, or as edging. The leaves are highly aromatic and frequently used as a culinary herb for their peppery flavor. Members of the mint family, they have square stems that bear clusters of two-lipped flowers that are highly attractive to bees.

Growing conditions and maintenance

Savories can be grown in ordinary garden conditions as long as the soil is not soggy. Propagate by seed sown indoors in early spring. Do not cover seed, as light is needed for germination.

Selected species and varieties

S. hortensis (summer savory)—1- to 1½-foot shrubby, branching annual with narrow, 1-inch-long finely hairy leaves and ¼- to ⅓-inch lavender, pink, or white two-lipped flowers in small clusters at the base of the top pairs of leaves from mid-summer to frost.

S. montana (winter savory)—9- to 15-inch woody species with narrow, ¾-inch shiny evergreen leaves and tiny lavender or white flowers dotted with purple spots in spikes at the end of branch tips from summer to early fall.

★ PRO'S PICK ★

S. montana 'Prostrate White' has white flowers atop a 3- to 6-inch-tall creeping mat of glossy leaves.

Sedum (SEE-dum)
STONECROP, SEDUM

Hardiness: Zones 3-10

Plant type: perennial

Height: 1 to 2 feet

Interest: flowers, foliage

Soil: well-drained

Light: full sun to partial shade

◀ *Sedum spectabile 'Brilliant'*

Stonecrops have thick, succulent stems topped by dense clusters of five-petaled, star-shaped flowers. The plants add color and texture in perennial borders and rock gardens, and the leaves often are covered with a white waxy bloom or tinged with copper or bronze. Stonecrops can be massed as a succulent ground cover that attracts numerous species of butterflies to its summer and fall flowers.

Growing conditions and maintenance

Stonecrops are heat and drought tolerant, and spread slowly. Space plants 1½ to 2 feet apart. Propagate species by seed, and all types by division in early spring or by stem cuttings in late spring through summer.

Selected species and varieties

S. spectabile (showy stonecrop)—round clumps of 18- to 24-inch stems lined with 3-inch fleshy, rounded, blue-green leaves and topped by flat clusters of white, pink, or red flowers from summer to frost; 'Brilliant' has deep red flowers.

S. telephium (orpine, live-forever)—1 to 2 feet with ob-long, toothed leaves and rounded clusters of pink, red, or some-times white flowers in late summer; 'Indian Chief' has coppery red flowers.

S. x 'Vera Jameson'—9- to 12-inch hybrid of **S. telephium** with coppery purple leaves cov-ered by a whitish bloom, bearing dusty pink or magenta flowers in early fall.

> ★ PRO'S PICK ★
>
> **S. x 'Autumn Joy'** is 15 to 24 inches tall with rosy pink flowers in mid-summer that turn dusky red in fall.
>
>

Silphium (SIL-fee-um)
ROSINWEED

Hardiness: Zones 3-9

Plant type: perennial

Height: 2 to 12 feet

Interest: flowers, foliage

Soil: well-drained

Light: full sun to partial shade

◀ *Silphium perfoliatum*

Bold plants native to prairies and woodland openings of eastern and central North America, rosinweeds raise their small, pure yellow, sunflower-like heads from summer to fall far above clumps of interesting foliage. When they are not in flower, their foliage provides a bold accent to the backs of borders, inter-planted with ornamental grasses, or naturalized in meadows. The ornate lower leaves of *S. laciniatum* point north and south to avoid the heat of the noonday sun, giving the plant its com-mon name of compass plant.

Growing conditions and maintenance

Rosinweeds require a lot of space to grow, so plant them 1 to 2 feet apart in sites where they will not dwarf other plants. *S. den-tatum* is the most shade-tolerant species. Propagate by seed, since the roots of these plants can be massive. Seeds require sev-eral months of chilling at 40° F before germinating, and benefit from having their hard coats nicked with a sharp knife before being planted ⅓ to ½ inch deep. It takes 2 to 3 years for seedlings to reach flowering size.

Selected species and varieties

S. dentatum (toothed rosin-weed)—2- to 8-foot smooth stems with narrowly oval, toothed leaves and a cluster of bright golden 3-inch flowers; Zones 6-9.

S. laciniatum (compass plant)—3- to 12-foot rough stems with 1- to 2-foot deeply pointed leaves and showy clusters of 5-inch flower heads.

S. perfoliatum (cup plant)—3- to 8-foot hairy stems clasping pairs of 6- to 12-inch leaves joined at the base to form a cup, and small clusters of 3-inch flowers.

S. terebinthinaceum (prairie dock)—3- to 9-foot smooth, slender stems bearing yellow daisylike flowers in summer above clumps of 1- to 2-foot-long rough, heart-shaped leaves.

Spiraea *(spy-REE-a)*
SPIREA

Hardiness: Zones 3-8
Plant type: shrub
Height: 2½ to 8 feet
Interest: flowers, foliage
Soil: well-drained
Light: full sun to partial shade

◀ *Spiraea x vanhouttei*

Spireas are deciduous shrubs with abundant clusters of tiny, roselike flowers in tight panicles along the entire length of their stems in spring, or at the tips of their branches in summer. Each of the small, pink or white flowers has five petals and a spray of stamens, often with colored anthers, at the center. Spireas are easy to care for and can be used as specimen shrubs, in shrub borders, or in beds.

Growing conditions and maintenance

Spireas are more vigorous and bear more flowers when grown in full sun. They grow well in all but the driest soil and benefit from moisture during the growing season. Prune summer bloomers in late winter and spring-blooming varieties immediately after they flower.

Selected species and varieties

S. x cinerea—4 to 5 feet with fuzzy, arching stems bearing downy green 1-inch leaves and 4- to 6-inch clusters of white flowers in spring; Zones 4-7.

S. japonica (Japanese spirea)— rounded, 5 to 6 feet tall with 1- to 3-inch toothed, pointed leaves and 5- to 8-inch clusters of pink flowers in late spring and early summer; 'Little Princess' has deep pink flowers and blue-green leaves tinted red in fall on 30-inch stems; Zones 4-8.

S. nipponica (Nippon spirea)— compact, 3 to 5 feet tall with 1-inch oval, blue-green leaves and an abundance of white flower clusters in mid-spring.

S. x vanhouttei (bridal-wreath)—6 to 8 feet tall, spreading in vase or fountain fashion to a width of 10 to 12 feet with 1- to 2-inch white flower clusters in spring; Zones 4-8.

Stewartia *(stew-AR-tee-a)*
STEWARTIA

Hardiness: Zones 5-9
Plant type: shrub, tree
Height: 10 to 40 feet
Interest: flowers, foliage, bark
Soil: moist, well-drained, organic, acid
Light: full sun to partial shade

◀ *Stewartia pseudocamellia*

Stewartias add year-round charm and grace to the landscape not only for their camellia-like flowers that bloom from mid- to late summer, but also for their colorful fall foliage and beautiful exfoliating bark in patches of cream, rusty red, and gray. These plants should be given a place of prominence in the landscape, where they can be viewed at every season. The smaller types combine well with other flowering shrubs.

Growing conditions and maintenance

These trees and shrubs are difficult to transplant, so carefully choose a location from which you do not plan to move them later. Dig a large hole and add copious amounts of compost and peat moss to maintain an acid soil. Stewartias require protection from drying winter winds and scorching summer sun. Provide extra moisture during dry spells. Once established, stewartias rarely need pruning.

Selected species and varieties

S. koreana (Korean stewartia)— pyramidal tree 35 to 45 feet tall with dark green foliage turning sunset red in fall, and 2- to 3-inch, wavy edged, creamy white flowers in late summer.

S. malacodendron (silky stewartia)—large shrub or small tree 10 to 15 feet tall bearing single 2½- to 4-inch white summer flowers with purple filaments and bluish anthers; Zones 7-9.

S. ovata (mountain stewartia)— bushy shrub or small tree 10 to 15 feet tall with spreading form, 2½- to 3-inch creamy white,

cup-shaped summer flowers with oval, 2- to 5-inch orange to red leaves in fall, and flaking bark.

S. pseudocamellia (Japanese stewartia)—oval tree 20 to 40 feet tall with showy, exfoliating bark and 2- to 2½-inch white flowers with white filaments and orange anthers in summer, and 1½- to 3½-inch leaves turning vibrant yellow, red, and purple in fall; Zones 5-7.

Syringa *(si-RING-ga)*
LILAC

Hardiness: Zones 3-8

Plant type: shrub, small tree

Height: 4 to 15 feet

Interest: flowers, foliage

Soil: moist, well-drained

Light: full sun

◀ *Syringa vulgaris 'Sarah Sands'*

Lilacs are sturdy, old-fashioned favorites with dense, grapelike clusters of fragrant flowers in late spring. They have pairs of pointed, oval, dark green leaves that add medium foliage texture after the flowers have faded. Lilacs make attractive specimens, or informal hedges, and contribute springtime elegance to mixed-shrub borders.

Growing conditions and maintenance

Lilacs grow best in loamy soil and benefit from annual additions of compost and extra moisture during dry spells. Prune older stems with reduced flower production immediately after flowering, and deadhead faded flowers as well. Lilacs often suffer from powdery mildew on their leaves during summer, so plant them where they will receive good air circulation.

Selected species and varieties

S. x chinensis (Chinese lilac)—graceful, spreading, 8- to 15-foot-tall shrub with arching branches bearing a profusion of fragrant purple-lilac flowers in 6-inch clusters in mid-spring; 'Alba' has white flowers; 'Saugeana' has reddish flowers; Zones 3-7.

S. meyeri (Meyer lilac)—wide-spreading, compact, 4- to 8-foot-tall shrub with dense ¾-inch to 1½-inch elliptical leaves, and abundant 4-inch clusters of long-lasting flowers.

S. reticulata (Japanese tree lilac)—wide-spreading, 20- to 30-foot shrub or small tree with rich mahogany-colored bark and large panicles of fragrant, antique white flowers in early summer; Zones 3-7.

S. vulgaris—erect, spreading, 8- to 15-foot shrub with 2- to 5-inch leaves concentrated near the top of the crown, and 4- to 8-inch clusters of extremely fragrant flowers in colors ranging from classic lilac to white and shades of blue, purple, or red; 'Albert F. Holden' is bicolored; 'Blue Boy' is heat tolerant and has blue flowers; 'Edith Cavell' has double white flowers; 'Sarah Sands' has purple flowers; Zones 3-7.

Thalictrum *(thal-IK-trum)*
MEADOW RUE

Hardiness: Zones 5-9

Plant type: perennial

Height: 2 to 7 feet

Interest: flowers, foliage

Soil: moist, well-drained

Light: full sun to partial shade

◀ *Thalictrum delavayi*

These graceful plants are grown both for their clusters of airy, fluffy blossoms displayed over several weeks, and for their deeply cut, lacy foliage that adds a soft accent to the garden the rest of the growing season. Plant both species of meadow rue listed below for a longer season of flowering in borders, rock gardens, and wild, informal gardens. They also make good cut flowers.

Growing conditions and maintenance

Meadow rues prefer morning sun and soil that never dries out. Space *T. aquilegifolium* 1 foot apart and *T. delavayi* 2 feet apart. Plants benefit from staking, especially if subjected to wind. Propagate by fresh seed sown in fall, or by division in spring.

Selected species and varieties

T. aquilegifolium (columbine meadow rue)—2 to 3 feet tall with delicate, rounded, dark green leaves and large clusters of creamy flowers with mauve centers in late spring and early summer.

T. delavayi [also listed as **T. dipterocarpum**] (Yunnan meadow rue)—clump-forming, 4 to 7 feet tall with showy clusters of lavender-blue or rose-purple flowers accented with bright yellow stamens in late summer and early fall; 'Hewitt's Double' has multipetaled flowers.

★ PRO'S PICK ★

T. aquilegifolium 'White Cloud' is slightly taller than the species, with dense foliage and clouds of white flowers.

Tiarella (ty-a-REL-a)
FOAMFLOWER

Hardiness: Zones 3-9

Plant type: perennial

Height: 6 to 12 inches

Interest: flowers, foliage

Soil: moist, well-drained

Light: partial to full shade

◀ *Tiarella cordifolia*

Foamflowers have spikes of white, frothy flowers that bloom in mid-spring, and are natives of moist woodlands and stream banks in eastern North America. These plants produce stalks that rise out of low-growing mounds of attractive, sharp-lobed, fuzzy, heart-shaped leaves that are medium green in summer, and reddish bronze or dark purple in fall, and remain visible over winter. They make an exceptional ground cover, edging, or rock garden plant for shady spots, and are especially effective when massed.

Growing conditions and maintenance

Foamflowers require additional water during dry spells. They grow best in slightly acid soil with a high organic content. Space plants 12 to 18 inches apart; they will spread quickly by runners. Propagate by digging and replanting runners in spring or fall, or by sowing fresh seed in the garden in fall.

Selected species and varieties

T. cordifolia (Allegheny foam-flower)—compact clusters of tiny, ¼-inch-wide, star-shaped, five-petaled white flowers with long white stamens on 6- to 12-inch-tall stalks above neat mounds of lobed leaves from mid-spring to early summer; 'Marmorata' has maroon flowers and bronze leaves that become marbled with purple in winter; 'Major' bears salmon-red or wine-colored blossoms; 'Purpurea' has purple flowers.

T. wherryi (Wherry's foam-flower)—6- to 12-inch-tall stalks covered with fine-textured white flowers from spring to early summer; Zones 6-9.

★ **Point of interest:** *The flower stems of foamflowers are decorated with leaves in the South, while those in the North are leafless.*

Tricyrtis (try-SER-tis)
TOAD LILY

Hardiness: Zones 4-8

Plant type: perennial

Height: 2 to 3 feet

Interest: flowers

Soil: moist, well-drained, fertile, slightly acid

Light: partial to full shade

◀ *Tricyrtis hirta*

Toad lilies are members of the lily family. Their unusually shaped white or pinkish flowers point upward from the leaf base along their arching stems or at the branch tips above clumps of dark green leaves. The bullet-shaped flower buds open in summer or fall to reveal six thin, flaring, spotted petals that are joined at the base. The blooming season is relatively long, lasting up to 6 weeks. Toad lilies are a good choice for shady perennial borders, and woodland or shady rock gardens.

Growing conditions and maintenance

Space rhizome pieces 12 to 18 inches apart in humus-rich loam. Remove dead leaves in late fall. In Zone 7 and colder regions, mulch plants after the ground freezes to protect from heaving. Propagate by division in spring or fall.

Selected species and varieties

T. formosana (Formosa toad lily)—1 to 2 feet tall with shiny, deep green, 5-inch leaves and clusters of 1-inch white to light pink flowers with yellow throats and dark purple spots at their tips.

T. hirta (hairy toad lily)—hairy, 2 to 3 feet tall with 6-inch lance-shaped leaves and 1-inch bell-shaped, waxy, creamy white flowers spotted with red or purple; 'Alba' has pure white flowers; 'Variegata' produces dark green leaves with white veins.

Tulipa (TEW-lip-a)
TULIP

Hardiness: Zones 3-8

Plant type: bulb

Height: 8 to 18 inches

Interest: flowers,

Soil: moist, well-drained, dry

Light: full sun

◀ *Tulipa 'Easter Fire'*

Tulips are available in almost every color but blue, and often are splashed with a second hue. They spring forth as single flowers or in clusters from clumps of fleshy, wavy-edged leaves, providing accents in borders and rock gardens, or naturalized in meadows. They come in many forms, including Darwins, with softly curved, cup-shaped petals; peony-flowered, with blossoms crowded with wavy petals; and species types with open, starry flowers. By selecting a diversity of tulips one can enjoy cheerful blooms continuously from early spring to early summer.

Growing conditions and maintenance

Plant tulip bulbs in late fall in a warm, sunny location at a depth equal to three times their diameter. They can withstand crowding with no ill effects—even five bulbs per square foot. Species tulips can provide years of beautiful blossoms, but the flower production of even well-tended hybrids declines after the second or third year.

Selected species and varieties

T. fosterana—18 inches tall with very large spring flowers and leaves often streaked or mottled with darker colors; 'Red Emperor' is an old favorite with brilliant red flowers edged with yellow.

T. greigii—8 to 16 inches tall with purple-lined foliage and flowers from early to mid-spring.

T. Hybrids—15 divisions, including single early, double early, Darwins, single late, lily-flowered, fringed, multiflowering, parrot, and double late, flowering from early spring to early summer;

'Easter Fire', a single late tulip, is one of the largest and sturdiest of tulips, and has deep red blossoms on 16-inch-tall stems.

T. kaufmanniana—urn-shaped buds opening into large flowers with curved petals on stems less than 12 inches tall in very early spring, and shiny green, sometimes mottled leaves.

Verbena (ver-BEE-na)
VERBENA, VERVAIN

Hardiness: Zones 4-10

Plant type: annual or tender perennial grown as an annual

Height: 6 inches to 4 feet

Interest: flowers, fragrance, foliage

Soil: moist, well-drained, dry

Light: full sun

◀ *Verbena rigida*

Verbenas provide vivid whites, reds, purples, and blues to the garden from late spring to frost. Their small, five-petaled, tubular flowers are often highly fragrant and borne in rounded or domed clusters on wiry stems. *V. canadensis* and *V. tenuisecta* form low mats of leaves and make an excellent ground cover. *V. bonariensis* and *V. rigida* have tall stems that provide a see-through effect useful in borders, in rock gardens, and as edging or replacement fillers with spring bulbs. They make good cut flowers.

Growing conditions and maintenance

Once established, these plants thrive in hot, dry sites and are effective in xeriscapes. They grow more vigorously and produce more flowers if given additional water during dry spells. Propagate by seed sown in spring spacing plants 1 foot apart. Or take cuttings in late summer, root them, and overwinter indoors for planting the following spring. Verbenas are short-lived perennials that will self-sow in warm climates, and are grown as annuals in northern regions.

Selected species and varieties

V. bonariensis—2 to 4 feet tall with branching, wiry, square stems with many clusters of purply lilac flowers from mid-summer to frost, and 2- to 4-inch rough, clasping leaves; Zones 7-9.

V. canadensis (rose verbena)—trailing, 6- to 12-inch stems forming dense mats of 4-inch leaves and rounded clusters of rosy pink flowers in summer; 'Candidissima' has white flowers; 'Rosea' bears long-lasting, highly fragrant pink flowers.

V. gooddingii (pink verbena)—18-inch mats of purplish stems

bearing bright purple-pink flowers in rounded clusters from summer to frost.

V. rigida [also listed as *V. venosa*]—1 to 2 feet with erect, branching stems and dense clusters of purple flowers in summer and fall, and narrow, 2- to 3-inch dark green leaves mostly at the bases of the stems; Zones 8-10.

V. tenuisecta (moss verbena)—spreading stems in 12-inch-tall clumps with blue, violet, or purple summer flowers in 2-inch clusters, and finely divided, triangular, ferny foliage; Zones 7-10.

Veronica (ve-RON-i-ka)
SPEEDWELL

Hardiness: Zones 4-8

Plant type: perennial

Height: 1 to 2 feet

Interest: flowers, foliage

Soil: well-drained

Light: full sun to partial shade

◀ *Veronica spicata* 'Rosea'

Speedwells form clumps of spreading stems lined with narrow, soft-textured leaves, and tipped with long spikes of tiny flowers densely packed into long, conical spires from spring to summer. They fit well into rock gardens and are a good choice for edging, as a filler, or for naturalizing in shady, informal gardens.

Growing conditions and maintenance

Space plants 1 to 2 feet apart. Speedwells will flower most abundantly in full sun where moisture is abundant. Deadhead withering flower spikes to encourage an extended season of bloom. Propagate by seed, by cuttings, or by division in spring or fall. Taller types may need support.

Selected species and varieties

V. austriaca ssp. ***teucrium*** (Austrian speedwell)—to 2 feet tall with ½-inch deep blue flowers from late spring to early summer and deeply cut leaves.

V. grandis—1 to 2 feet, sometimes erect or trailing, bearing 3-inch oblong leaves and 6-inch flower spikes in summer.

V. incana (silver speedwell, woolly speedwell)—12 inches tall with pale lilac-blue flowers in early summer and 6-inch-tall mats of woolly, silvery gray foliage.

V. latifolia [also listed as ***V. teucrium***] (Hungarian speedwell)—compact, 12 to 18 inches with wide spikes of deep blue, rose, or white flowers in summer.

V. spicata (spike speedwell)—18 inches tall with lavender-blue to pink flowers from late spring to mid-summer; 'Alba' has white flowers that persist all summer.

★ PRO'S PICK ★

V. austriaca ssp. ***teucrium*** 'Crater Lake Blue' has many flower spikes crowded in early summer with large, brilliant blue blossoms above compact mounds of dark green foliage.

Viburnum (vy-BUR-num)
VIBURNUM

Hardiness: Zones 2-8

Plant type: shrub

Height: 4 to 15 feet

Interest: flowers, foliage, fragrance, fruit

Soil: well-drained

Light: full sun to partial shade

◀ *Viburnum trilobum*

These deciduous or evergreen plants offer year-round interest to shrub borders, and also make effective backdrops, hedges, or specimen plants. All have clusters of white flowers in spring; the flowers of *V. plicatum* and *V. trilobum* are especially showy. Many species produce red, yellow, blue, or black berrylike fruit in late summer and fall. The leaves are borne in pairs, have interesting shapes, and turn attractive shades of red, orange, and purple in the fall.

Growing conditions and maintenance

Viburnums transplant easily and thrive in soil amended with organic matter. *V. acerifolium* grows best in dry, acid soil. *V. dentatum* and *V. trilobum* will tolerate damp, even waterlogged, soil. Propagate by cuttings made in early summer or by seeds planted in marked locations. Viburnum seeds have double dormancy and may take several seasons to germinate.

Selected species and varieties

V. acerifolium (maple-leaved viburnum)—low growing, 4 to 6 feet tall with 2- to 4-inch three-lobed, dark green maplelike leaves turning light purple in fall, modest 1- to 3-inch clusters of white flowers in spring, and blue-black fruit in early fall; Zones 3-8.

V. dentatum (arrowwood)—rotund, 6 to 15 feet with arrow-straight branches bearing attractive 2- to 4-inch, coarsely toothed, rounded green leaves turning glossy red in fall, 2- to 4-inch flat-topped clusters of creamy white flowers in spring, and blue-black fruit in fall.

V. plicatum var. ***tomentosum*** (double file viburnum)—6 to 10 feet tall bearing profuse, 2- to 4-inch white spring flowers with showy, sterile outer rings, and toothed oval leaves turning red-purple in fall, when red fruit matures; 'Shasta' grows 6 feet tall and twice as wide, with abundant clusters of pure white flowers; Zones 5-8.

V. trilobum (cranberry bush)—8 to 12 feet with thick, three-lobed, 2- to 5-inch leaves turning reddish in fall, and showy clusters of 3-inch creamy white mid-spring flowers surrounded by large sterile ones and edible red fruit; Zones 2-7.

Viola *(vy-O-la)*
VIOLET, PANSY

Hardiness: Zones 3-9

Plant type: hardy annual or perennial

Height: 2 to 10 inches

Interest: flowers, fragrance

Soil: moist, well-drained

Light: full sun to partial shade

◀ *Viola tricolor*

Violets and pansies have dainty, five-petaled flowers borne on thin stems. The flowers always have a prominent nectar-filled spur projecting back from the lower petal. These versatile plants often have attractive, heart-shaped leaves that form low mounds. Their rainbow of colors and long season of bloom make them perfect for edging or borders, and for growing in containers.

Growing conditions and maintenance

V. tricolor freely self-sows and grows best in shade. Space plants 8 to 12 inches apart. *V. tricolor* and *V.* x *wittrockiana* are short-lived perennials that can be grown as annuals if started indoors in late winter and planted in early spring. Propagate by seed or division.

Selected species and varieties

V. cornuta (horned violet, tufted pansy)—5 to 10 inches tall, bearing pale to deep violet-purple pansylike flowers in spring and early summer, and oval, toothed, evergreen leaves; 'Alba' has white flowers; 'Atropurpurea', dark purple blooms with small yellow centers; 'Chantreyland', pale orange flowers; Zones 5-8.

V. tricolor (Johnny-jump-up)—2 to 8 inches tall with ½-inch violet-blue-and-yellow flat-faced flowers from spring through early summer.

V.* x *wittrockiana (pansy)—6- to 8-inch bushy stems with 1- to 4-inch flowers in a wide range of colors, and hundreds of cultivars with flowers in solids or multicolors and with various flowering seasons.

How to: Deadheading pansies will prolong the bloom season. Cut withering flowers every few days before they set seed. At the end of the season allow the last crop to produce fruit capsules if you desire.

Vitex *(VY-tex)*
VITEX

Hardiness: Zones 6-9

Plant type: shrub, tree

Height: 8 to 20 feet

Interest: flowers, foliage, fragrance

Soil: moist, well-drained

Light: full sun

◀ *Vitex agnus-castus*

Vitex are vase-shaped shrubs or small trees with fragrant flowers and leaves. Their tiny lilac or pale violet flowers are borne in 6- to 12-inch spikes at the tips of new wood. The 4-inch-long, deep green deciduous leaves are aromatic when bruised, and have gray undersides. Vitex provide late summer to fall color in shrub borders, or can be pruned to specimen-tree form.

Growing conditions and maintenance

Vitex are woody plants that grow best in ordinary garden soil. Overfertilizing will reduce the intensity of flower color. Cold winters will kill tops to the ground in Zone 6, but these fast-growing plants will resprout in spring and flower in fall. Propagate by seed, by summer cuttings, or layering of shoots. Prune in early spring if needed.

Selected species and varieties

V. agnus-castus (chaste tree, hemp tree)—multistemmed, 8 to 10 feet tall in the North and to 20 feet tall in the southern part of its range, with 3- to 6-inch long racemes of fragrant lilac flowers in summer and compound leaves of five to seven leaflets arranged in maple-leaf fashion; 'Rosea' has pink flowers.

V. negundo—5-to 15-foot-tall shrub with four-angled stems bearing 5- to 8-inch terminal clusters of lavender flowers in summer, and compound leaves with three to five gray-green leaflets; 'Heterophylla' has highly divided ferny leaves and light lavender flowers.

★ PRO'S PICK ★

V. agnus-castus var. ***latifolia*** is more vigorous and hardy than the species, with large open clusters of fragrant lavender summer flowers.

Zinnia *(ZIN-ee-a)*
ZINNIA

Hardiness: hardy

Plant type: annual

Height: 8 inches to 3 feet

Interest: flowers

Soil: well-drained

Light: full sun

◀ *Zinnia angustifolia*

Zinnias have brightly colored, daisy- or pomponlike flowers accented with yellow or green centers. The old-fashioned species have maroon, purple, or orange flowers, but new hybrids and cultivars come in a staggering array of colors. Zinnias are perfect for adding color to beds and borders in summer and fall. *Z. angustifolia* is excellent in hanging baskets or containers.

Growing conditions and maintenance

Zinnias prefer hot, dry weather. Provide good air circulation to prevent mildew, a major problem for these plants. Propagate by seed sown in late spring or started indoors and transplanted after all danger of frost has passed. Space smaller plants 3 to 6 inches apart and larger ones 8 to 12 inches apart.

Selected species and varieties

Z. angustifolia (narrowleaf zinnia, Mexican zinnia)—compact, 8 to 12 inches tall with very narrow leaves and 1-inch orange blossoms from summer to fall.

Z. elegans—1 to 3 feet tall with 3-inch flat blossoms in nearly every shade but blue; 'Giant Cactus' has very large flowers; 'Mini Series' and 'Thumbelina Series' are dwarfs.

> ★ **PRO'S PICK** ★
>
> *Z.* 'Rose Pinwheel' has 3½-inch single rosy pink flowers on sturdy 18-inch-tall stems, and is resistant to mildew.
>
>

Zizia *(ZIZ-ee-a)*
ZIZIA

Hardiness: Zones 4-8

Plant type: perennial

Height: 1 to 2½ feet

Interest: flowers, foliage

Soil: moist, well-drained

Light: full sun to partial shade

◀ *Zizia aurea*

Zizia is a member of the parsley family. Its dark green compound leaves turn purplish in fall, and the clusters of tiny yellow flowers appear from mid-spring to early summer. *Z. aurea* is native to meadows and thickets in eastern North America. This plant is best used in informal wild gardens or for naturalizing in wet meadows.

Growing conditions and maintenance

Propagate by seed, or by division of forked, spreading rhizomes made in fall or very early spring. Replant the rhizome sections ½ inch to 1 inch deep, spacing them 8 to 12 inches apart.

Selected species and varieties

Z. aurea (golden alexanders)— 1 to 2½ feet with 2-inch flat-topped clusters of yellow flowers from spring to early summer, and compound leaves divided into three parts, with each leaflet further subdivided into three to seven segments.

★ **Point of interest:** *In beds and borders, the foliage of zizia gives the visual effect of goutweed or ground-elder without being aggressive or invasive.*

Acknowledgments and Picture Credits

The sources for the illustrations in the book are listed below. Credits from left to right are separated by semicolons; credits from top to bottom are separated by dashes.

Cover: ©Allan Mandell, Photographer, Inc./designed by/courtesy Ernie and Marietta O'Byrne.
Cover insets: Kevin Shields/New England Stock Photo—New England Stock Photo. Back Cover insets: Michael S. Thompson—Art by Susan Berry Langsten—Kathlene Persoff.
End papers: ©Crandall & Crandall/courtesy James and Mary McIntyre.
1: Lefever/Grushow/Grant Heilman Photography, Inc.2, 3: Derek Fell. 6, 7: Charles Mann Photography/designed by/courtesy Lauren Springer. 8: Art by Elayne Sears/designed by Elizabeth Heekin Bartels/based on design by Lauren Springer; Jerry Pavia—©Richard Shiell—Drawing by Luanne Urfer, Landscape Architect/designed by Elizabeth Heekin Bartels/based on design by Lauren Springer. 9: Art by Elayne Sears/designed by Elizabeth Heekin Bartels/based on design by Lauren Springer—©Richard Shiell—Joseph Strauch. 10, 11: ©Roger Foley/designed by/courtesy Oda Von Berg. 12: Art by Elayne Sears/designed by Elizabeth Heekin Bartels/based on design by Oda Von Berg—Jerry Pavia; Charles Mann Photography. 12,13: Art by Elayne Sears/designed by Elizabeth Heekin Bartels/based on design by Oda Von Berg. 13: Drawing by Luanne Urfer, Landscape Architect/designed by Elizabeth Heekin Bartels/based on design by Oda Von Berg—©R. Todd Davis Photography. 14, 15: Michael S. Thompson/designed by/courtesy Ernie and Marietta O'Byrne. 16: Jerry Pavia(2)—©Richard Shiell. 16,17: Art by Elayne Sears/designed by Elizabeth Heekin Bartels/based on design by Ernie and Marietta O'Byrne. 17: Drawing by Luanne Urfer, Landscape Architect/designed by Elizabeth Heekin Bartels/based on design by Ernie and Marietta O'Byrne—Charles Mann Photography. 18, 19: Kathlene Persoff/designed by/courtesy/Agatha Youngblood. 20: Art by Elayne Sears/designed by Elizabeth Heekin Bartels/based on design by Agatha Youngblood; ©Richard Shiell—Jerry Pavia. 21: Drawing by Luanne Urfer, Landscape Architect/designed by Elizabeth Heekin Bartels/based on design by Agatha Youngblood; Bill Johnson—Jerry Pavia; Art by Elayne Sears/designed by Elizabeth Heekin Bartels/based on design by Agatha Youngblood. 22, 23: Ken Druse/designed by/courtesy/Nancy Goodwin, Montrose. 24: Art by Elayne Sears/designed by Elizabeth Heekin Bartels/based on design by Nancy Goodwin—Bill Johnson; Joseph Strauch; ©Richard Shiell. 25: Drawing by Luanne Urfer, Landscape Architect/designed by Elizabeth Heekin Bartels/based on design by Nancy Goodwin—Jerry Pavia—Art by Elayne Sears/designed by Elizabeth Heekin Bartels/based on design by Nancy Goodwin. 26, 27: Lefever/Grushow/Grant Heilman Photography, Inc. 28: Kathlene Persoff/designed by/courtesy Pat Welsh, garden book author. 29: Art by Gordon Morrison. 30: Art by Gordon Morrison. 31: Art by Gordon Morrison. 33: Derek Fell—©Paddy Wales/courtesy Ann Buffam; Art by Gordon Morrison (2). 35: Art by Nancy Hull. 36: Art by Susan Berry Langsten. 38, 39: Ken Druse/courtesy Ruth Levitan. 40: Derek Fell. 41: Art by Nancy Hull. 42,43: Barry L. Runk/Grant Heilman Photography, Inc. 43: Christi Carter/Grant Heilman Photography, Inc. 45: ©Walter Chandoha; Art by Gordon Morrison (2). 46: Art by Joan Terese Child (2). 47: Art by Gordon Morrison (6)—Art by Joan Terese Child (4). 48, 49: Jane Grushow/Grant Heilman Photography, Inc. 50: Christi Carter/Grant Heilman Photography, Inc. 52: Art by Susan Berry Langsten (3). 54: Art by Susan Berry Langsten (3). 55: Jane Grushow/Grant Heilman Photography, Inc.—Carol Mackey/Visuals Unlimited—©R. Todd Davis Photography—Joseph Strauch (2)—Art by Susan Berry Langsten (2); Joanne Pavia. 56, 57: Kathlene Persoff. 59: ©Roger Foley/designed by Joanna McQuail Reed; Art by Gordon Morrison (2). 60: Art by Susan Berry Langsten (3). 61: Jerry Pavia. 62, 63: Kathlene Persoff. 64: Art by Susan Berry Langsten (2). 66: Christi

Carter/Grant Heilman Photography, Inc. 67: Art by Susan Berry Langsten (2). 68,69: ©Walter Chandoha. 69: ©Allan Mandell, Photographer, Inc. 70: ©Roger Foley/designed by Karen Burroughs. 72: Gay Bumgarner/courtesy Marjo and Al Price. 72,73: ©Jim Bleuer. 73: Art by Susan Berry Langsten (3). 74: ©Roger Foley/designed by Karen Burroughs. 76: Art by Susan Berry Langsten (3). 77: Joanne Pavia—Jerry Pavia (3)—Art by Susan Berry Langsten (2). 78, 79: Christi Carter/Grant Heilman Photography, Inc. 80: Michael S. Thompson. 81: Dency Kane/designed by/courtesy Nancy Goodwin, Montrose; Art by Gordon Morrison (2). 82: Jane Grushow/Grant Heilman Photography, Inc./courtesy Longview Farm. 83: Art by Susan Berry Langsten (5). 84: Art by Susan Berry Langsten—Michael Shedlock/New England Stock Photo. 85: Michael S. Thompson/designed by Lawrence Underhill, Landscape Architect. 86: Michael S. Thompson/designed by Barbara Thompson. 87: Art by Susan Berry Langsten (3). 88: ©Roger Foley/designed by Bill Harris and Carrie Dike. 89: J. Paul Moore/designed by/courtesy Susan and Stephen Felts. 90: Art by Susan Berry Langsten (2). 91: Lee Anne White/Positive Images—©Crandall & Crandall—Art by Susan Berry Langsten (2); judywhite/New Leaf Images—©Roger Foley—©Richard Shiell. 96: Map by John Drummond, Time-Life Books. 98: Thomas E. Eltzroth—Jerry Pavia. 99: Charles Mann Photography (2). 100: Art by Mike Wanke—Thomas E. Eltzroth; ©R. Todd Davis Photography—Art by Mike Wanke. 101: David Cavagnaro; Jerry Pavia. 102: Joanne Pavia—Joseph Strauch—©Richard Shiell—Art by Mike Wanke. 103: Thomas E. Eltzroth; Alan Detrick—©Mark Turner. 104: ©Mark Turner; Jerry Pavia. 105: Charles Mann Photography—Bill Johnson; Thomas E. Eltzroth—©Roger Foley. 106: Joseph Strauch—©Richard Shiell; ©Crandall & Crandall. 107: ©Roger Foley; Jerry Pavia—©Richard Shiell. 108: ©Crandall & Crandall; ©Richard Shiell. 109: Charles Mann Photography; Jerry Pavia—Joseph Strauch. 110: Thomas E. Eltzroth; David Cavagnaro. 111: David Cavagnaro—Thomas E. Eltzroth; Jerry Pavia. 112: Thomas E. Eltzroth—Art by Mike Wanke; ©Richard Shiell—Art by Mike Wanke. 113: ©Crandall & Crandall; Charles Mann Photography. 114: Joseph Strauch—Jerry Pavia; Bill Johnson—David Cavagnaro. 115: ©Mark Turner (2). 116: David Cavagnaro—Thomas E. Eltzroth; ©Crandall & Crandall. 117: judywhite/New Leaf Images; David Cavagnaro—Bill Johnson. 118: ©Richard Shiell; judywhite/New Leaf Images. 119: Joseph Strauch—©Roger Foley; judywhite/New Leaf Images. 120: ©Richard Shiell; ©Mark Turner. 121: ©Richard Shiell; Joseph Strauch—Jerry Pavia. 122: Joseph Strauch; Bill Johnson. 123: David Cavagnaro; judywhite/New Leaf Images—Jerry Pavia. 124: Jerry Pavia—Joseph Strauch; Thomas E. Eltzroth. 125: Thomas E. Eltzroth; ©Richard Shiell. 126: Bill Johnson; Charles Mann Photography. 127: Joseph Strauch (2); ©Richard Shiell. 128: ©R. Todd Davis Photography; Thomas E. Eltzroth. 129: David Cavagnaro—Art by Mike Wanke—Jerry Pavia—Bill Johnson. 130: Joseph Strauch; David Cavagnaro—©Richard Shiell. 131: Thomas E. Eltzroth (2); Charles Mann Photography—©Richard Shiell. 132: Jerry Pavia; Bill Johnson. 133: Jerry Pavia (2); Joanne Pavia. 134: Joseph Strauch; David Cavagnaro. 135: Joseph Strauch; Thomas E. Eltzroth—judywhite/New Leaf Images. 136: Bill Johnson—Jerry Pavia; Thomas E. Eltzroth. 137: ©R. Todd Davis Photography—©Roger Foley; Bill Johnson—Charles Mann Photography. 138: Thomas E. Eltzroth—©Richard Shiell; Thomas E. Eltzroth. 139: Joseph Strauch; ©Crandall & Crandall. 140: ©Crandall & Crandall—Bill Johnson (2)—©Richard Shiell. 141: Joseph Strauch—Thomas E. Eltzroth; ©Richard Shiell—David Cavagnaro. 142: David Cavagnaro; Joseph Strauch. 143: Thomas E. Eltzroth (2)—Jerry Pavia. 144: Joseph Strauch. 145: Charles Mann Photography; Joseph Strauch. 146: Bill Johnson (2); Joseph Strauch. 147: Joseph Strauch; Bill Johnson. 148: Bill Johnson. 149: Joseph Strauch—Bill Johnson; ©Richard Shiell. 150: Jerry Pavia; ©Richard Shiell (2). 151: ©Roger Foley—©R. Todd Davis Photography (2)

Bibliography

BOOKS:

Alexander, Rosemary, and Anthony du Gard Pasley. *The English Gardening School: The Complete Master Course on Garden Planning and Landscape Design for the American Gardener.* New York: Weidenfeld & Nicolson, 1987.

Appleton, Bonnie Lee. *Rodale's Successful Organic Gardening: Trees, Shrubs and Vines.* Emmaus, Pa.: Rodale Press, 1993.

Armitage, Allan M. *Herbaceous Perennial Plants.* Athens, Ga.: Varsity Press, 1989.

Art, Henry W. *A Garden of Wildflowers: 101 Native Species and How to Grow Them.* Pownal, Vt.: Storey Communications, 1986.
   The Wildflower Gardener's Guide: Northeast, Mid-Atlantic, Great Lakes and Eastern Canada Edition. Pownal, Vt.: Storey Communications, 1987.

Ashmun, Barbara. *The Garden Design Primer.* New York: Lyons & Burford, 1993.

Austin, David. *Old Roses and English Roses.* Woodbridge, Suffolk: Antique Collectors' Club, 1992.
   Shrub Roses and Climbing Roses. Woodbridge, Suffolk: Antique Collectors' Club, 1995.

Bailey, Liberty Hyde, Ethel Zoe Bailey and the Staff of the Bailey Hortorium, Cornell University. *Hortus Third* (rev. ed.). New York: Macmillan, 1976.
   Bailey, Liberty Hyde, and the Staff of the Bailey Hortorium, Cornell University. *Manual of Cultivated Plants* (rev. ed.). New York: Macmillan, 1951.

Bales, Suzanne Frutig. *Burpee American Gardening Series: Annuals.* New York: Prentice Hall, 1991.

Bloom, Alan, and Adrian Bloom. *Blooms of Bressingham: Garden Plants.* London: HarperCollins, 1992.

Brickell, Christopher, ed. *The American Horticulture Society Encyclopedia of Garden Plants.* New York: Macmillan, 1989.

Brookes, John. *The Complete Gardener.* New York: Crescent Books, 1994.

Buczacki, Stefan. *Creating a Victorian Flower Garden.* New York: Weidenfeld & Nicolson, 1988.

Chatto, Beth. *The Green Tapestry.* New York: Simon and Schuster, 1989.

Clark, Timothy. *Margery Fish's Country Gardening.* Newton Abbot, Devon: David & Charles, 1989.

Clausen, Ruth Rogers, and Nicolas H. Ekstrom. *Perennials for American Gardens.* New York: Random House, 1989.

Colborn, Nigel. *The Old-Fashioned Gardener (Lorenz Books).* London: Anness, 1995.

Consolino, Francesca, and Enrico Banfi. *Climbing Plants.* New York: Simon and Schuster, 1993.

Cowley, Jill. *Beds and Borders for Year Round Color (A Ward Lock Book).* London: Wellington House, 1995.

Cox, Jeff. *Landscaping with Nature.* Emmaus, Pa.: Rodale Press, 1991.
   Cox, Jeff, and Marilyn Cox. *The Perennial Garden: Color Harmonies through the Seasons.* Emmaus, Pa.: Rodale Press, 1985.

Crandall, Chuck, and Barbara Crandall. *Flowering, Fruiting, & Foliage Vines.* New York: Sterling, 1995.

Cravens, Richard H. *Vines (The Time-Life Encyclopedia of Gardening).* Alexandria, Va.: Time-Life Books, 1979.

Cresson, Charles O. *Charles Cresson on the American Flower Garden (Burpee Expert Gardener series).* New York: Prentice Hall, 1993.

Crockett, James Underwood, and the Editors of Time-Life Books:
   Annuals (The Time-Life Encyclopedia of Gardening). New York: Time-Life Books, 1971.
   Bulbs (The Time-Life Encyclopedia of Gardening). New York: Time-Life Books, 1971.
   Evergreens (The Time-Life Encyclopedia of Gardening). New York: Time-Life Books, 1976.
   Flowering Shrubs (The Time-Life Encyclopedia of Gardening). New York: Time-Life Books, 1972.
   Landscape Gardening (The Time-Life Encyclopedia of Gardening). New York: Time-Life Books, 1971.
   Perennials (The Time-Life Encyclopedia of Gardening). New York: Time-Life Books, 1972.
   Trees (The Time-Life Encyclopedia of Gardening). New York: Time-Life Books, 1972.

Crockett, James Underwood, and Ogden Tanner. *Herbs (The Time-Life Encyclopedia of Gardening).* Alexandria, Va.: Time-Life Books, 1977.

Cutter, Karen Davis, ed. *Vines.* Charlotte, Vt.: Camden House, 1992.

Damrosch, Barbara: *The Garden Primer.* New York: Workman, 1988.
   Theme Gardens. New York: Workman, 1982.

Dirr, Michael A. *Manual of Woody Landscape Plants.* Champaign, Ill.: Stipes, 1990.

Druse, Ken. *The Natural Garden.* New York: Clarkson N. Potter, 1989.

Edinger, Philip. *Flower Garden Plans.* San Ramon, Calif.: Ortho Books, 1991.

Elliott, Brent. *Victorian Gardens.* Portland, Oreg.: Timber Press, 1986.

Fell, Derek. *The Easiest Flowers to Grow.* San Ramon, Calif.: Ortho Books, 1990.

Foster, Gertrude B., and Rosemary F. Louden. *Park's Success with Herbs.* Greenwood, S.C.: Geo. Park Seed, 1980.

Frances Lincoln Limited (London), Editors of: *Best Borders.* New York: Viking Penguin, 1995.

Garden Way Publishing, Editors of. *The Gardener's Complete Q&A.* Pownal, Vt.: Storey Communications, 1995.

Gates, Galen, Chris Graham and Ethan Johnson. *American Garden Guides: Shrubs and Vines.* New York: Pantheon, 1994.

Genders, Roy. *The Cottage Garden: And the Old-Fashioned Flowers.* London: Pelham Books, 1984.

Greenlee, John. *The Encyclopedia of Ornamental Grasses (A Friedman Group Book).* Emmaus, Pa.: Rodale Press, 1992.

Griffiths, Mark, ed. *Index of Garden Plants.* Portland, Oreg.: Timber Press, 1994.

Halpin, Anne. *Morning Glories & Moonflowers.* New York: Simon and Schuster, 1996.

Harper, Pamela J.: *Designing with Perennials.* New York: Macmillan, 1991.
   Color Echoes. New York: Macmillan, 1994.

Hayward, Gordon. *Garden Paths: Inspiring Designs and Practical Projects.* Charlotte, Vt.: Camden House, 1993.

Heath, Becky, and Brent Heath. *Daffodils for American Gardens.* Washington, D.C.: Elliott & Clark, 1995.

Heriteau, Jacqueline, and Andre Viette. *The American Horticultural Society Flower Finder.* New York: Simon and Schuster, 1992.

Hill, Lewis. *Pruning Simplified.* Pownal, Vt.: Storey Communications, 1986.

Hillier Nurseries. *The Hillier Manual of Trees & Shrubs* (6th ed.). Newton Abbot, Devon: David & Charles, 1995.

Hobhouse, Penelope. *Color in Your Garden.* Boston: Little, Brown, 1985.

Jacobson, Arthur Lee. *North American Landscape Trees.* Berkeley, Calif.: Ten Speed Press, 1996.

Jekyll, Gertrude. *Colour Schemes for the Flower Garden.* Salem, N.H.: The Ayer Company, 1983.

Johnson, Hugh. *The Principles of Gardening.* New York: Simon and Schuster, 1979.

Lacy, Allen. *The Garden in Autumn.* New York: Atlantic Monthly Press, 1990.

Loewer, Peter: *The New Small Garden.* Mechanicsburg, Pa.: Stackpole Books,

1994.

Rodale's Annual Garden. New York: Wing Books, 1992.

Tough Plants for Tough Places. Emmaus, Pa.: Rodale Press, 1992.

Marston, Ted, ed. *Hearst Garden Guides: Annuals.* New York: Hearst, 1993.

McGourty, Frederick. *The Perennial Gardener.* Boston: Houghton Mifflin, 1990.

Moore, Charles W., William J. Mitchell and William Turnbull, Jr. *The Poetics of Gardens.* Cambridge: MIT Press, 1988.

Murphy, Wendy. *Beds and Borders: Traditional and Original Garden Designs.* Boston: Houghton Mifflin, 1990.

Murray, Elizabeth, and Derek Fell. *Home Landscaping.* New York: Simon & Schuster, 1988.

Nelson, William R., Jr. *Landscaping Your Home* (rev. ed.). Urbana, Ill.: Cooperative Extension Service, University of Illinois at Urbana-Champaign, 1993.

Obrizok, Robert A. *A Garden of Conifers* (2d ed.). Deer Park, Wis.: Capability's Books, 1994.

Ortho Books, Editorial Staff of. *Successful Flower Gardening.* San Ramon, Calif.: Ortho Books, 1990.

Ortloff, H. Stuart, and Henry B. Raymore. *The Book of Landscape Design.* New York: M. Barrows, 1959.

Phillips, C.E. Lucas, and Peter Barber. *Ornamental Shrubs.* New York: Van-Nostrand, Reinhold, 1981.

Phillips, Ellen, and C. Colston Burrell. *Rodale's Illustrated Encyclopedia of Perennials.* Emmaus, Pa.: Rodale Press, 1993.

Phillips, Roger, and Martyn Rix: *Perennials. 2 vols.* New York: Random House, 1991.

The Random House Book of Shrubs. New York: Random House, 1989.

Poor, Janet M., ed. *Plants That Merit Attention. Vol. 1. Trees.* Portland, Oreg.: Timber Press, 1984.

Reader's Digest, Editors of: *Reader's Digest Illustrated Guide to Gardening.* Pleasantville, N.Y.: Reader's Digest Association, 1978.

Reader's Digest Magic and Medicine of Plants. Pleasantville, N.Y.: Reader's Digest Association, 1986.

Roth, Susan A. *The Four-Season Landscape: Easy-care Plants and Plans for Year-round Color.* Emmaus, Pa.: Rodale Press, 1994.

Sinnes, A. Cort. *All About Perennials.* San Francisco: Ortho Books, 1981.

Smyser, Carol A., and the Editors of Rodale Press Books. *Nature's Design: A Practical Guide to Natural Landscaping.* Emmaus, Pa.: Rodale Press, 1982.

Springer, Lauren. *Waterwise Gardening (Burpee American Gardening series).* New York: Prentice Hall, 1994.

Squire, David. *The Complete Guide to Using Color in Your Garden.* Emmaus, Pa.: Rodale Press, 1991.

Still, Steven M. *Manual of Herbaceous Ornamental Plants* (4th ed.). Champaign, Ill.: Stipes, 1994.

Strong, Roy. *A Small Garden Designer's Handbook.* Boston: Little, Brown, 1987.

Sunset Books and Sunset Magazine, Editors of: *Sunset Garden & Patio Building Book.* Menlo Park, Calif.: Lane, 1983.

Sunset Western Garden Book. (rev. ed.). Menlo Park, Calif.: 1995

Trees and Shrubs. Menlo Park, Calif.: Sunset Books, 1994.

Tanner, Ogden, and the Editors of Time-Life Books. *Garden Construction (The Time-Life Encyclopedia of Gardening).* Alexandria, Va.: Time-Life Books, 1978.

Taylor's Guide to Annuals (Taylor's Guides to Gardening series). Boston: Houghton Mifflin, 1986.

Taylor's Guide to Perennials (Taylor's Guides to Gardening series). Boston: Houghton Mifflin, 1986.

Taylor's Guide to Roses (Taylor's Guides to Gardening series). Boston: Houghton Mifflin, 1995.

Tenenbaum, Frances, Rita Buchanan and Roger Holmes. *Taylor's Master Guide to Gardening.* Boston: Houghton Mifflin, 1994.

Thomas, Graham Stuart: *The Art of Planting: or The Planter's Handbook.* Boston: David R.Godine, 1984.

The Graham Stuart Thomas Rose Book. Portland, Oreg.: Sagapress/Timber Press, 1994.

Thompson, Sylvia. *The Kitchen Garden.* New York: Bantam Books, 1995.

Time-Life Books, Editors of: *Bulbs (Time-Life Complete Gardener).* New York: Time-Life Books, 1995.

Combining Plants (Time-Life Complete Gardener). New York: Time-Life Books, 1995.

Low Maintenance Gardening (Time-Life Complete Gardener). New York: Time-Life Books, 1995.

Perennials (Time-Life Complete Gardener). New York: Time-Life Books, 1995.

Shade Gardening (Time-Life Complete Gardener). New York: Time-Life Books, 1995.

Wildflowers (Time-Life Complete Gardener). New York: Time-Life Books, 1995.

Toogood, Alan. *Border Plants.* London: Ward Lock Limited, 1987.

Verey, Rosemary: *The Art of Planting.* Boston: Little, Brown, 1990.

Classic Garden Design. New York: Random House, 1989.

Wasowski, Sally, and Andy Wasowski. *Gardening with Native Plants of the South.* Dallas: Taylor, 1994.

Wilkinson, Elizabeth, and Marjorie Henderson. *Decorating Eden: A Comprehensive Source Book of Classic Garden Details.* San Francisco: Chronicle Books, 1992.

Williamson, John. *Perennial Gardens: a practical guide to home landscaping.* New York: Harper & Row, 1988.

Wilson, Andrew. *Garden Style Source Book (A Quarto Book).* Secaucus, N.J.: Chartwell Books, 1989.

Winterrowd, Wayne. *Annuals for Connoisseurs.* New York: Prentice Hall, 1992.

Wyman, Donald: *Shrubs and Vines for American Gardens.* New York: Macmillan, 1973.

Trees for American Gardens. New York: Macmillan, 1965.

Wyman's Gardening Encyclopedia. New York: Macmillan, 1971.

Wyman, Donald, and the Editors of Time-Life Books. *Easy Gardens (The Time-Life Encyclopedia of Gardening).* Alexandria, Va.: Time-Life Books, 1978.

Xerces Society. *Butterfly Gardening.* San Francisco, Calif.: Sierra Club Books, 1990.

Zeman, Anne M. *Fifty Easy Old-Fashioned Roses, Climbers, and Vines.* New York: Henry Holt, 1995.

PERIODICALS:

"American Cottage Gardens," *Plants and Gardens: Brooklyn Botanic Garden Record,* Vol. 46, No. 1. Brooklyn, N.Y.: Brooklyn Botanic Garden, 1990.

Beaubaire, Nancy, ed. *Brooklyn Botanic Garden Handbook No. 146: Native Perennials.* Brooklyn, N.Y.: Brooklyn Botanic Garden, 1996.

"Beds and Borders," *Plants and Gardens: Brooklyn Botanic Garden Record,* Vol. 42, No. 1. Brooklyn, N.Y.: Brooklyn Botanic Garden, 1986.

Burrell, C. Colston, ed. *Brooklyn Botanic Garden Handbook No. 145: Woodland Gardens, Shade Gets Chic.* Brooklyn, N.Y.: Brooklyn Botanic Garden, 1995.

"Ferns," *Plants and Gardens: Brooklyn Botanic Garden Record.* Brooklyn, N.Y.: Brooklyn Botanic Garden, Spring 1994.

Hyland, Bob, ed. *Brooklyn Botanic Garden Handbook No. 141: Shrubs, The*

New Glamour Plants. Brooklyn, N.Y.: Brooklyn Botanic Garden, 1994.

Irish, Mary F. "Diamonds of the Desert," *Horticulture,* January 1995.

Lawlor, Robert. "The Measure of Difference," *Parabola, The Magazine of Myth and Tradition,* November 1991.

Lewis, Alcinda, ed. *Brooklyn Botanic Garden Handbook No. 143: Butterfly Gardens.* Brooklyn, N.Y.: Brooklyn Botanic Garden, 1995.

Pelczar, Rita. 'The Prodigal Sunflower," *American Horticulturist*, Vol. 72, No. 8, August 1993.

Spaete, Peg. "Cacti," *American Horticulturist,* February 1992.

OTHER SOURCES:

Andre Viette Nursery catalog. Fisherville, Va.: 1994.
Appalachian Gardens catalog. Waynesboro, Pa.: 1996.
Beauty from Bulbs catalog. Bantam, Conn.: John Scheepers, Fall 1995.
Bluestone Perennials catalog. Madison, Ohio: 1995.
Breck's catalog. Peoria, Ill.: 1996
Chiltern Seeds catalog. England: 1996
Crownsville Nursery catalog. Crownsville, Md.: 1995.

Fairweather Gardens catalog. Greenwich, N.J.: 1995.
Jackson & Perkins Perennials catalog. Medford, Oreg.: 1996.
Joy Creek Nursery catalog. Scappoose, Oreg.: 1995.
Kurt Bluemel Nursery catalog. Baldwin, Md.: 1994.
Limerick Ornamental Grasses catalog. Port Matilda, Pa.: 1995.
McClure & Zimmerman catalog. Friesland, Wis.: Fall 1995 and Spring 1996.
Milaeger's Gardens Perennial Wishbook. Racine, Wis.: Spring 1996.
Niche Gardens catalog. Chapel Hill, N.C.: Spring 1996.
Nichol's Garden Nursery catalog. Albany, Ore.: 1996.
Oakes Daylilies catalog. Corryton, Tenn.: no date.
Park's Seed-Flowers and Vegetables catalog. Greenwood, S.C.: 1996.
Park's Springtime Planting Book catalog. Greenwood, S.C.: 1996.
Thompson & Morgan catalog, Jackson, N.J.: 1996
Wayside Gardens catalog. Hodges, S.C.: 1996.
WE-DU Nurseries catalog. Marion, N.C.: 1994.
Weiss Brothers Nursery catalog. Grass Valley, Calif.: 1996.
White Flower Farm Spring Garden Book catalogs. Litchfield, Conn.: Spring1995 and Spring 1996.

Index